STUDIES IN IMPERIALISM

general editor John M. MacKenzie

When the 'Studies in Imperialism' series was founded more than twenty years ago, emphasis was laid upon the conviction that 'imperialism as a cultural phenomenon had as significant an effect on the dominant as on the subordinate societies'. With more than sixty books published, this remains the prime concern of the series. Cross-disciplinary work has indeed appeared covering the full spectrum of cultural phenomena, as well as examining aspects of gender and sex, frontiers and law, science and the environment, language and literature, migration and patriotic societies, and much else. Moreover, the series has always wished to present comparative work on European and American imperialism, and particularly welcomes the submission of books in these areas. The fascination with imperialism, in all its aspects, shows no sign of abating, and this series will continue to lead the way in encouraging the widest possible range of studies in the field. 'Studies in Imperialism' is fully organic in its development, always seeking to be at the cutting edge, responding to the latest interests of scholars and the needs of this ever-expanding area of scholarship.

From Jack Tar to Union Jack

MANCHESTER
1824

Manchester University Press

AVAILABLE IN THE SERIES

CULTURAL IDENTITIES AND THE AESTHETICS OF BRITISHNESS ed. Dana Arnold

BRITAIN IN CHINA
Community, culture and colonialism, 1900–1949 Robert Bickers

RACE AND EMPIRE
Eugenics in colonial Kenya Chloe Campbell

RETHINKING SETTLER COLONIALISM
History and memory in Australia, Canada, Aotearoa New Zealand and South Africa ed. Annie E. Coombes

IMPERIAL CITIES
Landscape, display and identity eds Felix Driver and David Gilbert

IMPERIAL CITIZENSHIP
Empire and the question of belonging Daniel Gorman

SCOTLAND, THE CARIBBEAN AND THE ATLANTIC WORLD, 1750–1820 Douglas J. Hamilton

FLAGSHIPS OF IMPERIALISM
The P&O company and the politics of empire from its origins to 1867 Freda Harcourt

MISSIONARIES AND THEIR MEDICINES
A Christian modernity for tribal India David Hardiman

EMIGRANT HOMECOMINGS
The return movement of emigrants, 1600–2000 Marjory Harper

ENGENDERING WHITENESS
White women and colonialism in Barbados and North Carolina, 1625–1865 Cecily Jones

REPORTING THE RAJ
The British press and India, c.1880–1922 Chandrika Kaul

SILK AND EMPIRE Brenda M. King

COLONIAL CONNECTIONS, 1815–45
Patronage, the information revolution and colonial government Zoë Laidlaw

PROPAGANDA AND EMPIRE
The manipulation of British public opinion, 1880–1960 John M. MacKenzie

THE SCOTS IN SOUTH AFRICA
Ethnicity, identity, gender and race, 1772–1914 John M. MacKenzie with Nigel R. Dalziel

THE OTHER EMPIRE
Metropolis, India and progress in the colonial imagination John Marriott

IRELAND, INDIA AND EMPIRE
Indo-Irish radical connections, 1916–64 Kate O'Malley

SEX, POLITICS AND EMPIRE
A postcolonial geography Richard Phillips

IMPERIAL PERSUADERS
Images of Africa and Asia in British advertising Anandi Ramamurthy

GENDER, CRIME AND EMPIRE Kirsty Reid

THE HAREM, SLAVERY AND BRITISH IMPERIAL CULTURE
Anglo-Muslim relations, 1870–1900 Diane Robinson-Dunn

WEST INDIAN INTELLECTUALS IN BRITAIN ed. Bill Schwarz

MIGRANT RACES
Empire, identity and K. S. Ranjitsinhji Satadru Sen

AT THE END OF THE LINE
Colonial policing and the imperial endgame 1945–80 Georgina Sinclair

THE VICTORIAN SOLDIER IN AFRICA Edward M. Spiers

MARTIAL RACES AND MASCULINITY IN THE BRITISH ARMY, 1857–1914 Heather Streets

THE FRENCH EMPIRE BETWEEN THE WARS
Imperialism, politics and society Martin Thomas

ORDERING AFRICA eds Helen Tilley with Robert J. Gordon

BRITISH CULTURE AND THE END OF EMPIRE ed. Stuart Ward

'THE BETTER CLASS' OF INDIANS
Social rank, imperial identity, and South Asians in Britain 1858–1914 A. Martin Wainwright

From Jack Tar to Union Jack

REPRESENTING NAVAL MANHOOD IN THE BRITISH EMPIRE, 1870–1918

Mary A. Conley

MANCHESTER UNIVERSITY PRESS
Manchester and New York

distributed in the United States exclusively
by Palgrave Macmillan

Published by MANCHESTER UNIVERSITY PRESS
OXFORD ROAD, MANCHESTER M13 9NR, UK
and ROOM 400, 175 FIFTH AVENUE, NEW YORK, NY 10010, USA
www.manchesteruniversitypress.co.uk

Distributed in the United States exclusively by
PALGRAVE MACMILLAN, 175 FIFTH AVENUE, NEW YORK, NY 10010, USA

Distributed in Canada exclusively by
UBC PRESS, UNIVERSITY OF BRITISH COLUMBIA,
2029 WEST MALL, VANCOUVER, BC, CANADA V6T 1Z2

British Library Cataloguing-in-Publication Data
A catalogue record for this book is available from the British Library

Library of Congress Cataloging-in-Publication Data applied for

ISBN   978 0 7190 7534 6   *hardback*

First published 2009

18 17 16 15 14 13 12 11 10 09   10 9 8 7 6 5 4 3 2 1

Typeset
by SNP Best-set Typesetter Ltd., Hong Kong
Printed by the MPG Books Group
in the UK

To Jim

CONTENTS

General editor's introduction — ix
Acknowledgements — xi
List of figures — xiv
List of abbreviations — xv

Introduction: Gender, navy and empire   *page* 1

1 Imperial challenges and the modernisation of the fleet   19

2 For the good of the boys in blue: philanthropy, Agnes
   Weston and contested manhood   66

3 From powder monkey to admiral: social mobility,
   heroism and naval manhood   99

4 Strong men for a strong navy: naval scares, imperial
   anxieties and naval manhood   123

5 Lessons in manhood: boyhood, duty and war   160

Conclusion   193

Select bibliography — 197
Index — 211

GENERAL EDITOR'S INTRODUCTION

The later nineteenth century was a time of regulation and codification. Sports, societies, clubs, youth and other associations organised themselves with constitutions, rules, and sets of aspirations. All of this was part of the Victorian search for reliability and respectability. It is not surprising that this should also happen in the armed forces and the various bodies associated with them. As Mary Conley shows in this book, the structures and personnel arrangements of the navy were very much part of this organisational revolution. As a result, the image of the navy in society was very different in 1900 from that of 1800. This also reflected the great changes in technology that had taken place, the advances in educational provision, particularly after the 1870 Education Act, the developments in 'print capitalism' which had placed newspapers, magazines and books in almost every home in the land, as well as the more widespread use of various forms of illustrations and advertisements not only in such publications, but also in the domain of public space.

By the early 1880s, Empire shipping and cargoes were worth some £900 million per year. The Prime Minister Arthur Balfour described the trade routes carrying these goods as the 'arteries of empire', through which the lifeblood of the imperial system flowed. Consequently, as one author put it,

> 'the sea is much more than a trade route. It is the heart of Empire. The ebb and flow of its tides are the pulsating of the blood through the whole body. Without the strength which it gives every limb would atrophy and die.' (H.C. Ferraby, *The Imperial British Navy*, 1918, pp. 14–15).

With the exception of Canada, 'the only Continental Dominion', all colonies were vulnerable to direct naval attack. Another author suggested that on any given day, the British had some £250 to £300 million-worth of goods and ships on the high seas, imperial and non-imperial (Archibald Hurd, *Our Navy*, 1914, p. 253). The German equivalent was said to be a tiny fraction of that. It was not surprising, therefore, that such writers proposed that the navy continued to be most significant protective arm of the British imperial state. As Arnold White put it, 'Defeat at sea would starve these islands and reduce their inhabitants to compliance with the enemy's terms in far less time than was consumed by the sieges of Kimberley or Ladysmith.' (White, *Efficiency and Empire*, 1901, reprinted 1973, p. 262). Whether or not any of these assertions was true is irrelevant. What is significant is that they were propounded, and believed by many, in their day.

The Royal Navy thus held its own as the 'senior service' even when the focus and the weight of expenditure seemed to shift in favour of the military in the final decades of Victoria's reign. It was duly reformed in ways that were intended to help it meet the threats of a new world order. But such reform was in the hands of the private sector of philanthropy as well as the public domain of legislation, expenditure and regulation. Temperance and secure rest homes were seen as significant as reforms in pay, in the wearing of uniforms, in punishments and conditions, in service and pensions. And all this was reflected in new forms of social mobility as well as constructions of naval manhood that were designed to provide the social and cultural underpinning for the navy's role in the twentieth century. As Conley reveals, using a wide range of sources and innovative ideas, these conceptions fed into the images of heroism that seemed an essential part of the naval armoury in the dangerous times of the early twentieth century.

We find that by 1900 paintings, engravings and photography project a very different navy from that of the great battle canvases of the Napoleonic era. In the latter, the focus is on heroic officers backed by a polyglot crew, rugged men dressed in informal ways, conveying in their very forms the demands and mortal dangers of the naval life. A century later, the sailors are in uniforms, perfectly turned out, capable of taking on a range of technical and professional tasks. They, and their marine colleagues, become a central part of national and imperial pageantry, of state funerals and other occasions, suitably drilled and disciplined for their ceremonial roles. They become a visible expression of imperial power wherever they appear at naval bases in North America, the Mediterranean, southern Africa, the Indian Ocean and the Far East. Naval visits to colonial ports constituted a vital 'flying of the flag' for settler societies where naval league branches were founded and supported. They continued to be a vital expression of global and imperial power even after 'Jackie' Fisher embarked on his policy of concentrating more naval forces at home. Conley's book makes a very significant contribution to the study of this transformation.

John M. MacKenzie

ACKNOWLEDGEMENTS

The completion of this book offers a welcome opportunity for me to show my sincere appreciation to those who provided me with the intellectual, material and emotional support during the various stages of the development of this project. I am grateful to the many friends, teachers, colleagues and institutions who have made this book possible. My first thanks go to the history department at Boston College, where this project initially developed. I am indebted to the generosity, patience and friendship of Peter Weiler who has continued to serve as an assiduous editor, constructive critic and encouraging mentor. I also need to thank Jim Cronin for his abiding interest in this project and, in particular, for his insightful observations about the broader context of my work. In addition, I am appreciative of Kevin O'Neill's support and encouragement, which has endured despite my venture from Irish history. I am also particularly grateful to Robin Fleming for her intellectual and professional guidance throughout my graduate career.

This book has benefited from the generosity of colleagues who have shaped its development in numerous ways, whether from reading parts of the book, offering constructive criticism at conferences, or encouraging the project in its various stages. I am especially grateful to Daniella Sarnoff, John Mackey, Isaac Land, Minnie Sinha, Andrew Lambert, Robert Miller, Bill Fowler, John Hattendorf, Alston Kennerley, Lisa Norling, Ronald Spector, David M. Williams, Eugene Rasor, Leeann Lane, Peter Hansen, Olaf Janzen, Peter Burroughs, Jon Sumida, Mark Hampton, Dick Lourie and Alvin Jackson. In particular, special thanks go to Daniella Sarnoff who not only repeatedly edited this manuscript in its many stages, but also renewed my appreciation for Gilbert and Sullivan. I am also grateful to Susan Pennybacker, my adviser at Trinity College in Hartford, who first encouraged me to pursue graduate work in history and mentored my early development as a historian. While teaching at Emory and Marquette, I was fortunate to have colleagues who were supportive of both my teaching and research, particularly Phil Rosenberg, Judith Miller, Matt Payne and Wally Adamson at Emory and Jim Marten, Lance Grahn and Tim McMahon at Marquette. With Holy Cross as my academic home, I am privileged to work in a department whose members are committed, intellectually serious and always collegial. I am indebted to all my colleagues in the history department for their invaluable intellectual guidance, professional counsel and encouragement of this project, especially Lorraine Altreed, Sahar Bazzaz, Noel Cary, Theresa McBride, Gwenn Miller, Karen Turner and Stephanie Yuhl.

Without the assistance of many institutions, this book would not have been possible. A Boston College Dissertation Fellowship funded my initial research. Support from Holy Cross was instrumental to the completion of this project; a Batchelor Ford Fellowship and a research leave supported the later stages of my research and writing. I am especially grateful to the staff at the following libraries, archives, museums and organisations who shared their expertise with me: in London, the British Library (including the Newspaper Library at Colindale), the Public Record Office, the Imperial War Museum (including the Department of Documents, the Department of Art, the Photograph Archive and the Sound Archive), the National Maritime Museum, the Bodleian Library, the Scouting Association Archive, the archive at Madame Tussaud's and the Union Jack Club; in Portsmouth, the Royal Naval Museum, the Royal Sailors' Rest and the Portsmouth City Records Office; and, in Belfast, the Public Record Office of Northern Ireland. I would like to offer particular thanks to Matthew Sheldon at the Royal Naval Museum, Roderick Suddaby at the Imperial War Museum, Hugh Alexander at the National Archives and Paul Moynihan at the Scout Association. The library staff at Holy Cross, and Boston College have been very helpful, especially Holy Cross's inter-library loan office. I am also grateful for the help of Margaret Nelson and John Buckingham of Holy Cross who provided crucial technological support. I offer my special thanks to the anonymous readers for their useful suggestions and to the editorial staff at Manchester University Press for their patience and guidance in shepherding the publication of this book.

My friends and family deserve my deepest gratitude for their steadfast support and patient encouragement during this long journey. My special thanks go to Elisabeth Wengler, John Malone, Sarah O'Brien Mackey, Tom O'Shea, Anthony Cashman, Jen Terni, Antje Ricken and Matt Hannah. I am indebted to both my family and to my husband's family, who have become as dear to me as my own. Margaret Moore, Deb Bidwell, Gorka Sancho, Ryan and Marcie Demmy-Bidwell have helped in immeasurable ways, whether through the provision of familial comfort, practical advice, or outdoor adventures. Special thanks are due to my English 'cousins' the Feakes (Robert, Turi, Michael, Lynne, Gerry and Sue) who provided welcome diversions during my research trips to London.

As with most projects of any lengthy duration, the process of writing this book witnessed both the challenges and rewards entailed in research and life. While my husband's late mother Patricia Bidwell would have been gratified to witness the completion of this project, she would have been even more delighted by the birth of our first daughter, Astrid, in 2006. In fact, I am indebted to Astrid for her joyful disposition and, even more, her timely arrival, which enabled the completion of the manuscript. I am exceptionally grateful to my parents – my mother, Janet Conley, and my late father Timothy Conley. Apart from instilling in me his love of history, my father shared with me brief stories of his service as a naval corpsman in the Second World War. Since his death, those glimpses have offered me occasion to reflect broadly upon some of the themes of this book – about the relationship of war and society, war's allure, its immediate impact, and its sonorous reverberations. I have profound gratitude for my mother whose sacrifices have supported me in all life's endeavours. In particular, she has more than earned this modest recognition (as well as a rest) for helping with Astrid during those final weeks of manuscript preparation. Finally, I offer my utmost appreciation to my husband Jim Bidwell who has been a partner in this project since its inchoate beginnings at graduate school. Whether in editing successive drafts, giving constructive criticism, offering constant friendship, or providing primary childcare duties in the last months, Jim has made this book possible. For these reasons, I dedicate this book to him.

LIST OF FIGURES

1.1   'Royal Navy Stokers', Cat. No. IWM PST/0805. By
       permission of the Department of Art, Imperial War
       Museum.   46

1.2   'A Sailor and his Lass', *Navy & Army Illustrated* 8,
       No. 127 (8 July 1899). By permission of the Bodleian
       Library, University of Oxford.   51

2.1   'A Home without the Drink', *Ashore and Afloat*, XXV,
       No. 5 (May 1901). By permission of The British Library.
       © British Library Board. All rights reserved (P.P.1138.o). 86

2.2   'A Sad Hobby', *Ashore and Afloat*, XXV, No. 2
       (February 1901). By permission of The British Library.
       © British Library Board. All rights reserved (P.P.1138.o). 88

3.1   A children's board game, 'From Sailor-Boy to Admiral'.
       Courtesy of the Royal Naval Museum, Portsmouth.   108

4.1   Carr & Co. biscuit advertisement, 1899. Ref: Copy
       1/146 (ii), f. 442. By permission of the National
       Archives, UK, and United Biscuites Ltd. © United
       Biscuits (UK) Ltd.   126

4.2   Bovril advertisement, 1902. Ref: Copy 1/195 f. 221.
       By permission of the National Archives, UK, and
       Unilever. © Unilever.   127

4.3   'Making and Mending Clothes on the Lower Deck',
       Navy & Army Illustrated, 27 November 1896, 285,
       NMM 59/332. © National Maritime Museum.   129

4.4   'Gymnastics on board the Battleship *"Howe"*',
       Navy & Army Illustrated, 15 May 1896, 238,
       NMM 59/160. © National Maritime Museum.   143

4.5   Colman's Starch advertisement. By permission
       of Unilever. © Unilever.   146

5.1   Reproduced poster of Robert Baden-Powell's portrait of
       Cornwell, Autumn 1916. By permission of the Scout
       Association.   178

5.2   Reproduced poster of Frank Salisbury's portrait
       of Cornwell, Spring 1917. © Estate of Frank O.
       Salisbury/DACS 2007.   179

LIST OF ABBREVIATIONS

ADM   Admiralty
CDA   Contagious Diseases Act
IML   Imperial Maritime League
IWM   Imperial War Museum
NMM   National Maritime Museum
PRO   Public Record Office (National Archives, UK)
RNTS   Royal Naval Temperance Society
RNVR   Royal Naval Volunteer Reserve
SPCK   Society for the Promotion of Christian Knowledge
SSFA   Soldiers' and Sailors' Family Association
WRNS   Women's Royal Naval Service

INTRODUCTION

Gender, navy and empire

In 1895, Arthur Quiller-Couch asked, 'Can anyone believe that the Empire was won by the sort of drunken, stupid mountebank who pervades the sea songs of that period, bawling for grog or "swizzy", talking rubbish about Poll, Sue and Nancy, and even greater rubbish about marling spikes and maintopbraces?'[1] What disturbed Quiller-Couch, the editor of *Story of the Sea* and the *Oxford Book of English Verse*, was the incongruity between empire building and the alleged buffoonery of the sailor. In arguing that the British naval man was no caricature of the 'Jolly Jack Tar', 'Q.', as Quiller-Couch signed his work, recognised the centrality of naval manliness to both the success of the navy and the expansion of the empire. For 'Q.', Victorian naval seamen had little in common with the imagined sailors of earlier ballads. His query points to the interconnectedness of empire, naval manhood and British society that is the focus of this book. Its aim is to uncover how naval manhood came to be aligned with imperial manliness by studying the relationship between navy, empire and society from the Victorian period through the years leading up to the First World War.

In *The Wooden World: An Anatomy of the Georgian Navy*, Nicholas Rodger argues that the eighteenth-century public image of Jack Tar was of the 'sailor on a run ashore, probably drunk and riotous'.[2] In depictions from the eighteenth and early nineteenth centuries, popular representations of sailors noted the disjuncture between the sailor's character afloat and ashore. While the sailor might be brave and heroic at sea and praised for being a 'heart of oak', William Boyce's song from 1759, according to Henry Fielding, the eighteenth-century writer, 'All these good qualities, however, they always leave behind them on shipboard: the sailor out of water is, indeed, as wretched an animal as the fish out of water'.[3]

In reality, such portraits were exaggerations of sailors' lives afloat and ashore. Personnel conditions rather than the sailor's innate

[1]

criminality best accounted for any lapses of disorderly behaviour by naval men in port. Since naval captains rarely granted leave to their crews, naval men spent long periods at sea without contact with women or home society. Port towns, whether in Britain or across the globe, were sites where young seamen enjoyed freedom from ship's discipline and, being recently paid, released themselves to the 'pleasures' of the town. Although such incidents occurred irregularly in their individual careers, seamen were heralded in ballads for their lust for women and their unquenchable thirst for grog.[4] Because they spent their time in the homosocial world of the all-male navy and their money on such ephemeral pleasures, seamen were depicted as social dangers who promoted industries of 'sin and vice' in port towns like Portsmouth and Plymouth.

As a result, 'Jack in Port' was feared as a disruptive influence, a drunken carouser and a sexual menace. Within popular depictions, the sailor's rugged manhood, which could be unleashed effectively aboard ship, betrayed him ashore since his rough temperament clashed with the mores of the mainland. According to Rear-Admiral W. Edward Parry, the Arctic explorer, the naval man ashore was 'a slave to drunkenness and every other sensual passion which tends to degrade and defile the body and to destroy the soul; rushing headlong into the wildest excesses, abandoning himself to the indulgence of every sin; he became an easy prey to the vilest of both sexes, who are always lying in wait to pounce upon the warm-hearted and unguarded sailor'.[5] His unrefined language, his flights to violence, his rootlessness and his strong passions for women and drink characterised the sailor of ballad, burlesque and legend as a social danger and deviant ashore.

Although the disruptive sailor was certainly a commonplace image, by the late eighteenth century, there were competing visions of naval manhood. State and pronatalist interests promoted naval domesticity by encouraging sailors to marry, in the hope that it would raise the national birthrate, curb incidents of venereal disease and produce what eighteenth-century maritime philanthropist Jonas Hanway coined a 'race of seamen' able to defend wartime Britain.[6] In 1756, at the start of the Seven Years War, Hanway established the Marine Society, which trained orphaned or destitute boys for merchant and naval service, in order to secure more naval recruits for active service. These practical goals were infused with the spiritual and patriotic aims of redeeming both men and the nation: 'If we instruct these young persons in the fear of God and at the same time teach their hands to war and their fingers to fight in the cause of their country, in the cause of real and substantial virtue, we may hope such a conduct will draw down the mercies of heaven on this nation'.[7]

By the early nineteenth century there were signs that the sailor's image ashore had improved. Margarette Lincoln has argued that the romanticisation of the domestic attachments of sailors in the post-Napoleonic era perhaps responded to the perception that they posed a 'threat to social order on land', so that sailors were 'increasingly represented in prints, ballads and on chinaware, as faithful to their loved one at home'.[8] While married seamen only represented approximately 25 per cent of the Georgian fleet, all seamen could cherish the home through their familial attachments to sisters and mothers.[9] Women's longing for their sons, brothers and husbands thus helped to produce sympathetic depictions of the sailor as a figure longing for home and family. In addition, sailors like John Bechervaise began to defend the character of the 'British sailor' arguing that they were often models of respectable behaviour.[10] Although not by design, national concerns and familial interests worked concurrently to produce a more domestic vision of naval manhood aligned to the values of the mainland and the needs of the empire.

By the mid-nineteenth century, the process of taming the perceived deviance of the sailor was by no means complete. Popular allusions to the sailor's domesticity had increased by the post-Napoleonic period, but it was the experience of empire, the far reach of Victorian domestic ideology and the transformation of the mid-nineteenth-century navy that led to the dramatic refashioning of naval manhood by the late-Victorian period. By the late nineteenth century, popular depictions no longer cast naval men in such dichotomous terms as heroes afloat and deviants ashore. Portrayals of naval manhood were not simply characterised by flights to excess as was typical of late eighteenth-century imagery – to women, to drink, or to violence – rather representations of naval manhood, both afloat and ashore, began to assert a cohesive masculinity that was endowed with self-restraint, respectability and bravery.

While the men of the Royal Navy extended and defended the empire, representations of naval men increasingly reflected and informed British masculine ideals in Victorian and Edwardian Britain. Popular imagery cast naval men as symbols of respectable British manhood celebrating their duty to nation and empire and their devotion to the family. The construction of the naval man's image as both patriotic defender and dutiful husband and father stood in sharp contrast to the image of the brave but bawdy tar of the Georgian navy whose bravery afloat was only matched by his licentiousness ashore. Even the sailor afloat was lauded for his skills as a 'handy man' – as much at ease sailing, coaling and fighting as cooking, cleaning and mending. A historical examination of sailors' domesticity afloat disrupts the neat expectations of public and private spheres as masculine and feminine spaces and bolsters Anne McClintock's claims of a distinctive 'imperial domesticity' marked as 'a domesticity without women'.[11] The transformation of the image of 'Jack Tar' into a respectable symbol of empire was not simply the exchange of one stereotype for another; doubtless many Britons were still entertained by the rollicking image of the Jolly Jack Tar at the turn of the century, but now these representations faced the proliferation of positive depictions of naval manhood that were increasingly aligned to imperial masculine ideals.

One should wonder why this period effected such a transformation in depicting naval manhood. The answer lies partly in understanding the import of gender to the social, economic and political order. Like other historians of gender, I argue that masculinity, like femininity, was neither natural nor innate but was a social construction. As R. W. Connell has noted, 'gender is not fixed in advance of social interaction, but is constructed in interaction'.[12] The specific meanings of masculinity and manhood in nineteenth-century imperial Britain were changeable, multiple, potentially contradictory, and always dependent upon specific historical contexts.[13] While this book concentrates primarily on depictions of naval manhood in Victorian and Edwardian Britain, its representations clearly shifted before and after this period.[14]

Portrayals of naval men were not static but were cultural creations that interacted, reflected and responded to a variety of different contexts, underscoring how domestic concerns and imperial experiences shaped representations of British manhood.[15] To understand how naval manhood was refashioned, we need to examine the historical context of intense political, social and cultural changes in Victorian and Edwardian Britain. A host of conditions arising from imperial exigencies, charitable missions, naval reforms, political strategies and an emergent mass market provided crucial settings that refashioned naval manhood over the course of the late 1800s and early 1900s.

In particular, the changing nature of imperialism, marked by territorial expansion and justified by social Darwinist rhetoric and challenges from France, Russia and Germany to Britain's industrial, commercial and imperial dominance, enhanced the navy's role as the key protector of British interests at home and abroad. Muriel Chamberlain's admission that the navy's importance 'to British policy throughout the nineteenth century can hardly be overstressed' serves as a starting point to consider the ways in which the navy informed many different aspects of British society during the Age of Empire.[16] The promulgation of Christian militarism in the Victorian period contributed both to the popularisation of army and navy and to the addition of new models of manhood that emphasised Christian sensibilities, self-control and duty. Naval expansion during the late-Victorian period as well as the implementation of far-reaching personnel reforms improved the reputation of the navy and the status of its men. As a consequence of widespread criticism about Britain's military performance in the Boer War, national and imperial identities became even more sharply aligned to Britain's naval heritage. By the Edwardian age, the popular image of the naval man came to symbolise the strength of the navy, the stability of Britain and the health of the British empire. During the First World War, despite the unexpected subordination of naval warfare to land combat, popular celebrations of naval manhood offered respite from the challenges that trench warfare posed to romanticised visions of heroic manhood.

A close examination of naval manhood during the height of British empire provides a useful context to understand the relationship between British and imperial identities, militarism and masculinity. Cast in the similar rhetoric of duty, heroism and adventure, empire and manhood were concomitant pursuits achieved most gloriously in battle. Celebrations of militaristic definitions of manhood came to the fore at the moment that imperial expansion captured the public imagination.[17] Historians like Michael Paris have revealed the extent to which Victorian and Edwardian Britain were consumed by a martial spirit and how this manifested itself in the promulgation of a masculine warrior ideal.[18] In particular, studies have focused upon the increased popularity of the Tommy Atkins figure and the improved reputation of the British army in late-Victorian Britain.[19] To what extent was this martial spirit embodied by a reformed image of the Jack Tar?

By the late-Victorian period, with greater national prominence given to the navy's role in securing empire, naval men came to be increasingly represented within this nationalist discourse not only as defenders of British interests at home and abroad but also as exemplars of Britishness and manliness. By the late nineteenth century, naval manhood, characterised by military sacrifice and masculine prowess, would reflect and inform British and imperial masculine ideals. Empire and war were both sites that influenced, and were influenced by, the construction of naval manhood. As Connell has argued, 'masculinities are not only shaped by the process of imperial expansion, they are active in the process and help to shape it'.[20] As this book demonstrates, the circulation of stalwart portrayals of naval manhood assisted the Admiralty in recruiting more men, philanthropists in spreading a national temperance movement and navalists in lobbying for higher naval budgets. The alignment of naval manhood with British masculine ideals promoted social acceptance of both war and empire and prepared Britain's youth to sacrifice themselves for imperial ideals.

Public depictions of naval men as emblems of national, naval and imperial strength were only one component of a panorama of military, imperial and royal symbols that were dispersed throughout Britain and the Empire in ritualistic displays, exhibitions and consumer spectacles.[21] Late-Victorian and Edwardian celebrations of the Royal Navy intensified in popularity as marked by the frequency of, and public attendance at, fleet reviews, naval exhibitions and launches of warships.[22] Representations of British bluejackets, like those of Britannia and Tommy Atkins, projected the strength of the British empire through pageantry and spectacle. Naval races between Britain and foreign nations, increased fears of invasion after the 1880s, and heightened imperial anxieties over Britain's performance in the Boer War not only led to ever-increasing naval estimates but also contributed to the diffusion of representations of the brave, dauntless, dutiful British bluejacket within advertisements, song, boys' stories and exhibitions. Imperial exploits often found their way into songs such as 'The Gallant Blue Jackets of England', which celebrated the navy's bombardment of Alexandria in 1882.[23] These late-Victorian popular songs also increasingly heralded sailors en masse rather than treating them as individual subjects as previous generations of sea songs had done.[24]

By highlighting the martial and imperial influences upon constructions of gender, this book brings new relevance to Joan Scott's now canonical observation that concerns about social and political issues displace themselves onto concerns about gender.[25] This martial spirit, which elevated naval manhood, did not necessarily reflect confidence in the empire but rather signalled imperial anxiety and disunity within British society. In fact, historians such as Catherine Hall, Philippa Levine and Kathleen Wilson have argued that a gendered analysis of empire reveals the uncertainty of imperial control.[26] While hardy and healthy patriotic representations of naval men, who were ever ready to protect Britain and its empire, projected an image of the inviolability of Britain's strength, they also revealed popular anxieties about the vulnerability of Britain's naval superiority, the unity of its empire and the permanence of its status as an industrial, imperial and world power.

Celebrations of naval power like naval reviews and launches of warships increasingly emphasised the Britishness of the navy by the turn of the century. Jan Rüger has argued that by the twentieth century the navy had come to represent imperial unity as politicians attempted to diffuse competing 'subnational' identities that challenged the empire, like Irishness during the conflict over Home Rule.[27] Although the navy could simultaneously be considered both 'British' and 'English' within cultural discourse, the Admiralty and Parliament consciously worked to make the navy more appealing to a wider voting British public in the United Kingdom.[28]

Such debates about the status of British bluejackets were marked by similar uncertainty and fluidity. As crowds in music halls marked the Diamond Jubilee by singing Felix McGlennon's popular 'Sons of the Sea', they heralded naval sailors who were 'All British born!' and who were 'Boys of the bulldog breed/Who made old England's name'.[29] While the conflation between the British and English character of the navy and its men was increasingly challenged in public discourse, there was no easy resolution – references heralding British bluejackets like Thomas Campbell's 'Mariners of England' abounded.[30]

Determining the actual geographic composition of naval ratings (sailors of non-commissioned rank) in late-Victorian and Edwardian Britain is an even more difficult undertaking. Although the navy increasingly drew recruits from the industrial centres of England, from Scotland and from Ireland with the expansion of the fleet and changes in technology, uncovering those numbers is a challenge of naval research.[31] While 20 per cent of Britain's merchant marine was born outside the confines of the United Kingdom, by the 1890s, the Royal Navy was becoming more 'British' with the introduction of continuous service. Formally, the Royal Navy prohibited the entry of 'foreigners' into naval ranks without the sanction of the Admiralty at home or commanders-in-chief abroad. In practice, when ships docked in stations across the empire, supernumeraries of African, Indian, Asian and the West Indian descent were added to ship's complement to serve in a variety of positions from skilled seamen, carpenters, artificers, servants and coalers.[32]

Historians have noted both how the British army rose in popularity and how gender ideals were infused with a martial spirit in late-Victorian Britain, yet few studies of this period have differentiated this imperial manliness by class.[33] And many of these important studies of late-Victorian British masculinities have focused on constructions of middle-class and elite manhood.[34] For example, J. A. Mangan has argued that the culture of New Imperialism, fuelled by rising militarism, helped to breed the 'cultural creation of a self-sacrificial warrior – an imperial elite', 'on the public school playing fields of the privileged'.[35] Whether on the playing field, in the public-school classroom, or at university, young privileged Britons were trained to assume the mantle of imperial manhood. Heroic accounts of empire targeted middle-class readers and celebrated the bravery, duty and sacrifice of subalterns and officers on the battlefield. Yet as Kelly Boyd has shown, such popular heroic accounts of manliness were increasingly democratised within late-Victorian boys' story papers with the expansion of a working-class readership that resulted from rising literacy rates, educational reforms and cheaper publishing costs. The intent of this book is to shed light upon social and cultural constructions of working-class rather than elite masculinities by focusing on portrayals of non-commissioned naval men, the 'lower deck', rather than naval officers. While it would be worthwhile to uncover 'what it meant to be a sailor' during this period, it would be difficult to gauge either how naval men made sense of popular representations of naval manhood or how these images might have informed their own gendered identities.[36] What is clear is that naval men had limited agency in producing or countering these images within popular culture, especially given that the Queen's Regulations forbade naval personnel to speak publicly about naval affairs.[37] For the most part, these images still remained the domain of elites who controlled popular discourse produced within press, literature and advertisements. By the end of the century, non-commissioned naval men would find more opportunities to articulate their own interests but the problems of censorship and media access continued to stifle naval men's voices.

Although popular culture was saturated with representations of this new naval manhood, a development that suggests both the popularity of the navy and its sailors, it is difficult for the historian to determine what the public knew and felt about the navy and its empire. Both the pioneering work of John MacKenzie and the studies of the 'new imperial history' have demonstrated convincingly the imperial reach upon domestic Britain.[38] Andrew Thompson's recent study of empire's impact on modern Britain historicises the complex and contradictory ways that empire shaped British identities, offering sound counterargument to Bernard Porter's recent polemic against imperial social formation.[39] Like the empire, the navy represented a world seemingly inaccessible to most of the public, but popular and political discourse brought the navy closer to home. By the late nineteenth century, revolutions in printing, a cheaper press and rising literacy rates helped to produce entertainments, publications and advertisements that reached out to a mass audience and informed the public about the navy.[40]

While it is difficult for the historian to evaluate what individuals read or bought, never mind what they believed (especially in the days before polls), there can be little doubt that these various cultural vehicles – whether it be boys' magazines, advertising, or naval reviews, were popular and persuasive. In fact, Cecil Eby has argued that for English youth growing up in the late-Victorian period, 'infatuation' with empire and war 'was as natural as breathing'.[41] The ubiquity of the sailor suit as typical children's dress (not only in Britain but in Europe and the United States) attested to the popularity of all things naval in Victorian Britain and marked how the sailor's image had become domesticated for mass consumption.[42] The (more than) two million spectators who attended the 1891 Royal Naval Exhibition at Chelsea affirmed the popularity of the navy for the exhibition's planning committee. Through the films of Alfred West, Pathé Frères and Eclair Film, pictures of naval subjects and reviews reached an audience in the millions across the empire by the early twentieth century.[43] The *Daily Telegraph* heralded Alfred West's 'Our Navy', an animated picture show, as an 'effective recruiting agency' as it travelled across the country illustrating the training of young naval recruits who had 'their muscles strengthened and developed, their nerves tested and tempered and ... fitted physically, mentally and educationally for their duties'.[44] George Orwell remembered the Edwardian years which 'were the great days of the navy's popularity. Small boys wore sailor suits and everyone belonged to something called the Navy League and had a bronze medal which cost a shilling and the popular slogan was "We want eight (dreadnoughts) and we won't wait!" '[45] In fact, Orwell was no exception, joining the Navy League at seven and wearing 'a sailor suit with HMS *Invincible* on my cap'.[46]

Looking back on their reasons for joining the navy, sailors themselves recalled the impact of popular imperialism and the longstanding allure of the sea. One naval rating, James Cox, who grew up in London and whose father was a grocer, joined the navy in 1900 for a variety of reasons, but he acknowledged the influence of literature, 'And of course I used to read the *Boys' Friend, Boy's Own Paper, Union Jack* and *Chums* and all those very romantic boys' books which were sold in those days for halfpenny or a penny ... I wanted to lead a life of adventure'.[47] 'An urge for the sea' and posters like 'Join the Navy, See the World' led Albert Heron to join the navy as a boy in 1918.[48] Naval recruiters capitalised on impressionistic young boys captivated by the 'free spirit' of the sailor. Sam Noble, an able seaman from Dundee, recalled that when he joined in 1875, the recruiting sergeant had drawn a picture of the sea that was hard to resist, 'how I should have nothing to do but sit and let the wind blow me along ... seeing the world the while and meeting and chatting with princesses and all the beautiful ladies of other lands'.[49] Although the realities of shipboard life and discipline most likely cured men of romantic delusions, memoirs from the period, which often chronicled their travels across the globe, suggest that sailors retained their wanderlust.[50]

[9]

In light of the navy's popularity, its role in the expansion and maintenance of empire and its status as an all-male institution, the late-Victorian and Edwardian navy offers an ideal opportunity to interrogate the masculine nature of the British imperial project. While historians have increasingly employed gender as a central category to analyse and illuminate the history of the British empire, British naval history has escaped close gendered scrutiny. While informing European definitions of civilisation and barbarism, gender helped to distinguish between coloniser and colonised, to justify imperial rule and to order the imperial structures of power. For example, mid-century perceptions of the unrestrained masculinity of imperial pioneers led Britons to introduce programmes to transport British women to domesticate white settler areas and introduce a familiar and familial domestic order.[51] Similarly, the perceived licentiousness of naval manhood became increasingly incompatible with the rhetoric of civilising empire by mid-century and sailors became renewed objects of concern for philanthropists and missionaries.

A gendered study of navy and society shows just how enmeshed late-Victorian and Edwardian ideals of masculinity were with martial and naval concerns. Yet, few of the valuable social histories of the navy have even attempted to detail the relationship between navy and society.[52] There are signs of hope. In her examination of naval life in Georgian Britain, Margarette Lincoln's *Representing the Royal Navy* offers a good example of how to approach a social and cultural history of the navy and places the navy as squarely important to British domestic politics and society.[53] Jan Rüger has demonstrated the cultural and political significance of the British and German fleets to their respective societies in his comparative study, *The Great Naval Game: Britain and Germany in the Age of Empire*.[54]

Most work that examines the relationship between the military, imperialism and society focuses upon public attitudes towards the British army rather than the navy. A wealth of scholarship has shown how popular representations and public attitudes towards the British army improved over the course of the nineteenth century.[55] While the late eighteenth-century army was viewed by contemporaries as an 'unpopular excrescence', within a hundred years, 'the reputation of the military in Britain was transformed', according to John MacKenzie.[56] In particular, Olive Anderson's work has shown how the combination of the Crimean War and the attempted Christianisation of the military by evangelical organisations recast the army's public image as a venerable heroic service.[57] Others have argued how imperial conquest, Social Darwinism and imperial instabilities like the Indian Mutiny of 1857 or the Jamaican revolt of 1865 not only contributed to the expansion of the military but also romanticised the British army as a distant force justified by a moral imperial mission.[58] By focusing upon the navy, *Jack Tar to Union Jack* makes visible the navy's long-standing influence upon British domestic and imperial culture and, in turn, reveals further contours in the militarisation of pre-war Britain.

In his introduction to *Popular Imperialism and the Military*, John MacKenzie has asserted that the image of the British soldier 'came to rival, even overtake, the reputation of the naval "Jack Tar" in the popular imagination'.[59] Similarly, Jeffrey Richards has focused his attention on the dynamic popularity of 'Tommy Atkins' in late-Victorian Britain. In addition, Richards has argued that the eighteenth-century portrayal of Jack Tar, which depicted a 'robust and down-to-earth Englishness' marked by courage, simplicity and prodigality, remained ever popular and unchanged throughout the nineteenth century.[60] Both MacKenzie and Richards, who have provided insightful work on the way the image of the army was culturally constructed, have overlooked the possibility that the Jack Tar stereotype could also be recast within late-Victorian British society.

Nearly forty years ago, American social historian Jesse Lemisch issued an entreaty to historians to 'do better than these [Jack Tar] stereotypes' and opened up a whole field of history devoted to understanding the experiences of mariners and their roles within wider domestic, economic and political contexts. Lemisch was among the first historians not only to argue that common seamen were worthy of serious study but also to recognise that the image of 'Jack Tar' had distorted the way that social maritime history had been written.[61] Colin Howell and Richard Twomey have argued that the 'concept of "Jack Tar" concealed as much as it disclosed'.[62] In a study of merchant labour, Valerie Burton recognised that the 'Jack Tar' stereotype was 'a projection of seafaring life half-glimpsed and filtered through a myriad of prejudices'.[63] Now that maritime historians have begun to study sailors in earnest, the debate is now to determine the extent to which Atlantic seafaring shaped a distinct maritime culture, community and consciousness at any particular period.[64] *Jack Tar to Union Jack*, it should be confessed, is not a social history of the lives of the non-commissioned men who formed the lower deck of the navy, but more a cultural history seeking to explain how representations of their manhood were imbricated in larger narratives of naval and imperial manhood. This book seeks to lay bare the distortion, concealment and filters that produced and disseminated the different iterations of 'Jack Tar' within late-Victorian and Edwardian Britain and to reveal the contested nature of constructing and reforming 'Jack Tar'.

To chart the complex process of constructing naval masculinities, the book is divided into five main chapters that explore the historical refashioning of naval manhood. Chapter 1, 'Imperial challenges and the modernisation of the fleet', sets the foundation for the book, explaining how imperial challenges, technological changes and domestic pressures transformed the navy and naval service from the wake of the Crimean War to the First World War. The consequent expansion of the British navy promoted the professional development of non-commissioned naval personnel. In part, it is argued that the refashioning of naval manhood was contingent upon the transformation of the navy both in terms of its structural reforms and its diplomatic, strategic and imperial roles. While new portrayals of naval manhood served naval recruiting efforts, the navy was not alone responsible for the emergence of more positive depictions of the bluejacket but it was crucial in making that reconstruction possible.

Chapters 2–5 follow a chronological and thematic order that explore the influence of domesticity, class, empire and war upon naval manhood. Chapter 2, 'For the good of the boys in blue: philanthropy, Agnes Weston and contested manhood' examines how the Victorian cult of domesticity reached the lower decks of the navy through the ministrations of charitable middle-class women like Agnes Weston, considered by contemporaries to be the navy's equivalent of Florence Nightingale. In particular, the chapter considers how female-run naval philanthropic organisations domesticated the reputation of naval men by refashioning the imagery of the drunken debauched sailor through temperance and evangelical campaigns. By the early twentieth century, naval men attacked the benevolence of women like Weston, arguing that their ministrations reduced them to children who required constant guidance and protection rather than respecting them as imperial defenders, responsible husbands and dutiful fathers. This chapter concludes that the marriage of domestic and martial virtues found best expression in this philanthropic discourse, whether for reformers to justify their campaigns or for sailors to defend themselves.

Chapter 3, 'From powder monkey to admiral: social mobility, heroism and naval manhood', argues that late-Victorian portrayals of naval manhood were preoccupied with class distinctions that both elided realities of class tensions and affirmed the patrilineal nature of manhood, in which birthright assured one's masculine stature. Within a ripening consumer culture, the image of the heroic British bluejacket was widely disseminated in advertisements, theatre, music-hall songs, juvenile literature and imperial ephemera. For example, in popular boys' writer G. A. Henty's *Do Your Duty: With Nelson at Trafalgar*, the heroic actions of Harry Langley, a common sailor's adopted son, save England from defeat at Trafalgar. Rather than attribute Harry's bravery or sense of duty to manly lessons learned during Harry's humble childhood, Henty reveals that Harry's real parents had perished at sea and his father had been a ship's captain. Such depictions of naval manhood revealed that the attainment of proper masculinity was bound by questions of class and patrimony. By seamlessly resolving questions about class and masculinity within the safe confines of the ship, these stories ignored real class obstacles of Victorian society and presented their boy readers with the illusion of a unified egalitarian Britain.

Chapter 4, 'Strong men for a strong navy: naval scares, imperial anxieties and naval manhood', explores how portrayals of naval manhood adapted to the imperial challenges Britain faced by the turn of the century. This chapter argues that Britain's imperial position in the early twentieth century contributed to depictions of a rugged naval manhood. Such emboldened visions of naval manhood grew in stature as Germany's new navy threatened British naval supremacy, the difficulties of fighting the Boer War called into question Britain's imperial future, and fears of racial degeneracy intensified after the publication of the 1902 report of the Interdepartmental Committee on Physical Deterioration. In particular, this chapter reveals how British navalists relied on such depictions of naval manhood as they lobbied both Parliament and the British public to spend more for a stronger navy.

The chapter highlights the writings of Navy League members and writers such as Arnold White, Rudyard Kipling, Frank Bullen and Fred T. Jane, whose writing emphasised the physical prowess and straightforward integrity of British naval men. Their writings not only refashioned naval masculinity but also democratised naval manhood as a model that would protect the health and future of the British empire. The rhetorical strategy of personifying the navy contributed not only to more positive images of naval men within popular culture but also to the passage of exorbitant naval expenditures in the early 1900s and to a climate of militarism within British society.

The final chapter (Chapter 5), 'Lessons of manhood: boyhood, duty and war' considers through a case study whether the experience of the First World War, which transformed so much in British society, resulted in noticeable changes in the representations of naval manhood. The wartime commemoration of Jack Cornwell, a boy seaman whose death at the 1916 Battle of Jutland won him a Victoria Cross, Britain's highest honour for bravery, offers a telling and complex finale to this larger project. In a war of devastating losses, the commemoration of Cornwell reinforced Victorian masculine ideals that emphasised duty, obedience and passive sacrifice rather than Edwardian constructions of a rugged manhood defined by action, strength and individualism. Although the battle of Jutland did not prove to be that war's Trafalgar as hoped for by navalists, admirals and politicians found in Jutland their Nelson – resurrected as boy seaman Cornwell, who had answered his call to duty. While the reality of trench warfare was irreconcilable with the rhetoric of rugged manly heroism, the celebration of British naval manhood as embodied by Jack Cornwell's dutiful sacrifice served to reinvigorate the wartime British manly ideal.

Notes

1 Arthur Quiller Couch ['Q.', pseud.], ed., *Story of the Sea*, vol. 1 (London: Cassell, 1895), 743. 'Q.' also served as the assistant editor of the liberal weekly *The Speaker* between 1890 and 1899.
2 N. A. M. Rodger, *The Wooden World: An Anatomy of the Georgian Navy* (Annapolis, Md.: Naval Institute Press, 1986), 15.
3 C. H. Firth, *Naval Songs and Ballads* (London: Navy Records Society, 1908), 220; *The New Oxford History of Music: The Age of Enlightenment, 1745–1790*, ed. Egon Wellesz and Frederick Sternfeld (London: Oxford University Press, 1973); Michael Lewis, *The Navy of Britain: A Historical Portrait* (London: George Allen & Unwin, Ltd, 1949), 297.
4 Songs like 'A Jolly Jack Tar', 'The Seamen's Wives' Vindication', 'Saylors for my Money' and 'Jack's Disaster' all describe sailors' celebrated penchant for carousing. See Firth, *Naval Songs and Ballads*, and John Ashton, ed., *Real Sailor-Songs* (London: Leadenhall Press, 1891). See also Terence M. Freeman, *Dramatic Representations of British Soldiers and Sailors on the London Stage, 1660–1800: Britons, Strike Home* (Lewiston, NY: Edwin Mellen Press, 1995).
5 W. H. G. Kingston, *Popular History of the British Navy from the Earliest Times to the Present* (London: Gall and Inglis, 1876), 465.
6 Isaac Land, 'Domesticating the Maritime: Culture, Masculinity and Empire in Britain, 1770–1820' (unpublished dissertation, University of Michigan, 1999), 114; Donna Andrew, *Philanthropy and Police: London Charity in the Eighteenth Century* (Princeton: Princeton University Press, 1989).
7 Jonas Hanway, *Letter to the Marine Society* (2nd edition, 1758), 4, quoted in Linda Colley, *Britons: Forging the Nation 1707–1837* (New Haven: Yale University Press, 1992), 91.
8 Margarette Lincoln, *Representing the Royal Navy, British Sea Power, 1750–1815* (Aldershot: Ashgate, 2002), 32; Land, 'Domesticating the Maritime', 102; James Stephen Taylor, *Jonas Hanway: Founder of the Marine Society, Charity and Policy in Eighteenth-century Britain* (London: Scolar, 1985).
9 Lincoln, *Representing the Royal Navy*, 147.
10 John Bechervaise, *Thirty-Six Years of a Seafaring Life by an Old Quarter Master* (Portsea: W. Woodward, 1839), 336. See also Isaac Land, 'The Many-tongued Hydra: Sea Talk, Maritime Culture and Atlantic Identities', *Journal of American Culture* 25, 3–4 (September 2002), 412–17.
11 Anne McClintock, *Imperial Leather: Race, Gender and Sexuality in the Colonial Contest* (New York: Routledge, 1995), 32. For discussion of domesticity and manhood, see John Tosh, *A Man's Place: Masculinity and the Middle-Class Home in Victorian England* (New Haven: Yale University Press, 1999).
12 R. W. Connell, *Masculinities* (Berkeley: University of California Press, 2005), 35.
13 George L. Mosse, *Nationalism and Sexuality: Respectability and Abnormal Sexuality in Modern Europe* (New York: Howard Fertig, 1985); J. A. Mangan and James Walvin, eds, *Manliness and Morality: Middle-Class Masculinity in Britain and*

America, 1800–1940 (New York: St Martin's Press, 1987), 3; Mrinalini Sinha, *Colonial Masculinity: The 'Manly Englishman' and the 'Effeminate Bengali' in the Late Nineteenth Century* (Manchester: Manchester University Press, 1995), 7–8; John Tosh, *Manliness and Masculinities in Nineteenth-Century Britain: Essays on Gender, Family and Empire* (Harlow, England: Pearson Longman, 2005).

14 Lincoln, *Representing the Royal Navy*, 29–31; Quintin Colville, 'Jack Tar and the Gentleman Officer: The Role of Uniform in Shaping the Class- and Gender-Related Identities of British Naval Personnel, 1930–1939', *Transactions of the Royal Historical Society*, 13 (2003), 105–29.

15 Sinha, *Colonial Masculinity*, 7–8; Catherine Hall, *Civilising Subjects: Metropole and Colony in the English Colonial Imagination, 1830–1867* (Chicago: University of Chicago Press, 2002); Philippa Levine, 'Introduction', in *Gender and Empire* (Oxford: Oxford University Press, 2004), 1–13; Angela Woollacott, *Gender and Empire* (Houndmills, Basingstoke: Palgrave Macmillan, 2006), 1–13.

16 Muriel Chamberlain, *'Pax Britannica'? British Foreign Policy, 1789–1914* (London: Longman, 1988), 8.

17 Woollacott, *Gender and Empire*, 11, 76; John Horne, 'Masculinity in politics and war in the age of nation-states and world wars, 1850–1950', in *Masculinities in Politics and War*, ed. Stefan Dudink, Karen Hagemann and John Tosh (Manchester: Manchester University Press, 2004), 22–40.

18 Michael Paris, *Warrior Nation: Images of War in British Popular Culture, 1850–2000* (London: Reaktion Books, 2000), 27–8; Stefan Dudink, Karen Hagemann and John Tosh, eds, *Masculinities in Politics and War*; Graham Dawson, *Soldier Heroes: British Adventure, Empire and the Imagining of Masculinities* (London: Routledge, 1994); Cecil D. Eby, *The Road to Armageddon: The Martial Spirit in English Popular Literature, 1870–1914* (Durham: Duke University Press, 1988).

19 John Peck, *War, the Army and Victorian Literature* (London: Macmillan, 1998); Jeffrey Richards, 'Popular Imperialism and the Image of the Army in Juvenile Literature', in *Popular Imperialism and the Military*, ed. John M. MacKenzie (Manchester: Manchester University Press, 1992), 88.

20 Connell, *Masculinities*, 185.

21 John MacKenzie, *Propaganda and Empire* (Manchester: Manchester University Press, 1985), 7; Eric Hobsbawm and Terence Ranger, eds, *The Invention of Tradition* (Cambridge: Cambridge University Press, 1983); McClintock, *Imperial Leather*.

22 Jan Rüger, 'Nation, Empire and Navy: Identity Politics in the United Kingdom 1887–1914', *Past & Present* 185 (2004), 159–87.

23 John Winton, *Hurrah for the Life of a Sailor: Life on the Lower-Deck of the Victorian Navy* (London: Michael Joseph, 1977), 266–7.

24 Penelope Summerfield, 'The Effingham Arms and the Empire: Deliberate Selection in the Evolution of Music Hall in London', in *Popular Culture and Class Conflict 1590–1914*, ed. Eileen and Stephen Yeo (Sussex: The Harvester Press, 1981), 236.

25 Joan Scott, 'Gender: A Useful Category of Historical Analysis', in *Gender and the Politics of History* (New York: Columbia University Press, 1988), 42–3, 49.

26 Hall, *Civilising Subjects*; Philippa Levine, *Prostitution, Race and Politics: Policing Venereal Disease in the British Empire* (New York: Routledge, 2003); Kathleen Wilson, *The Island Race: Englishness, Empire and Gender in the Eighteenth-Century* (London: Routledge, 2003).

27 Rüger, 'Nation, Empire and Navy', 163.

28 Rüger, 'Nation, Empire and Navy', 167.

29 Felix McGlennon, 'Sons of the Sea', quoted in Penelope Summerfield, 'The Effingham Arms and the Empire', 236. See also Anthony Bennett, 'Music in the Halls', in *Music Hall: Performance and Style*, ed. J. S. Bratton (Milton Keynes: Open University Press, 1986), 8–9.

30 Herbert Hayens, *Ye Mariners of England: A Boy's Book of the Navy* (London: Thomas Nelson and Sons, 1901).

31 Public Record Office, Kew (hereafter PRO), ADM 1/6272, 'Remarks on the Manning'. Apart from occasional references to the recruiting of sailors from the United Kingdom and the colonies, it is difficult to determine the geographical composition of the fleet at any particular time because the statistics are embedded within Admiralty records from recruiting stations, port stations, ship's muster books and naval ratings certificates of service. Michael Lewis has noted in his discussion about assessing the origins of sailors for an earlier period that the problem is a 'surfeit of knowledge' that is 'so overwhelming indeed that to analyse it in tabular form would be a matter, probably, of many years' labour. And it would not repay the doing'. See Michael Lewis, *A Social History of the Navy, 1793–1815* (London: Allen & Unwin, 1960), 81. The historian of the later Victorian period is also faced with a lack of crucial records that would record the background of sailors because most quarterly ledgers (ADM 117), which recorded pay and allotments for all ratings and officers from 1878 were destroyed by fire during the Second World War. However, research that could be done in former imperial ports to study recruiting patterns in the navy might 'pay' in myriad ways. For example, Bob Nicholls has recounted the problem of naval desertion in Australian ports and the attempts by the Admiralty to increase recruitment in Australia by the turn of the century. See Bob Nicholls, '"Sailors to citizens, citizens and sailors, citizens to sailors": Naval men and Australia from 1788–1914', in *The Navy and the Nation: The Influence of the Navy on Modern Australia*, ed. David Stevens and John Reeve (Crows Nest, Australia: Allen & Unwin, 2006), 271–86.

32 *Queen's Regulations and Admiralty Instructions* (London: HMSO, 1879), 91; Rozina Visram, *Ayahs, Lascars and Princes: Indians in Britain, 1700–1947* (London: Pluto Press, 1986), 34–54; Paul Gilroy, *The Black Atlantic: Modernity and Double Consciousness* (Harvard: Harvard University Press, 1993). Sailors' memoirs mention the presence of foreign-born seamen like 'Kroomen' from West Africa, 'Lascars' from India and 'Seedies' from East Africa. See Sam Noble, *Sam Noble, Able Seaman: 'Tween Decks in the Seventies* (New York: Frederick Stokes, 1926), 96–100. More work needs to be done, whether using Admiralty papers, sailors' accounts, or records from port towns, to assess the role of colonial supernumeraries on ship complements. Melvin Hendrix, 'The British Admiralty Records as a Source for African History', *History in Africa* 13 (1986), 161–75.

33 Kelly Boyd, *Manliness and the Boys' Story Paper in Britain: A Cultural History, 1855–1940* (Houndmills, Basingstoke: Palgrave Macmillan, 2003); Patrick F. McDevitt, *May the Best Man Win: Sport, Masculinity and Nationalism in Great Britain and the Empire, 1880–1935* (Houndmills, Basingstoke: Palgrave Macmillan, 2004), 4–6; Levine, *Gender and Empire*, 2. For United States history, see Gail Bederman, *Manliness and Civilization: A Cultural History of Gender and Race in the United States, 1880–1917* (Chicago: University of Chicago Press, 1995), 11.

34 See Mangan and Walvin, *Manliness and Morality*; John Tosh, *A Man's Place: Masculinity and the Middle-Class Home in Victorian England* (New Haven: Yale University Press, 1999); Paul R. Deslandes, *Oxbridge Men: British Masculinity and the Undergraduate Experience, 1850–1920* (Bloomington: Indiana University Press, 2005).

35 J. A. Mangan, 'Duty unto Death: English Masculinity and Militarism in the Age of the New Imperialism', *International Journal of the History of Sport* 12, no. 2 (1995), 12.

36 Sonya Rose, *Limited Livelihoods: Gender and Class in Nineteenth-Century England* (Berkeley: University of California Press, 1992), 18.

37 *Queen's Regulations and Admiralty Instructions* (London: HMSO, 1879), 210.

38 John MacKenzie, ed., *Imperialism and Popular Culture* (Manchester: Manchester University Press, 1986); Hall, *Civilising Subjects*; Antoinette Burton, *At the Heart of the Empire: Indians and the Colonial Encounter in Late-Victorian Britain* (Berkeley: University of California Press, 1998); Sinha, *Colonial Masculinity*, Catherine Hall and Sonya Rose, eds, *At Home with the Empire: Metropolitan Culture and the Imperial World* (Cambridge: Cambridge University Press, 2006).

39 Andrew Thompson, *The Empire Strikes Back? The Impact of Imperialism on Britain from the Mid-Nineteenth Century* (Harlow, England: Pearson Longman, 2005); Bernard Porter, *The Absent-Minded Imperialists: Empire, Society and Culture in Britain* (Oxford: Oxford University Press, 2004).

40 See Kirsten Drotner, *English Children and their Magazines, 1751–1945* (New Haven: Yale University Press, 1988), 80–4; Patrick A. Dunae, 'Boys' literature and the idea of empire, 1870–1914', *Victorian Studies*, 24 (1980); John R. Gillis, *Youth and History: Tradition and Change in European Age Relations* (New York: Academic Press, 1975), 95–131.

41 Eby, *The Road to Armageddon*, 3.

42 Sailor suits for children rose in popularity after a painting by Franz Xaver Winterhalter in 1846 depicted future King Edward in sailor dress, a costume that he wore on the royal yacht that summer. See Phillis Cunningham and Anne Buck, *Children's Costume in England from the Fourteenth to the end of the Nineteenth Century* (London: Adam and Charles Black, 1965), 182 and Alison Lurie, *The Language of Clothes* (New York: Random House, 2000), 41–2.

43 Rüger, 'Nation, Empire and Navy', 166.

44 *Daily Telegraph*, 24 December 1902, 4.

45 George Orwell, 'Review of Penguin Books', *New English Weekly*, 5 March 1936, in *The Collected Essays, Journalism and Letters of George Orwell: An Age Like this, 1920–1940*, vol.1, ed. Sonia Orwell and Ian Angus (New York: Harcourt, Brace and World, 1968), 166–7. Orwell evaluated the persuasive power of fiction: 'To what extent people draw their ideas from fiction is disputable. Personally I believe that most people are influenced far more than they would care to admit by novels, serial stories, films and so forth, and that from this point of view the worst books are often the most important, because they are usually the ones that are read earliest in life'.

46 Orwell, 'Review of Penguin Books', 166–7.

47 James George Cox, 000728/21, Oral History Recordings: Lower Deck, 1910–1922, Department of Sound Records, Imperial War Museum. Drotner, *English Children and their Magazines*, 148–9, 179; J. S. Bratton, *The Impact of Victorian Children's Fiction* (London: Croom Helm, 1981), 134; David Vincent, 'The Domestic and the Official Curriculum in Nineteenth-Century England', in *Opening the Nursery Door: Reading, Writing and Childhood, 1600–1900*, ed. Mary Hilton, Morag Styles and Victor Watson (London: Routledge, 1997), 161.

48 Albert A. Heron, Leading Seamen, 000681/20, Oral History Recordings: Lower Deck, 1910–1922, Department of Sound Records, Imperial War Museum.

49 Noble, *Sam Noble*, 3.

50 Published memoirs and unpublished journals of non-commissioned men who served the late-Victorian and Edwardian periods featured descriptions of their travels across the globe, sharing anecdotes about geography, climate, culture, flora and fauna. Although these writings are great resources, there are too few sources on which to base a social study. For examples of published memoirs, see Patrick Riley, *Memories of a Blue-Jacket, 1872–1918* (London: Sampson Low, Marston: 1927); Noble, *Sam Noble*; Henry Capper, *Aft-from the Hawsehole: Sixty-Two Years of Sailors' Evolution* (London: Faber & Gwyer, 1927). Men's shipboard logs structured themselves around their ship's voyages and ports of call; for examples covering the period, see diaries held at the Royal Naval Museum of William Joyce [98 45/88 (1)], Herbert Arthur Lynch, [74/355/85], Robert Percival [120/1995 9.2.1 19156].

51 Philippa Levine, 'Sexuality, Gender and Empire', in *Gender and Empire*, 137; A. James Hammerton, 'Gender and Migration', in *Gender and Empire*, 158–61.

52 Christopher McKee, *Sober Men and True: Sailor Lives in the Royal Navy, 1900–1945* (Cambridge: Harvard University Press, 2002); Anthony Carew, *The Lower Deck of the Royal Navy, 1900–1939* (Manchester: Manchester University Press, 1981); Henry Baynham, *Men from the Dreadnoughts* (London: Hutchinson, 1976); Eugene Rasor, *Reform in the Royal Navy: A Social History of the Lower Deck,*

1850–1880 (Hamden, Conn.: Archon Books, 1976); Michael Lewis, *The Navy in Transition, 1814–1864: A Social History* (London: Hodder & Stoughton, 1965); and N. A. M. Rodger, *The Wooden World: An Anatomy of the Georgian Navy* (Annapolis, Md.: Naval Institute Press, 1986).

53 Lincoln, *Representing the Royal Navy*. For another example of an integrative study examining the relationship between navy and society, see Tim Jenks, *Naval Engagements: Patriotism, Cultural Politics and the Royal Navy 1793–1815* (Oxford: Oxford University Press, 2006).

54 Jan Rüger, *The Great Naval Game: Britain and Germany in the Age of Empire* (Cambridge: Cambridge University Press, 2007).

55 Paris, *Warrior Nation*; Kenneth E. Hendrickson, *Making Saints: Religion and the Public Image of the British Army, 1809–1885* (Madison, NJ: Fairleigh Dickinson University Press, 1998); Peck, *War, the Army and Victorian Literature*; Douglas H. Johnson, 'The death of Gordon: a Victorian myth', *Journal of Imperial and Commonwealth History* 10 (1982), 185–310; Allen J. Frantzen, *Bloody Good: Chivalry, Sacrifice, and the Great War* (Chicago: University of Chicago Press, 2004).

56 John M. MacKenzie, ed., *Popular Imperialism and the Military* (Manchester: Manchester University Press, 1992), 1; Correlli Barnett, *Britain and Her Army, 1509–1970* (New York: William Morrow, 1970), 170.

57 Olive Anderson, 'The Growth of Christian Militarism in mid-Victorian Britain', *English Historical Review* 86 (January 1971), 46–72. Michael Paris has argued that public interest in war and the popularity of the military began much earlier, fostered by fighting wars on foreign soil in the eighteenth century and intensified by the imperial battles of the nineteenth century. See Paris, *Warrior Nation*, 13–48.

58 Jeffrey Richards, 'Popular Imperialism and the Image of the Army in Juvenile Literature', in *Popular Imperialism and the Military*, 84–5; MacKenzie, *Popular Imperialism and the Military*, 12.

59 MacKenzie, *Popular Imperialism and the Military*, 1. It is interesting to note that the 1924 illustration, 'Defenders of the Empire' chosen to accompany the introduction of *Propaganda and Empire* featured a British naval man leading a military parade of soldiers from across the Empire.

60 Jeffrey Richards, 'Popular Imperialism and the Image of the Army in Juvenile Literature', in *Popular Imperialism and the Military*, 88.

61 Jesse Lemisch, 'Jack Tar in the Streets: Merchant Seamen in the Politics of Revolutionary America', *William and Mary Quarterly* 25 (July 1968), 371–407.

62 Colin Howell and Richard J. Twomey, eds, *Jack Tar in History: Essays in the History of Maritime Life and Labour* (Fredericton, New Brunswick: Acadiensis Press, 1991).

63 Valerie Burton, 'The Myth of Bachelor Jack: Masculinity, Patriarchy and Seafaring Labour', in *Jack Tar in History*, ed. Howell and Twomey, 179.

64 Markus Rediker, *Between the Devil and the Deep Blue Sea: Merchant Seamen, Pirates and the Anglo-American Maritime World, 1700–1750* (Cambridge: Cambridge University Press, 1987); Eric Sager, *Seafaring Labour: The Merchant Marine of Atlantic Canada, 1820–1914* (Kingston: McGill-Queen's University Press, 1989); Margaret Creighton and Lisa Norling, eds, *Iron Men, Wooden Women: Gender and Seafaring the Atlantic World, 1700–1920* (Baltimore: Johns Hopkins University Press, 1996); W. Jeffrey Bolster, *Black Jacks: African American Seamen in the Age of Sail* (Cambridge: Harvard University Press, 1997); Marcus Rediker and Peter Linebaugh, *The Many-Headed Hydra: Sailors, Slaves, Commoners and the Hidden History of the Revolutionary Atlantic* (London: Verso, 2000); Isaac Land, 'The Many-tongued Hydra', *Journal of American Culture* 25, 3–4(2002), 412–17.

CHAPTER ONE

Imperial challenges and the modernisation of the fleet

Between 1850 and 1913, the navy almost quadrupled in size, from 39,000 to 146,000 men. British naval expansion during the late nineteenth century resulted from a variety of developments – diplomatic tensions, naval scares, imperial uncertainties, internal domestic pressures and new technologies – which forced the navy to modernise its ships and to professionalise its men. While the dramatic expansion began in the 1880s, significant internal reforms were under way in the 1850s. By the mid-Victorian period, the pressure to achieve a navy that could be mobilised quickly for war resulted in a new personnel system in which men were recruited for long-term service rather than discharged after a ship's commission.[1] The implementation of continuous service and the introduction of a naval uniform in 1857 reinforced the distinctiveness of the naval man and created the 'British Bluejacket'. No longer able to rely upon its older schemes of hire-and-discharge and impressment, the Admiralty was forced to rely on new methods to recruit men and to improve conditions of service in order to retain them. Fiscal constraints and conservatism within the Admiralty, particularly over personnel issues, accounted for the uneven pace of reforms throughout the Victorian period.[2] Yet the reforms transformed the structure and status of naval personnel by the twentieth century, helping to solve the manning question in the late-Victorian and Edwardian navy and to produce a navy with an unprecedented number of trained and qualified men in service by the beginning of the First World War.

This chapter argues that Victorian naval reforms forced the navy to improve lower-deck conditions in order to recruit more men. In many cases, external threats forced the Admiralty to seek and implement innovative solutions in order to acquire and retain vast numbers of qualified naval personnel. By the early 1900s, the lower deck reflected a better educated, trained and disciplined community than those who had served under Nelson. While this chapter does not claim that naval men in the late nineteenth century were really 'sober men and true', like W. S. Gilbert's sailors serving aboard the HMS *Pinafore*, or that representations mimicked the reality of life aboard ship, naval reforms had cast off the possibility that the navy was a prison afloat as contended by Samuel Johnson a century earlier. The chapter argues that these personnel reforms facilitated the professionalisation of the service and the transformation of popular representations of naval manhood.

This chapter also provides a context for the chapters that follow. It explains how and why the navy expanded in the nineteenth century, and then how this expansion affected manpower and personnel reforms. This latter part of the chapter focuses upon the passage of the Continuous Service Act, which effectively introduced a standing navy, the challenges of raising and meeting manning levels by recruiting from the merchant marine, and the training of boys for service. In addition, this chapter examines the rationale and development of lower-deck reforms in pay, pensions and promotions over the course of the late-Victorian and Edwardian period.

The close of the Napoleonic Wars confirmed the might of British seapower and ushered in what has been called the *Pax Britannica*.[3] The end of the Napoleonic wars also meant the demobilising of troops and the decommissioning of ships and men to peace-time levels. Between 1814 and 1818, the number of commissioned ships declined from 713 to 121, and the number of sailors and marines serving in the navy decreased from 140,000 to only 20,000.[4] Clearly a peace-time navy did not require an exorbitant budget to meet wartime demands, but reduced naval estimates could not meet the logistical and strategic needs of a navy poised for war. Rather, the parliamentary reduction of naval estimates reflected national budgetary pressures to reduce the swollen national debt, which had paid for the long years of war.

While the size and finances of the navy diminished in the wake of the Napoleonic Wars, the expectations put upon it had not. The purported *Pax Britannica* existed so long as peace served British interests and so long as these interests went unchallenged by major European powers. But Britain faced numerous challenges to its commercial, diplomatic, and imperial interests in the decades following the Congress of Vienna. In fact, barely a year elapsed in which the British military did not face combat somewhere.[5] Yet, for nearly the next thirty years, naval estimates hovered between £4.4 and £6 million despite the rising costs created by periodic naval engagements, the navy's increasing global presence and the implementation of new ship technologies. In an era of tightening budgets, this meant that the Admiralty had to do more with less.

Between 1819 and the 1850s, the navy was deployed to advance British commercial and imperial interests in the Mediterranean, Latin America, China and Africa. The British navy enjoyed a reputation as an international policeman safeguarding the seas whether by stamping out piracy on the Algerian coast or suppressing the slave trade in the waters off the Atlantic and Indian oceans. Justified by the language of freedom – individual liberty and freedom of the seas – this use of seapower sought to protect British commercial and imperial interests in the Mediterranean and in the southern hemisphere. Although naval efforts at suppressing the African slave trade, a venture that the British had once dominated, had negligible impact on slowing the number of slaves traded, British patrols served as physical reminders of British dominance of the seas. After the Napoleonic Wars, Britain expanded its fleet presence in Africa, in the Mediterranean, in Asia, and in Latin America and the Caribbean. By 1848, the British had 129 warships on foreign stations with only 35 in commission at home.[6] The percentage of ships on foreign stations had risen steadily since the late eighteenth century when only 54 British warships were active on foreign stations. The international presence of the British navy both reflected the absence of any significant European threat to Britain at home and the increasing commitment and ability of the state to protect British commerce as it spread across the globe.

The Mediterranean was arguably the navy's most important station in the wake of the Napoleonic Wars as the British sought to defend their commercial claims to the region and prevent the proliferation of Russian influence in the area. The destruction of the Turkish fleet at Navarino in 1827 was not so much the consequence of British public sympathy with Greek independence nor political disdain for Turkish imperial overreach so much as the reflection of a British desire to prevent the possibility of a Russian Aegean base. For the next thirty years, in an effort to constrain Russian influence, monitor French designs and strengthen British interests, the government repeatedly deployed the navy to aid the Ottoman empire. For example, the British navy's bombardment of Acre in 1840 defended Turkish imperial claims on Syria and Egypt, which had been threatened by Mehemet Ali, and sought to maintain the delicate balance of power, which favoured British commercial and imperial interests in the Mediterranean and in India. The success of the heavy coastal shelling by naval warships at Acre not only led to the defeat of Mehemet Ali but also signalled to the world the capabilities and consequences of British seapower.

By the early 1850s, Britain readied for a Russian war to defend Turkey and ensure Britain's predominance in the region. Despite a marked increase in British naval expenditures in 1851, as Parliament responded to public fears of France's new military and naval capacity under Louis Napoleon, naval expenditures rose dramatically to meet the threat of war. The Admiralty inaugurated a massive shipbuilding programme, accompanied by extensive manning reforms to mobilise a navy to meet the new danger. In 1852, Parliament supported raising manning levels to 45,500, an increase of nearly 6,000 men from the previous year.[7] As the French crisis passed in 1853, war with Russia became imminent and Britain and France became allies, formally declaring war on Russia in March 1854. Britain's past ability to mobilise its fleet for discrete short engagements was challenged by the Crimean War, which was waged on two fronts in the Baltic and Black Seas.[8] The war had tested both navy and army requiring not only naval bombardment and blockades but also military campaigns that engaged British forces for over two years. One of the main consequences of the Treaty of Paris in 1856 was to put an end to Russian hopes in the Mediterranean by forcing its exit from occupied Ottoman territories and declaring the neutrality of the Black Sea. But there was a cost to Britain's victory – the war, with the help of extensive newspaper coverage, had exposed the weakness of its army and the difficulty of mobilising a navy for battle.

Despite its limited resources, the navy also helped to extend British imperial interests in Asia. In China, naval power served as a weapon of foreign policy that advocated military solutions to develop British commercial interests and secure a stable cost-effective informal empire. The coercive force of the navy achieved commercial diplomatic ends during the 'Opium Wars' in the 1840s and 1850s as Britain forced China to open its major ports to trade and to surrender Hong Kong. By the late 1850s, Britain also secured a formal presence in southern Asia. Implementation of formal control of India after the failed 1857 Indian Rebellion also meant that the British navy would now have increasing responsibilities in patrolling the Indian Ocean. Engagements in the Mediterranean, Black Sea and in Chinese waters demonstrate that the so-called *Pax Britannica* was not the result of indifferent lassitude but rather was the consequence of British diplomatic coercion backed by naval engagement. While the navy had continually defended this peace, it had also helped to secure the foundations of an informal and formal British empire.

Despite its increasing significance to Victorian British policy, the navy had not undergone any thorough reform until mid-century. As the responsibilities of the navy had broadened in the forty years after the Napoleonic Wars, technological advances made the modernisation of the British fleet possible, but not certain. In particular, state fiscal constraints slowed the implementation of new technologies. New innovations in screw propulsion, armaments and gunnery were initially developed in the first half of the nineteenth century but their practical application in foreign stations like Africa, China, and the Mediterranean, as well as the competitive pressure from foreign navies including France, Russia and the United States, ultimately determined the extent of their implementation. In particular, the Crimean War was crucial in swaying the Admiralty to modernise its fleet. The war witnessed the success of newer ship technologies like screw propulsion, rifled guns and gunboats. In addition, French naval progress, evident during the war, worried the Admiralty, which feared that a French naval threat would emerge in the wake of Russian hostilities.

Anxiety about French naval advances appeared justified as technological competition between the two navies intensified in the late 1850s. In 1859, France grabbed the headlines with the launch of the 36-gun *Gloire*, the world's first ironclad seagoing ship. The Admiralty had experimented with iron-hulled designs in the 1840s but the shattering of the iron upon a shell's impact had relegated these ships to non-combat duty. The response to the *Gloire*, whose plating still clad a wooden hull, was immediate. Within a year, the Admiralty commissioned Isaac Watts to design the *Warrior*, Britain's first iron-hulled screw-propelled masted warship. The HMS *Warrior*, launched in 1861, was superior in nearly all respects to the *Gloire* and ushered in an era of innovation of ship, armament and gunnery design. With ten new 110-pounder Armstrong rifled breech loaders and twenty-eight 68-pounder smooth-bore guns, the *Warrior* assured Britain's technological superiority over the French.[9] As ever newer technologies superseded older designs, the Admiralty would find itself reinventing its fleet over the next twenty years to be ever faster, stronger and more destructive. By 1869, the Admiralty laid down the first mastless screw ironclad, the HMS *Devastation*, designed for naval warfare in European waters, capable of steaming up to fourteen knots and travelling for long distances. Commissioned in 1871, the *Devastation*, with armour plating a foot thick and buttressed by 18-inches of wooden backing, was notable for its innovations in firepower with twin 12-inch muzzle-loading rifles in turrets located fore and aft on the ship.[10]

The steady integration of new technologies into the fleet also meant that the Admiralty faced new pressures in training its men for a modern navy. Standardised instruction, which began in training hulks in Portsmouth and Plymouth for boys, continued through a seaman's career so that every commissioned ship became 'a training ship'.[11] The ascendancy of steam and steel, signalled by the launch of the *Devastation*, also put additional strains on naval manning since the navy no longer trained seamen to be sailors but to be industrial workers afloat. These new technologies required larger ship complements as greater numbers of men were required to work the engine room and the stoke hold.[12] As a consequence, active personnel during this period increased from 68,000 at the end of the Crimean War to 79,000 in 1860, before declining under financial pressures and manning difficulties to 67,000 in 1867.[13]

The decision to embrace new technologies not only committed the British navy to redesign its fleet but also made its older ships redundant, leading to the criticism that foreign powers could catch up with British designs and threaten its naval supremacy. Technological innovation by Russian and French navies, in particular, helped to fuel British naval and invasion scares in the late 1850s and early 1860s. Even the First Lord of the Admiralty, perhaps posturing for the need for greater estimates, admitted to Parliament that the navy was not 'in a proper and adequate state for the defence of our coasts'.[14] By 1859, French naval building and rumours that a 'steam bridge' would ferry French troops across the Channel to launch an invasion led Lord Palmerston, as Prime Minister, to allocate £9 million on British and Irish coastal fortifications.[15]

During the last third of the nineteenth century, the size of the navy expanded alongside rising British anxieties over trade, empire and domestic security. By the 1870s, Britain's 'splendid isolation' was jeopardised by increasing diplomatic tensions with Russia and by the consolidation of German political and economic strength on the continent. At the same time, imperial expansion fuelled arguments for a strong navy and legitimated increased naval expenditure. As other European powers committed themselves to naval building, by the 1880s, British naval strength once again seemed vulnerable. Rumours that France now planned to build a tunnel under the Channel increased British mistrust of French naval intentions. In addition, new technologies like Whitehead's self-propelled torpedo jeopardised the stability of Britain's naval supremacy by imperilling Britain's battleships.

In 1884 in the midst of these diplomatic tensions and rumours about invasion, W. T. Stead, editor of the *Pall Mall Gazette*, published a series of articles, 'The Truth about the Navy', ostensibly exposing the precariousness of British naval superiority and thus the vulnerability of British interests at home and abroad.[16] With the help of naval sources like Captain Jackie Fisher, later to become Admiral Fisher, of the HMS *Excellent*, Stead warned his readers that the sudden increase and strength of French and Russian navies had caught the Admiralty off guard and would challenge Britain's command of the seas if not redressed. Other periodicals and papers like *The Times* and the *Daily Telegraph* followed Stead's lead and reported on the deficiencies of the Royal Navy. Naval critics charged that the British fleet was outdated in terms of its ship construction, armament and gunnery when compared to the advances of European navies. As a result of this 1884 panic about the state of the navy, William Gladstone, the Liberal Prime Minister, who had been reluctant to expand military spending, allocated an extra £3.5 million to the Admiralty.[17] Over the next decade, naval budgets increased by more than 50 per cent.[18]

Justifications for a big navy in the 1880s often revolved around the navy's role in defending both national and imperial interests. British naval advocates echoed the popular theories of Alfred T. Mahan, a retired American naval captain, that naval supremacy historically distinguished state power and that a strong navy served as the best guardian of peace.[19] As European powers committed themselves to naval programmes, continental interest in empire-building and in overseas trade further added to British anxieties over the safety of its empire, trade and naval supremacy. While the British army was instrumental in expanding the empire, the navy's role was to annex colonies, secure the empire and protect commerce during this age of 'new imperialism'.[20] The objective of the navy, argued Philip and John Colomb, brothers and naval strategists, was 'to keep open the great sea routes to and from the heart of the Empire – the islands of Great Britain'.[21] As such, the navy's bombardment of Alexandria in 1882 enabled British occupation of Egypt, protected trade routes through the Suez Canal, and solidified the navy's reputation as Britain's imperial defender. Vice-Admiral Humphrey H. Smith, for example, argued that a strong navy was needed to 'police' the *Pax Britannica* in order 'to safeguard law and order throughout the world – safeguard civilisation, put out fires on shore, and act as guide, philosopher and friend to the merchant ships of all nations'.[22] In the words of the *London Quarterly Review*, everything dear to Britain rested upon naval supremacy:

> Our social progress, our international influence, our power 'to help the right and heal the wild world's wrongs', our missions as the leaders and organisers of the backward and chaotic races that have come beneath our rule, and what is dearer to the hearts of Christian Englishmen, the opportunity to give to all the world the Gospel that has made us all free; all these, and every good we can desire ourselves or wish to share with men, depend upon our maritime supremacy.[23]

Debates about the strength of Britain's navy were much more than a logistical calculus of fleet strength but rather were imbricated in a larger imperial discourse about the vitality of British notions of civilisation, progress and empire.

In 1889, the Conservative administration under Lord Salisbury committed the government to even heavier investment in the navy in order to affirm British naval superiority. Responding to rising French and Russian military expenditures, domestic concerns over the safety of sea-borne trade, and renewed criticism over the state of the navy, in March 1889 Salisbury signed the first Naval Defence Act, which established the two-power standard, requiring the Royal Navy to be as powerful as the combined strength of the next two largest navies (excluding the United States).[24] Despite the overwhelming cost entailed by the Defence Act, it was passed with relative ease and with strong public approval and ushered in intense naval construction in which a new fleet of first-class battleships, cruisers and torpedo gunboats was ordered at a cost of £21,500,000.[25] The size of the British fleet had grown dramatically by the turn of the century, but the size of foreign fleets had also expanded; in 1883 Britain had 38 capital ships to 40 for France, Russia, Germany, Italy, the USA and Japan combined – by 1897 the ratio was 62 to 96.[26] The passage of the Naval Defence Act in 1889 assured the government's commitment to increased naval expenditure, but the efficacy of such expenditures was debated since incessant innovations in armament, gunnery and warship design made implementation expensive and new technologies provisional.

Nevertheless, in 1894 the Admiralty called for another long-term campaign of ship construction under the proposed Spencer Programme, named after Lord Spencer, the First Lord of the Admiralty. Although both Conservatives and many Liberals firmly committed themselves to a heavily funded navy, Gladstone, once again prime minister, refused to approve the 1894 estimates because he believed that exorbitance was a 'stimulus to militarism' which corrupted Liberal principles. On 20 January 1894, Gladstone outlined his objections to the costly expenditures:

> I cannot and will not add to the perils and the coming calamities of Europe by an act of militarism which will be found to involve a policy, and which excuses the militarism of Germany, France or Russia. England's providential part is to help peace and liberty of which peace is the nurse.[27]

However, Gladstone's objections to the naval expenditures stood in sharp contrast to mounting parliamentary support for the Spencer Programme.

Gladstone's resignation in 1894, which marked his final departure from parliamentary leadership, was intended as a protest to awaken

Parliament to the dangers of ever-increasing military estimates and jingoistic militarism. However, his resignation meant that his Foreign Secretary, the fifth Earl of Rosebery, a Liberal-Imperialist and big navy supporter, would succeed him as prime minister. Lord Rosebery was more sympathetic to the Admiralty than his predecessor and supported the exorbitant Spencer Programme.[28] By the turn of the century, navalist programmes formed the basis of consensus politics between the two main parties. Under Lord Salisbury's government naval expenditures grew even more dramatically; and between 1895 and 1901, nearly doubled from £18 million to over £30 million.[29]

The state of the navy was central to both political discourse and public spectacle in late-Victorian Britain. At the same time that politicians and navalists urged the nation and public to commit themselves to maintaining naval supremacy, the Admiralty and government paraded the navy, its fleet and its men, through such events as the Jubilee Naval Reviews at Spithead in 1887 and 1897, annual naval manoeuvres, and 'hurrah trips'. During 'hurrah trips', naval ships would cruise along the British coast, stopping in ports along the way in attempts to raise popular support for the navy and to recruit boys from the local population.[30] In port, the ships would be open to the public to review the ship and its men, who would be wearing their best uniforms. The popularity of Admiralty-sponsored events was not guaranteed, however. For example, the first annual naval manoeuvres held in 1888, which were intended to publicise the readiness of the navy, met with unfavourable reviews by naval correspondents.[31]

Inspired by the 1890 Royal Military Exhibition, the Royal Naval Exhibition, opened at the Chelsea grounds on 2 May 1891, was the grandest naval spectacle organised by the Admiralty for public consumption.[32] The goal of the exhibition was to popularise the navy with the voting public, whose approval could ensure the maintenance and expansion of naval budgets.[33] As president of the exhibition, the Prince of Wales admitted the advantages of the exhibition, 'though our Navy is very popular, and bound to be very popular throughout the country, anything to make it still more popular is our bounden duty to promote, in every sense of the word'.[34] The motto of the exhibition, extracted from the preamble of the Articles of War, which governed the conduct of the navy, underscored its importance to the nation: 'It is on the Navy, under the Good Providence of God, that our Wealth, Prosperity, and Peace depend'.[35] At the opening ceremony of the exhibition, Lord George Hamilton, First Lord of the Admiralty, proclaimed that the exhibition would be 'the cause of renewed interest in the Navy, whereon under the good providence of God the wealth, safety, and strength of the kingdom chiefly depend'.[36]

The exhibition, which covered fifteen acres of the Chelsea Hospital grounds and the Thames embankment, featured historical displays of the Royal Navy from the medieval period until 1891, a full-scale replica of Nelson's *Victory*, daily combat on an artificial lake between two large-scale model ironclads, the HMS *Majestic* and the HMS *Edinburgh*, and daily cutlass and gunnery drills performed by actual seamen and marines. *The Times* praised the sailors' drills, noting that 'all who have seen them and are competent to judge will agree that smarter and finer bodies of men cannot be shown by any country in the world'.[37] The exhibition ran for 151 days and was attended by over two million visitors, making a profit of nearly £48,000, which was allocated to the Royal Naval Fund to alleviate the financial distress of naval widows and orphans.[38]

Public celebrations of the navy increased amidst the imperial and domestic challenges of the new Edwardian age. The death of Queen Victoria and the difficult campaigns of the Boer War confirmed for some that the turn of the century signalled an empire in crisis.[39] Investigation into the high rejection rates for military recruits from industrial towns, such as the 1904 Report of the Inter-Departmental Committee on Physical Deterioration, which described the 'degeneracy' of the urban working classes, not only confirmed the inefficiency of the British army but also deepened imperial anxieties.[40] In addition, the rise of trade unionism, the militancy of feminist suffragism, and the pressure of Irish Home Rule appeared to deepen internal divisions. But the consensus about the navy was that it was 'one of the fixed points of the universe, admitting of no question or discussion'.[41]

Faith in the navy was expressed in ritualised ways throughout the Edwardian age as observant masses attended fleet reviews, the launchings of warships, and popular films. The spectacle and innovation of the coronation naval review of 1902 at Spithead had exceeded even Victoria's diamond jubilee review in 1897, prompting the *Daily Express* to note that 'nothing on a similar scale has ever been previously attempted by the Admiralty'.[42] While thousands attended the 1902 review, the cinematographic company Pathé Frères claimed that 'more than 10 million people all over the world' would see the review through its shows.[43] Similarly, the 'Our Navy' series by Alfred West, one of Britain's cinematographic pioneers, toured Great Britain and the Empire, but was based at Regent Street Polytechnic, where West had claimed that over two million had seen his performances.[44]

In this new Edwardian age, the navy may have served as both the strategic and moral bulwark of Empire, but the enormous debt incurred by the cost of the Boer War forced closer parliamentary scrutiny of naval estimates, despite the strident claims by ardent navalists that such financial prudence compromised Britain's naval supremacy.[45] With stagnant tax revenues, even Conservatives like Michael Hicks-Beach and Austen Chamberlain urged financial restraint and called for naval reductions. As Chancellor of the Exchequer, Hicks-Beach, had argued in 1901 for a slow-down in budgetary growth, and in 1904, his successor, Chamberlain urged spending cuts, especially in the bloated army and naval estimates, in exchange for tariffs on non-imperial goods.[46] However, loans facilitated the expansion of naval estimates from £27,522,000 in 1900 to £36,889,000 in 1904 and contributed to the sharp increase in the national debt.[47]

The financial difficulties of maintaining a policy of isolation contributed to the decision by successive British governments to negotiate with potential allies and to reduce their commitments abroad. A friendly relationship with the United States and an alliance with Japan enabled the Admiralty to reduce the presence of British warships in the Caribbean and in the Far East and to allot more ships to home waters. In terms of European diplomacy, war between Russia and Japan in 1904 served as the backdrop to negotiations between Britain and France that culminated in the *Entente Cordiale*. The Russian threat to British interests diminished as Britain and Russia negotiated a settlement over colonial antagonisms in 1907. An important consequence of such friendships with France and Russia was the realisation that fewer British warships were needed to police the Mediterranean. With improved relations with France and Russia, the Admiralty, under Admiral Fisher's leadership as First Sea Lord, consolidated most of its fleet in home waters off the North Sea in order to meet the new challenge from Germany.[48] Without the demonstration of sea power across the globe, navalists and pro-navy journalists in the *Daily Mail*, *The Times* and the *Pall Mall Gazette*, argued that alliances and the redistribution of the fleet had effectively destroyed British command over the seas. To these writers, too much was at stake to sacrifice naval supremacy to budgetary constraints.

When Jackie Fisher began his term as First Sea Lord in 1904, his two main objectives included 'the sufficiency of strength and the fighting efficiency of the fleet' and 'absolute instant readiness for war', and these were to be achieved 'with a great reduction in the Navy Estimates!'[49] His emphasis on 'naval efficiency' prioritised naval readiness, initiated reforms which eliminated redundancy and waste, and claimed to offer a more efficient and powerful navy at less cost, all steps which initially pleased both Conservatives and Liberals struggling to solve the budgetary crisis of the early 1900s.[50] Fisher's push for naval efficiency occurred within a larger progressive political movement that lobbied for national efficiency in government.[51] Considered by some

Liberals as a way of reducing state costs, national efficiency emphasised professionalism, economy, and discipline in the management of the state bureaucracy. Fisher's application of efficiency within the navy won the support of Liberals who were impressed by his ability to cut naval estimates by £3.5 million in 1905.[52]

All of Fisher's reforms aimed to mobilise the navy for the changing political climate of the early twentieth century.[53] He encouraged new technologies like battlecruisers and submarines, stressed the importance of gunnery, and demanded the better organisation and administration of naval resources. To respond to the growing threat of Germany, Fisher redistributed the fleet in 1905, which entailed scrapping 154 obsolete ships docked at foreign stations, reorganising naval stations across the globe, and concentrating active warships in home waters.[54] In terms of fleet distribution, Fisher formed the Channel Fleet, which acted as the main defence against any German threats from the North Sea from its strategic centre at Dover. Fisher also created the Atlantic Fleet with its home base in Gibraltar; its goal was to patrol the western Mediterranean and to offer quick reinforcement, if needed, to the Channel Fleet. The Mediterranean Fleet was still to be based in Malta, but the emphasis on the Channel Fleet had taken the lustre from the Mediterranean command, which traditionally had been considered by the Admiralty as the most strategically important of all fleets. In addition, Fisher increased the efficiency and readiness of the naval reserve by commissioning reserve ships, manned by nucleus crews of naval reserves sufficient in numbers and skills to take ships to sea and fight if needed for a limited time.[55]

Despite budgetary concerns, the rapid growth of the German navy in the early twentieth century committed the Admiralty to submit ever greater naval estimates. The choice of investing in the navy was clear; Viscount Esher, who served on the Committee of Imperial Defence and founded the navalist society 'The Islanders', argued that 'Britain either is or is not one of the Great Powers of the World. Her position in this respect depends solely upon sea-command'.[56] To Fisher, maintaining naval supremacy against the Germans meant investing in new technologies, whether it was battleships, battlecruisers, or submarines. The introduction of the HMS *Dreadnought*, the first 'all-big gun' battleship, in 1906, revolutionised battleship design and gave Britain the technological advantage momentarily.[57] With its fire power, speed, and armoured strength, the *Dreadnought* dwarfed its competition and, inadvertently, made the older ships of the British fleet obsolete, thus levelling the naval race between foreign navies and the British. The introduction of the HMS *Invincible* followed the *Dreadnought* and introduced the first line of battlecruisers that ushered in swift big-gun warships designed for imperial defence and trade protection. Investment in torpedo boats and submarines helped to define Fisher's stategy of 'flotilla defence' that could both impose heavy losses on enemy shipping and protect home waters.[58] To many naval proponents, Fisher's embrace of new technology only exacerbated Germany's threat to British security. Even Fisher thought that the *Dreadnought* would 'mark the beginning of a new naval epoch for all existing battleships – even the most modern – will be practically obsolete . . . today all nations start *de novo*'.[59] While Fisher received considerable criticism from his contemporaries for allegedly undermining British naval supremacy, most other navies had designs like the *Dreadnought* in the works.[60]

The Liberals' impressive victory over the Conservatives in 1906 brought a reappraisal of the debt, budgetary priorities and naval estimates. Although the Liberal Party had been a supporter of qualified naval programmes since Rosebery's administration, elected Liberals faced with demands for debt reduction and the desire for greater social expenditure grew increasingly critical of militaristic and imperialistic programmes.[61] Henry Campbell-Bannerman, the new Liberal Prime Minister, had been a critic of an expanding navy and, while he was not 'anti-Navy' like certain Radicals, he disparaged political strategies that offered big naval estimates merely as a popular platform.[62] In fact, during the 'navalist age' marked by the passage of the Naval Defence Act in 1889 until the beginning of war in 1914, the only period when naval estimates remained stable occurred between 1905 and 1908 during Campbell-Bannerman's government. And even during this period, navalist programmes were hardly dismantled; expenditures never fell below £30 million per year.[63] Any moderation in naval spending ceased during Asquith's administration with the McKenna naval programme of 1909, which responded to widespread alarm over German naval building and resulted in the immediate construction of eight dreadnoughts and the promise of ten more.[64] With Winston Churchill's guidance as First Lord of the Admiralty, naval estimates rose to nearly £45 million by 1913.[65]

The First World War may have confirmed the prophecies of warmongers but it dashed decades of planning by 'blue-water' school strategists who had anticipated the next war as a showdown of naval strength. The navy found itself well prepared for battle. Although Jutland was not the decisive victory hoped for by navalists, it served strategic ends for the British navy by containing the German High Seas Fleet. The Grand Fleet, so named in August 1914, carried out a substantive but less dramatic role in its later blockade of the German Fleet and German shipping and in its convoy protection of British trade.[66]

[31]

weak on
naval
history

Although perceived as ancillary to the land campaigns, the navy's role in the war, by providing transport supplies and reinforcements, protecting trade and containing the High Seas Fleet proved crucial to the success of the war effort. In a secret memorandum, the Admiralty contended that the 'Navy and Mercantile Marine of Great Britain have, in fact, been the spearshaft of which the Allied armies have been the point'.[67]

Manpower, the navy and continuous service

At the close of the Napoleonic Wars, over 140,000 sailors had served on ninety-nine ships of the line. The end of hostilities shrank the number of commissioned ships and men as the Royal Navy contracted to a shadow of its former size; by 1817, the number of active seamen had been reduced more than sevenfold. No longer in need of impressment, the Admiralty supplied its fleet with volunteers who signed on for short-term service. This was known as the 'hire-and-discharge' system because men were recruited only for the commission of the ship, which was usually between two and four years. In this system, sailors could move back and forth between merchant and naval ships. Since this practice allowed the Admiralty to maintain the minimum number of seamen necessary during peacetime and enabled the merchant marine to train potential naval men in sail, the practice brought significant savings to the naval budget.

Short-term service perhaps saved the navy money by hiring men only when needed but left it scrambling in time of war for trained skilled seamen. Such a system was inefficient because it released a man from service just as he had become well trained in a given field. In addition, the hire-and-discharge system had the unintended result of keeping the navy at a consistently low level of war readiness since trained naval men, once discharged, often did not return to another naval ship but rather joined a merchant ship or sometimes entered the army. The problem was made worse since technological changes in steam power and gunnery reduced the interchangeability of the skills shared between the navy and merchant marine. The transition to a modern navy required increased training and specialisation of men.

In addition to the problems posed by 'hire and discharge', the Navy List in the 1830s consisted of a distended and aging officer class whose battle experience had been gained during the Napoleonic Wars. By the 1840s, the Admiralty finally took steps to reform personnel issues that faced both lower deck and quarter deck. In 1847, the Admiralty effectively retired 200 senior captains by appointing them to rear admiral and placing them on half-pay. The percentage of unemployed post captains by 1865 was down to 55 per cent, a reduction of 30 per cent in twenty years.[68] Admiralty reforms to the quarter deck were intended to produce a professionalised officer class that could meet the changing needs of the fleet without compromising leadership ability or bankrupting naval budgets. The effect was to reduce dramatically the number of idle or unemployable officers on the Navy List.

The need for lower-deck manning reforms would become apparent during the mounting diplomatic crisis between Russia and Turkey in 1853. As the possibility of war in the Crimea loomed, the Admiralty faced difficulties in maintaining and recruiting trained personnel for the navy. The press gang, used widely during the Napoleonic Wars, had been unpopular (and was suspended at the end of the wars); yet, it had the benefit of securing skilled seafarers to serve on Her Majesty's ships. The easiest solution might have been to return to the coercive efficiency of the press gang, but impressment was not viable given popular disdain for its practice and the reform-minded nature of British politics. Instead, the Admiralty created the first Committee on Manning the Navy in 1852 during Lord Derby's Conservative administration. The committee's recommendations, submitted in 1853 to the First Lord of the Admiralty, Sir James R. G. Graham, resulted in the passage of the path-breaking Continuous Service Act, which effectively established a permanent standing navy. The Admiralty now took over, from captains, the responsibility of filling out ships' complements. The Continuous Service Act introduced a long-term service system of manning that relied on British-born volunteers who agreed to serve for commissions of ten years at a time; by the 1860s, recruits enlisted for twelve-year periods.[69] The creation of a standing navy offered the Admiralty greater security and flexibility than hire-and-discharge and standardised the training of recruits as sailors, stokers and gunners.

The development of a long-term service system also helped to resolve the many problems associated with hire-and-discharge and the unpopularity of impressment. With the voluntary long-service system, the Admiralty had to entice men to volunteer for the navy rather than join the mercantile marine. The Continuous Service Act forced the Admiralty to restructure all aspects of recruitment and to consider the means by which to retain men. For example, one way was to initiate a new programme to recruit and train boys for the navy. To entice men to serve and naval men to reengage, the Admiralty reluctantly granted reforms that had the effect of making service afloat less like a prison and more like a disciplined profession. To attract recruits, the navy also increased pay and offered long-term pensions. For ordinary seamen, pay increased from £1 6s 0d to £1 13s 7d a month, and for able seamen from £1 14s 0d to £2 1s 4d.[70] To induce men to re-engage, the navy offered new avenues to promotion and advancement like the new ratings of chief petty officer and leading seaman, both of which were accompanied by higher pay rates.[71] The Admiralty also created new categories of qualifications for specialists; a seaman gunner, for example, was now able to rise to the warrant office of 'gunner'. Additional pay, promotions and pensions offered the strongest inducements for men to stay in the navy. The new terms of service and the standardisation in 1857 of the sailor's uniform, which he had to pay for and make himself, signalled the professionalisation of the fleet and the creation of a distinguishable breed of 'British Bluejackets'.[72]

These personnel reforms made naval men's pay nearly competitive with merchant men's in peacetime.[73] Unfortunately for the Admiralty, these reforms appeared too late to have an effect on wartime mobilisation for the Crimean War. The strains on naval manning during the war were evident since many ships in its newly formed Baltic squadron were either undermanned or underskilled. Although its ships in the Mediterranean fleet were well manned, the Admiralty had to accept all types of men for its warships stationed in the Baltic; Second Sea Lord Admiral Sir Maurice Berkeley admitted to Admiral Charles Napier, who commanded the Baltic fleet, that the navy had to accept even 'butchers' boys, navvies, cabmen, etc. – *not* men of the standard of the Guards'.[74]

The war's end meant that the Admiralty was faced with the prospect of inheriting this wartime fleet of underskilled men of questionable character for the reduced needs of peacetime. This transition proved that the Admiralty was still faced with the problem of mobilising and maintaining a skilled British navy for both war and peace.[75] As a solution, the Admiralty offered returning non-commissioned men the opportunity to take complementary discharges from their continuous service engagement and to force compulsory discharges of sailors deemed bad characters. Even with a reduced fleet, the Admiralty's inability to solve the manning crisis and ameliorate shipboard conditions in part contributed to the intensification of lower-deck discontent and an outbreak of shipboard disturbances by the late 1850s.

The challenges of wartime and peacetime prompted Parliament to consider further reform. The 1859 report of the Royal Commission on Manning, led by First Lord of the Admiralty, Sir John Pakington, affirmed the merits of the newly established continuous-service system but recommended reforms to strengthen manning. Among its proposals were additional training and provision of training ships for boy seamen, free bedding, further concessions regarding clothing and mess allowances, small improvements in dietary rations, and the extension of pensions.

Specifically, the committee acknowledged and sought to bridge the rift between the naval and the merchant services that had resulted from the implementation of the continuous-service system. The Commission found that the merchant man steered clear of naval service to avoid long-term commissions under poor conditions. According to an Admiralty report, a typical merchant sailor viewed the navy as 'a black nightmare in which he would be scrubbed till clean and then flogged to death'.[76] Although the suspension of impressment and the end of hire-and-discharge had severed the navy's reliance on the merchant service to supply men in wartime, the Admiralty and parliamentary commission believed that a reserve could solve the navy's temporary manning in wartime. To this end, the government introduced a Royal Naval Reserve in 1859, which was intended to draw experienced able-bodied seamen of British descent from the merchant navy. In return for committing to five years' service and twenty-eight training days a year, reservists would enjoy the same pay, benefits and conditions, and prospects for promotion and pension as continuous service men.[77] However, such inducements are unlikely to have persuaded merchant sailors that the navy was no longer a prison afloat; by 1860 only about 3000 men had volunteered.

The navy's reputation for adamantine discipline was in part reinforced by contemporary events. Although the French war scare of 1859 prompted the Admiralty to reintroduce a temporary bounty scheme to raise manning levels, the bounty unintentionally triggered the resentment and wide-scale desertion (and then re-engagement) of skilled ratings who had previously volunteered without such financial incentives. The new bounty scheme, which ushered in 'bounty crews' generally poorly trained and disciplined, coupled with long-standing complaints about inadequate shore leave provisions, constituted the main grievances that prompted shipboard disturbances across the fleet in 1859. The disturbances, which recalled the mutinies at Spithead and the Nore, forced the Admiralty to re-examine the state of naval discipline and shipboard conditions throughout the fleet and contributed to the passage of a series of disciplinary reforms during the 1860s.

Disciplinary reforms

The Naval Discipline Act, which was initially passed in 1860 before being repealed, modified and re-enacted in 1861, offered the most comprehensive reform of naval regulations since the 1749 Articles of

War.[78] The 1861 act, which was amended over the next several years until its final revision in 1866, standardised disciplinary procedures and practices intended to promote good conduct of ratings and to avoid wanton abuses by commanding officers. Among its notable reforms, the act established a leave policy that recommended monthly leave determined by the character of the rating and the status and location of his ship. To curb leave-breaking, the act increased the distinctions between leave-breaking and desertion, charging a man with desertion after twenty-one days of intentional and unauthorised leave from his ship. Modifications to naval leave policy continued until 1890 when shore leave became an uncontested right of non-commissioned men.[79]

The Naval Discipline Act also curbed the authority of a ship's commanding officer to award punishments without court martial and rationalised those summary punishments at his disposal.[80] The type of punishment awarded was now contingent upon whether a rating belonged to the first or second 'class', a distinction that separated ratings by conduct. With the act's passage, the Admiralty now counselled against the use of corporal punishment, advising a sentence of confinement instead. Even the navy's long-held tradition of flogging, reserved only for the lower deck, was to be practised with increasing discretion by the 1860s; the navy reluctantly followed the 'enlightened' lead of the army by limiting the maximum number of lashes awarded to forty-eight. In part, it was hoped that moderation in disciplinary practices would aid recruitment, retention and attract merchant seamen who continued to resist naval service.[81] Lord Goschen, First Lord of the Admiralty, celebrated the Admiralty's plans to suspend flogging in a speech to Parliament in July 1871. He boasted that the reforms would be a boon to the fleet, 'we have great confidence that the higher education of our seamen and the general condition of the Navy will enable us to make these changes without detriment to the efficiency of our fleets and with much advantage to the popularity of the service'.[82] In December 1871, the Admiralty suspended flogging in peacetime and extended its suspension to wartime in 1879. These measures reflected both Admiralty's enlightenment to achieve discipline through other means and its reticence to forsake naval custom. A difficult tradition to abandon, flogging was suspended but never abolished.

Reforms to court-martial procedure were intended to rationalise the judicial process and its concomitant punishments. Depending upon the offence, punishments could include forfeiture of pay, reprimand, dismissal from ship or service, disrating, corporal punishment, penal servitude, or death. Reflecting contemporary British attitudes towards punishment, court-martial reforms in the 1860s advocated penal servitude in place of corporal or capital punishment. In 1862, the Admiralty modified the Lewes county gaol in Sussex to serve as the navy's first naval prison. By isolating its prisoners from the rest of Britain's convicted criminals, the Admiralty may have hoped 'to save our seamen from the contamination of prisoners in civil jails', but it also intended to keep the spectacle of naval discipline from public scrutiny.[83] To such ends, by 1867 the Admiralty had discontinued the tradition, begun in 1853, of submitting annual punishment statistics to Parliament.

The Naval Discipline Act was particularly ground-breaking because it reduced the number of offences that either called for or required a death sentence.[84] The number of offences for which possible punishments might include death decreased from 22 to 17, and with the act's passage, only two offences from an original ten now mandated a compulsory death sentence – treason and murder. Convictions on charges of sodomy no longer warranted death; defendants guilty of sodomy or indecent assault, which in 1828 had been defined more narrowly in civil law as comprising anal penetration, now received sentences that could range from five years to life imprisonment.[85] Capital punishment for sodomy was also removed from the civil statute books in 1861 with the passage of the Offences Against the Persons Act, which awarded life imprisonment or a term not less than ten years for the crime.[86]

The Admiralty's punishment for the offence of sodomy may have diminished with the mid-Victorian reforms, but its revulsion of the practice did not moderate. Despite Churchill's alleged declaration that the traditions of the navy could be summed up as 'rum, sodomy, and the lash', the Admiralty historically treated sodomy as a 'detestable' and 'abominable' offence whose 'unnatural' practice threatened to disturb the maintenance of shipboard discipline and to destroy the navy's reputation for duty, manliness, and honour.[87] Although both civil and naval codes condemned sodomy, the navy enjoyed a fierce reputation in its punishment of sodomitical acts. Sodomy had been a capital offence since the 1533 Act of Henry VIII. The Articles of War of 1661 had specifically stipulated punishment of death 'without mercy' for 'the unnaturall and detestable sin of Buggery or Sodomy'.[88] The rate of courts martial for sodomy as with most serious naval crimes intensified in war and trailed off in peacetime. The number of cases and convictions contracted considerably in the nineteenth century in the wake of the Napoleonic Wars. In fact, the last naval-rating hanging for sodomy occurred in 1829.[89] The challenge of conviction probably led many captains to avoid court-martial proceedings altogether and mete out their own summary punishments to the sailor guilty of such offences as 'uncleanliness', 'unnatural offence' or 'indecent behaviour'.

The task of the historian either to track the pervasiveness of homosexual acts in the fleet at any particular period or even to chart the frequency of charges related to sodomy is complicated by a host of challenges.[90] Although it seems reasonable to conclude that homosexual acts occurred throughout the fleet and throughout the history of the navy; whether rates of occurrence remained steady throughout the period of this study or whether these incidents reflected situational practices or affirmed sexual identities of sailors who committed them is debatable.[91] Long commissions combined with all the things that a ship lacked – privacy, leave and women – most likely fostered male intimacies that transcended the bounds of typical male camaraderie. Noting the prevalence of situational homosexuality in the early twentieth-century fleet, Able Seaman Walter Basford frankly recalled that when 'you take perhaps a thousand men in a battleship and you don't go ashore and all that kind of thing, the sexual urge comes on'.[92] Leading Seaman Bert Heron admitted that one 'could be easily drawn into this sort of thing because you had no leave ashore and no women'.[93]

Despite these anecdotal remembrances collected in oral history interviews from the 1970s, few ratings or officers left contemporary candid accounts about the prevalence and nature of homosexuality in the navy. This is certainly not surprising given the recriminalisation of homosexuality in the 1885 Criminal Law Amendment Act, and the increasing social reproach for homosexuality by the 1880s and 1890s as evidenced by scandals like the Cleveland Street and Oscar Wilde trials.[94] Social fears cast homosexuality as a danger to the very foundations of Victorian virtues of domesticity, work and duty. John Tosh notes that the figure of the homosexual represented 'someone who struck at the roots of the family, flouted the work ethic and subverted the camaraderie of all-men association'.[95] Within the navy, the spectre of same-sex indecency threatened to unravel the moral fabric that bound men together in service, to undermine the discipline of the fleet and, as a consequence, to enervate the overall strength of the fleet.

Instead, historians have tried to glean meaning from courts-martial records of sodomy and indecency, but challenges abound. In 1902, the Admiralty noted in its correspondence that not one case of sodomy had resulted in imprisonment between 1891 and 1902; however, the absence of a conviction did not necessarily indicate a lack of homosexual activity.[96] Arthur Ford, a leading seaman who volunteered in 1908, remembered that 'there's a lot more goes on than is ever caught'.[97] The cryptic language of Admiralty and officers obscured the true nature of offences and a diffident press rarely covered cases concealing the details of crimes from public inspection.[98] The draconian punishments imposed and the evidence required to convict a man of buggery probably deterred ratings from pressing charges. In addition, there was increasing reticence on the part of officers who worried that a potential scandal would tarnish the reputations of their ships and the future of their careers. These challenges are compounded further by the survival of few detailed Victorian and Edwardian courts-martial cases in Admiralty records.[99]

Although the Admiralty historically considered sodomy as one of the gravest threats to the maintenance of naval discipline, it was difficult for the Admiralty not only to define what constituted sodomy but also to discuss it candidly. Instead, the Admiralty obliquely referred to homosexual acts in its correspondence in such ambiguous terms as 'uncleanliness, 'lewd acts', 'nasty acts', and 'disgraceful conduct'.[100] Its reticence to categorise homosexual acts uniformly did not deter the Admiralty from punishing decisively when either sodomy or 'gross indecency' were proved. Although convictions of sodomy cases were fewer than for serious naval crimes of mutiny, desertion, or striking an officer, sodomy convictions rarely received the clemency more often accorded to these other charges. In the years 1700 to 1861, sodomy executions comprised 'thirty-one per cent of all probable executions'.[101] Even before the 1861 act, which established that a prisoner charged with sodomy could be found guilty of indecent assault, courts-martial boards relied upon an 'in part prov'd' verdict when the offence of sodomy could not be substantiated.[102] In fact, eighteenth and nineteenth-century punishments for lesser charges of 'indecency' routinely awarded more lashes than for mutiny or desertion.[103] In a study of buggery in the British navy, Arthur Gilbert discovered that the mutiny lash average was 283 for the period between 1755 and 1797, dramatically lower than the average rates of 527 awarded for homosexual offences.[104] All of this suggests that the Admiralty viewed homosexuality, in whatever its forms, as a graver danger to the fleet because it believed that homosexual acts had the ever-present potential to disturb shipboard hierarchies, camaraderie and discipline more thoroughly than the occasional incident of mutiny.

In addition to the punitive measures to deter indecent behaviour, the Admiralty also emphasised positive reforms like 'healthy' recreation, education and moral suasion. The provision and extension of educational opportunities, religious services, libraries, magic lantern entertainments and athletic facilities all sought to promote 'healthy' recreational alternatives for men afloat and ashore. Significantly, naval medical officers offered periodic shipboard hygiene lectures that informed ratings about the 'dangers of venereal disease', urged diseased men to seek help upon discovery, admonished them about the abhorrence of indecent behaviour, and even warned boys to avoid forming close relations with older seamen. In particular, the Admiralty worried about the harmful impact that close friendships between older ratings and younger recruits would have on discipline and boys' future prospects.[105]

At the end of 1913, around fifty years after the passage of the Naval Discipline Act, the Admiralty, 'concerned at the large number of cases of immorality', confidentially advised commanding officers to increase surveillance of all acts of indecency. The Admiralty counselled officers to investigate complaints of indecency and 'uncleanliness' more thoroughly, by employing the aid of a medical examination to detect disease caused by an 'unnatural vice', and to encourage younger ratings to report complaints as early as possible. The Admiralty strongly advised that officers attend to the 'moral well-being of the ship's companies' by emphasising 'the horrible character of unnatural vice and its evil effects in sapping the moral fibre of those who indulge in it' as well as the physical dangers to those who submitted themselves 'to the desire of vicious men'.[106]

While the Admiralty was anxious about the spread of 'unnatural vice', it recognised that those 'natural' vices concomitant with a ship's arrival in port were inevitable. Admiralty concerns about conduct ashore did arise when venereal disease threatened naval efficiency. Nothing enervated fleet strength more than the prevalence of venereal disease. In 1863, roughly 10 per cent of naval ranks had been stricken by a sexually transmitted disease.[107] By the early 1860s, military officials in both army and navy argued that controlling the health of prostitutes in garrison and port towns would curb the spread of venereal disease through the ranks of soldiers and sailors, increasing the efficiency of Britain's military forces. In an effort to recover the number of lost man-hours resulting from the spread of syphilis and gonorrhoea, Parliament approved the passage of a series of Contagious Diseases Acts (CDA) in the mid- to late 1860s, which regulated the health of prostitutes in port and garrison towns through intrusive medical inspections.

Despite Admiralty claims that they had succeeded in halving disease rates by the early 1870s, these Acts had generated outrage from social purity campaigners like Josephine Butler who had argued that the CDA had not only spread immorality by, in effect, legalising prostitution through its regulation, but that it also missed an opportunity to control the immoral conduct of soldiers and sailors. In an 1870 letter to the Admiralty that was later published in the *Shield*, the official newspaper for the repeal of the acts, Butler admonished the Admiralty to 'endeavour to deter men from vice, not to throw wider the door, to them'. She claimed the efforts to regulate the bodies of prostitutes would be brought to nought since men would 'infect each other', citing a case where seventy men who had not 'seen the face of a woman for more than year' had acquired venereal disease during a ship's commission.[108] By targeting bodies of prostitutes rather than of sailors, Admiralty efforts in the 1860s and 1870s revealed that it considered it easier to control women's bodies than curb men's passions especially when critical interests of fleet efficiency were concerned. In the end, despite the Admiralty lamenting the repeal of the CDA in domestic ports in the 1880s, the rates of venereal disease would gradually decline by the Edwardian period as a result of the spread of hygiene education and the use of prophylactics.

A naval nursery: boy ratings in the fleet

One of the most innovative solutions to the manning problem in the mid-Victorian period was the extensive recruitment and formal training of boys for service. The presence of boys on ships was nothing new. Boys had served aboard naval and merchant ships in the eighteenth century in apprentice-like positions as servants and 'powder monkeys', giving them time to 'learn the ropes'. In addition, eighteenth-century maritime charities like Jonas Hanway's Marine Society had prepared boys for a life at sea.[109] However, before the 1850s, there had been no specific rating for boys serving in the Royal Navy other than 'boy'. Likewise, the Admiralty previously had neither actively recruited boys nor provided formal training for boy volunteers. With the pressures to fill ships' complements after the passage of continuous service, the Admiralty was 'forced to nurture its own seamen' since merchant seamen were reluctant to join the navy.[110] But by mid-century, the recruitment and training of boys was seen by the Admiralty as a way to bypass the difficulties in luring seamen into the navy and away from the merchant marine.

Following the recommendations of the 1853 Manning Committee, the Admiralty formally introduced the rating of 'boy seaman' for recruits between the ages of 15 and 18. Recruited boys agreed, with the permission of their parents, to serve out their contract as boys until the age of 18 when they would begin their ten years of 'continuous and general service'.[111] In order to prepare boys for the navy and especially for service in the Crimea, Sir James Graham, the First Lord of the Admiralty, established the HMS *Illustrious* in Portsmouth in 1854 as the first training ship for boy seamen. Known as 'Jemmy Graham's

*) Put this into relation with efforts of constructing new-style union jack sailors? (i.e. reality on board + in ports drastically different from new image!)

Novices', these boys were trained in seamanship and provided with an essential knowledge of reading and writing. Already trained as seamen by the age of 18, these boy ratings had the opportunity to serve the navy for at least another two decades, providing a cost-effective and efficient investment for the Admiralty.

Recruiting boys not only helped alleviate manning pressures by creating an internal feeder programme for naval personnel; it also allowed the Admiralty to be selective in its choice of boys, seeking boys of 'good character' who demonstrated reading, writing and mathematical skills. The formal provision of boys in the navy gave the Admiralty the opportunity 'to grow seamen' and rebuild the fleet from its foundation. In addition to instructing boys in seamanship, the Admiralty also intended to 'break them into naval discipline'.[112]

In contrast to the way it recruited men, when recruiting boys the Admiralty had to consider the interests and motivations of parents who released their sons into the service. For those interested in a naval career, the Admiralty stressed good pay and good chances for promotion, and promised parents that boys would 'when abroad remit home a large proportion of their pay for the support of their relations'.[113] By the 1880s, the Admiralty depicted naval service in its recruiting propaganda as an honourable and respectable career for a young man. One pamphlet, detailing all of the various facets of naval life for boys, portrayed the navy as if it were a public school rather than a military institution. In such publications, the Admiralty assured parents that their sons would also be well educated, noting that 'voluntary study of a more advanced nature than the ordinary school course is encouraged'.[114] Recruiting literature celebrated boys' free time 'both on board and on shore' – boys could join bands, read in the large lending library, play shipboard games like bagatelle, chess and dominoes and, once ashore, cricket, skittles, football and quoits. The Royal Navy also promised boys magic lantern lectures and field trips where 'boys are taken for pleasure parties and to suitable public entertainments, free of expense to themselves, as opportunities offer'.[115] The Admiralty reassured parents that their sons would receive generous leave, medical care, spiritual guidance, and be kept clear of drink and tobacco.

With such attractions, life in the Royal Navy for the boy rating provided both adventure and prospects. The willingness of boys to enter the navy under such rigorous and stark conditions was not necessarily unusual since boys from working-class families would have been expected to contribute to the family economy. In such perspective, the romanticised vision of a life at sea, no doubt reinforced by recruiting agents, perhaps appeared more exotic and appealing than work either as an apprentice, an errand boy, or as a farmhand.[116] Whether it lived up to its expectations for those who served is debatable, but many of the men who had served in the late-Victorian and Edwardian navy agreed that the reality of the naval life was more arduous than depicted in the recruiting literature. Naval men complained about the harshness of discipline for boys and the frequency of birching for minor offences. Able Seaman Sam Noble mused that within three months of joining the navy had he met the recruiting sergeant who had promised him that life in the navy would be a pudding-filled carefree adventure, and that he 'would gladly have stood by and seem him half murdered'.[117] The lower-deck service paper the *Bluejacket* complained about the Admiralty's claims that: 'While not departing from the letter of the truth, they frequently violate the spirit of it . . . They say for instance that a boy who joins the Navy may attain to a commission, and retire with a pension of £200 a year. So he may, and so may the errand boy in the Army and Navy stores, live to become Prime Minister. And he may not'.[118]

It appears that the effect of demanding highly qualified boy applicants brought its rewards by the 1870s and 1880s.[119] Although most boys continued to be drawn from the southwest and south of England (especially London, Plymouth and Portsmouth), increasing numbers came from merchant ports, rural areas and industrial towns, as well as from Ireland, Scotland and Wales. Liverpool was an important naval recruitment centre because of its numbers of boys with sea experience and because of its convenient location to receive entries from Ireland and Scotland. In the early 1870s, Ireland and Scotland provided around 350 of the 600 boys that the Liverpool station supplied annually to the training establishments in Plymouth. According to Admiralty officials, the increasing geographic diversity of boys in the Victorian navy was in part proof of the growing popularity of the navy throughout British society.[120]

By the early 1880s, the training of boys appeared to have solved the Admiralty's manning problems to the point that the Admiralty was faced with the possibility that there were too many active personnel.[121] Satisfaction with manning levels was short-lived, however, as the Naval Defence Act forced the Admiralty to seek more recruits and more boys by the late 1880s and 1890s. According to Admiral A. C. Key, the navy had to outdo the merchant service in recruiting boys for service: 'It may be safely assumed, that the system of entering and training boys is the only mode by which we could compete with the Merchant Service on such nearly equal terms'.[122] Although the Admiralty actively recruited boys from merchant training ships – even offering monetary bounties to boys and to the managers of the training ships – it prohibited the entry of boys from reformatory ships.

[43]

Manning issues for a new navy

The seventy new warships commissioned after the 1889 Defence Act required a recruiting campaign to secure more men into active service to peacetime levels that exceeded the numbers maintained by the navy during most of the Napoleonic Wars.[123] Fifteen years after the Naval Defence Act was passed, naval personnel had nearly doubled to over 125,000 officers and men.[124] Fisher is best known for revolutionising naval armaments and materiel through the introduction of the *Dreadnought* class. Yet, as Jon Sumida has shown, the Fisher revolution also encompassed key structural changes in personnel and manning.[125] As Second Sea Lord (1902–03), Fisher did much more than simply manage everyday personnel affairs; he brought about sweeping changes in the manning, education and training of the navy's personnel.[126] Within six months of his arrival in 1902, Fisher had introduced the Selborne Memorandum, named after his senior, Lord Selborne, the First Lord of the Admiralty, which modernised the education and training of naval officers, much to the resentment of some senior officers who viewed it as a threat to naval traditions. In addition, Fisher also made noticeable structural changes to the lower deck that included reforming naval instruction at all levels. Although the navy had abandoned sail for at least a decade, only in 1903 did the Admiralty finally cease sailing instruction in 1903.[127] In its place, men and boys were now subject to physical training and gymnastics as well as to mechanical training.[128] To keep manning levels high, experienced naval men, who had nearly qualified for their pension, were encouraged to re-engage for a period of ten years or until reaching the age of 50.

During most of this period of expansion, the Admiralty was always looking for more volunteers to fill the massive complements required by its modern ships as well as to recruit more men into the reserve programme. The Admiralty also sought to staunch the losses to manning caused by sailors deserting, purchasing discharge before their contract ended, or failing to re-engage after their twelve-years' service.[129] Much of the training for the new navy focused on the new skills required in engineering, signalling and telegraphy, and gunnery. As Second Sea Lord, Fisher helped to professionalise the lower deck by adding training centres like the HMS *Fisgard* in Portsmouth to train new branches in gunnery and engineering and new schools to train new branches like Physical Training (a branch devoted to training gymnastic instructors added in 1900) and Signalling and Wireless Telegraphy. As a result, the proportion of skilled men in the navy rose dramatically by the turn of the century; around one-third of naval men were considered skilled in the 1898–99 programme and that ratio increased to at least three-quarters skilled men by 1905–06.[130]

The development of a modern navy and faster ships also led to a greater need for stokers and engine-room ratings.[131] Nearly half the ship's complement of the *Dreadnought* and *Invincible* classes was devoted to the engine-room and stokehold. The exhausting work of stokers coupled with their comparatively low pay contributed to the difficulty in manning stoker complements. These recruiting challenges led Fisher to include engine-room and stokehold duties in the instruction of boy ratings and ordinary seamen, so that seamen would be capable of augmenting engine-room staff when warranted. To procure more skilled engine-room artificers, the Admiralty created special civilian recruiters who offered a substantial bounty for suitable candidates in this category.[132] Deliberations about converting to oil-fired ships were in part driven by manning concerns. Fisher admitted that 'at one stroke, oil fuel settles half our manning difficulties! We should require fifty per cent less stokers'.[133] The introduction of oil-fired boilers in the early 1900s meant that ships would neither be beholden to coal nor to stokers. By 1912, Churchill had committed the Admiralty to complete the transfer of the fleet to oil with the production of the *Queen Elizabeth*-class battleships; however, the expense of retrofitting battleships and the uncertainty of oil supplies meant that both coal and stokers would remain in high demand.

In order to add more men for the engine-room, the Admiralty amended the continuous-service system in 1900 by adding the choice of short service in order especially to attract potential stokers. Ordinary seamen and stokers (between the ages of 18 and 23) could now sign on for a reduced contract of five years in active service, followed by seven years in the reserves. The shortening of terms of service led to an influx of naval entries by the early twentieth century; within two years of its establishment nearly 20,000 men were added to the service.[134] The changes in service engagement further distinguished the work of the stoker rating from that of the typical seaman. Friction existed between the engineering and regular contingents of both lower deck and quarter deck. Discontent over work, pay and discipline in part accounted for the widely publicised stokers' mutiny that took place in Portsmouth in 1906.[135]

In addition, the Admiralty targeted engine-room recruits from working families in interior industrial areas and advertised the navy as a desirable occupation for those eager to get on. In 1913, the Admiralty produced a recruiting poster entitled, 'Royal Navy Stokers', idealising life in the stokehold and in the navy (see figure 1.1). Having approved the distribution of 10,000 posters and postcards, the Inspec-

1.1   A recruiting poster for stokers, *c*.1913.

tor of Recruiting noted that the attractive advertisement could serve as an antidote to the shortage of stoker recruits and that only 'good can result in the navy from pictures of this kind'.[136] Although stoking was gruelling dirty work, the navy depicted the stokehold as a pleasant, clean, bright space where coaling and conversation went hand in hand. The amount of work required by stokers appeared to be minimal as the Admiralty emphasised stokers' freedom; stokers were shown with plenty of time to 'make and mend clothes' when off duty, to play football with their mates ashore, and to enjoy the exotic pleasures of empire by being driven around in a rickshaw in the China station. As shown in these captions, life in the stokehold was one part of a rewarding life in the navy. If men worried about the stability of employment and the ability to maintain a family on stokers' wages, the Admiralty claimed that 'good pay and good prospects' awaited men who were 'desirous of getting on' and for those who exhibited 'good conduct'. Aside from anecdotal evidence, it is difficult to determine the effect that posters like these had on men's decisions to serve in the navy but such recruiting campaigns reveal an Admiralty intent on meeting pressing personnel needs.[137] Alongside parades, naval reviews, West's 'Our Navy' films, these posters and postcards presented the public with romanticised images of the navy where hard work was balanced by exciting adventures and compensated by lucrative wages.

Although the navy was well prepared for the First World War, the war would challenge the navy's ability to mobilise for battle and would usher in far-reaching personnel changes. The multiple demands placed on the navy by the war dramatically increased the Admiralty's need for men. In terms of raw numbers, naval ranks increased from 250,000 in 1914 to 350,000 a year later, with most of the additional men volunteering as 'hostilities only' ratings. The pressure to recruit military personnel for the war front led to the introduction of general conscription in 1916 with the passage of the Military Service Acts. Since many naval reserves waited to be activated for naval service, the Admiralty diverted many ratings and reservists in the Royal Naval Division to contribute to military campaigns in Belgium, France and Gallipoli. Of course, the navy's demand for men paled into insignificance when compared with the ceaseless consumption of soldiers in land campaigns. In the Battle of the Somme in 1916, British and imperial forces lost 415,000 casualties, a figure which also included naval contingents. Despite conscription, the Admiralty still faced a manpower shortage in 1917. Full mobilisation for the war effort led the Admiralty to recruit women temporarily into its ranks with the formation of the Women's Royal Naval Service (WRNS). Organised as a separate service within the navy, the WRNS provided supplementary female personnel wherever needed in order to free male naval ratings from shore duties.[138] By the end of the war there were over 7000 women serving in the WRNS. With all able naval men activated for service, wartime naval personnel exceeded 450,000 by 1918.

[47]

Pay

Monetary compensation was perhaps the best way to entice more men to serve and to stay in the navy. With the introduction of continuous service in 1853, the daily pay for an able seaman had been secured at 1s 7d. Although the basic wage would not change until the early twentieth century, there were a variety of ways for sailors to augment their pay. The Admiralty awarded monetary benefits through a variety of incentives that rewarded good behaviour and specialised training; naval men boosted their wages by becoming 'trained men' or passing specialised qualifications in branches like gunnery, or earning good conduct badges. These non-substantive wages were not permanent or secure increases since both badges and qualifications could be stripped for poor conduct or performance.[139] By the Edwardian period, the combination of economic structural changes, lower-deck discontent and manning pressures forced the Admiralty to increase pay rates.

Although difficult to measure, men's overall income, including benefits, had improved since the introduction of the continuous-service system, even if the basic rate of pay had remained static or stagnant until wage increases were implemented in 1913.[140] After continuous service was introduced in 1853, off-periods between commissions became periods of paid leave, unlike the older hire-and-discharge system in which sailors were only paid for work afloat. In 1858, the administration of pay had been rationalised, enabling seamen to receive their wages regularly and to allot pay home to wives and families, all of which reduced financial worries for seamen and their families.[141] By the 1870s, the Admiralty established naval banks in port towns to make allotments easier, to encourage thrift among naval families, and to reduce men's temptations to spend freely ashore.[142] The implementation of these programmes reflected the Admiralty's main desire to recruit dependable men for service; but the consequence was also to strengthen sailors' ties to family ashore.

Instead of altering basic rates of pay, the Admiralty introduced a series of half-measures. By the early 1870s, monetary compensation for good behaviour increased a man's wages by an additional 7d per week.[143] Rewards for conduct and character were not inducements to enlist; rather they aimed to provide incentives for good behaviour. In addition, the Admiralty introduced supplementary pay in 1859 for those qualified as naval gunners.[144] Increasing men's pay periodically came under review in the late-Victorian period and the Admiralty realised that increasing wages would offer the best way to induce men to join the service. Captain George Tryon commented in an Admiralty Committee investigating pay and pensions in 1882 that 'to get good workmen good pay must be offered, pay that does not compare unfavourably with that which is offered on shore'.[145] Admiral A. C. Key, First Sea Lord of the Admiralty, argued that poor pay still stood in the way of recruiting the merchant sailor whose compensation exceeded his counterpart in the navy who faced the discipline and privations of naval life especially 'the long separations from their families and homes'.[146]

Despite the addition of supplementary pay and the recognition that higher base wages were necessary, seamen's basic pay did not increase until 1913. Falling prices as a result of a general economic depression beginning in the 1870s had benefited or had at least sustained wage labourers like naval seamen.[147] However, by the early 1900s, the recovery of prices in the British economy debased seamen's wages, even when supplementary pay was included, and decreased living standards for naval families. Given the sailor's poor wages, the rise in prices in the first twelve years of the twentieth century, which had reduced real wages by 15 per cent, made naval men with families just as vulnerable as other workers ashore.[148] In comparison to other trades, naval men were poorly compensated even with the inclusion of such benefits as pensions and room and board.[149] The naval man's responsibility to provide his own kit and to keep up with an elaborate list of uniform requirements was, by the Edwardian period, financially onerous. When compared to their counterparts in the army, which passed a 50 per cent wage increase in 1902, naval men received paltry wages. It should not be surprising that lower-deck discontent became more vocal and organised in its calls for reform and redress by the early twentieth century, especially as trades unionist activity within industrial Britain intensified and more men from industrial areas joined naval ranks.[150]

In addition, by the early 1900s, the real wages of seamen ratings had declined in relation to other ratings on the lower deck.[151] The introduction of, and demand for, new ratings like stokers, signalmen and engine-room artificers, among others, added new rates of pay that were often higher than an able seaman's wages. By the early twentieth century, the swelling numbers on the lower deck required more than ninety different rates and allowances.[152] In 1906, Admiral John Fisher as First Sea Lord established a Pay Revision Committee, which overhauled the swollen bureaucracy of personnel administration and streamlined pay scales for ratings, but did not recommend any significant changes to pay rates.

The work begun by Fisher was completed in 1912 by Churchill as First Lord who introduced the first real pay increase in sixty years.[153] After considering seamen's living and working conditions, Churchill proposed increases in pay for specific groups most in need: young men near marrying age and senior ratings with established families.[154] With input from Lionel Yexley, the leading lower-deck advocate and founder of the service papers the *Bluejacket* and the *Fleet*, Churchill advocated a substantial pay increase for all ratings that included a 4*d* increase for ratings with three years' service. Faced with the Treasury as an adversary, he exhorted the Cabinet that an increase would defuse lower-deck discontent, which was 'rendered more dangerous by every successful strike for higher wages which takes place on shore'.[155] Opposition by David Lloyd George, the Chancellor of the Exchequer, led to a compromise scheme that would raise an able seaman's wages by 3*d* per day but only after six years' service, representing, at best, a 15 per cent increase. With hopes for a 20 per cent increase, naval men reacted to the concessions with both disappointment and relief.

Churchill had even taken up the cause of marriage allowances for naval men; after all, the army and Royal Marines already granted separation allowances. Fisher's redistribution of the fleet in 1904 had stationed more men in home waters and had reduced the length of foreign-service commissions. Redistribution was popular with personnel, 60 per cent of whom would now be stationed in home waters and thus be closer to their families.[156] It also meant that naval personnel, whether stationed at home or abroad, now had greater opportunities to maintain a family (see figure 1.2). The difficulties in maintaining a family on a seaman's income led to lower-deck demands for a marriage allowance, a benefit enjoyed by soldiers and marines.[157] Despite the lack of an allowance, around 60 per cent of petty officers and 10 per cent of junior ratings had married by the Edwardian period.[158]

The marriage allowance was introduced only after the start of the First World War when wartime necessitated government action. In early September 1914, the Cabinet agreed to Churchill's proposal for a 'separation allowance' that allotted married men beneath the rank of petty officer 6*s* per week, plus 2*s* for the first two children and 1*s* for each subsequent child.[159] Although naval men's substantive pay had not changed since the insufficient increase implemented in 1913, the separation allowance effectively increased some men's pay by 50 per cent. And by early 1915, the allowances targeted for children were doubled. Together, these additional allowances represented a substantial pay raise for most ratings.

Pensions

Like pay, pensions were fundamental to the Admiralty's strategy of recruiting and retaining men in the nineteenth century. Although the formal provision of pensions for naval men began in 1831, actual relief

VOL. VIII.—No. 127.]   *SATURDAY, JULY 8th, 1899.*

1.2   'A Sailor and his Lass', *Navy & Army Illustrated* 8, No. 127
(8 July 1899).

to disabled or retired naval men had been provided by Parliament since 1696 in order to promote 'the Encouragement and Increase of Seamen'. Hopes that pensions could offer a means to boost naval recruitment initially animated mid-nineteenth-century pension reform. However, by the 1870s the Admiralty gradually realised that pensions, by providing longer-term security for naval men and their families, encouraged retention rather than stimulated recruitment.

With the introduction of continuous service in 1853, the Admiralty expected that a more comprehensive pension scheme would induce men to volunteer for service and that naval men, nearing the completion of their first engagement, would re-engage for another ten-year period in order to receive their pension. The pension was considered by Admiralty officials and others to be the naval man's great benefit, a scheme not enjoyed by men in the merchant marine. The personnel reforms that accompanied the introduction of continuous service in the 1850s simplified eligibility requirements for pensions to twenty years' service and increased the pay rates of pensions. A naval man could expect 10*d* per day for a basic pension when he retired. But, not everyone stayed to qualify for a pension; one in three men left the mid-century navy before qualifying.[160]

Although the new scheme had focused on providing financial relief to pensioners, the Admiralty continued to fund the Greenwich Hospital, which cared for disabled and transient sailors. The hospital had been an object of both pride and satire for Londoners since its establishment in 1705. While the grandeur of its buildings, designed by Christopher Wren, and its prominent location on the south bank of the Thames evoked Britain's rich naval heritage, the hospital had inspired William Hogarth's famous sketches of debauched and disfigured pensioners that, in part, parodied state paternalism. Within twenty years of the passage of continuous service, the expense of maintaining both the hospital and the pension schemes led the Admiralty to close access to Greenwich Hospital to pensioners and to allocate the additional space and grounds for its naval school for boys; the last pensioner left in 1869.[161] After its closure, the Admiralty increased the pension fund by £30 million in December 1871 to accommodate greater numbers of retiring men.[162] In this process, the implementation of a formal pension scheme had the unintentional consequence of contributing to the professionalisation of the navy by severing the perception of a pension as charity and structuring a pension as equitable compensation for hard-earned service.

By the 1880s, the Admiralty considered how to reform its pension schemes, and particularly debated whether to extend pension benefits to the naval man's family after his death.[163] The debates considered the extent to which the Admiralty owed responsibility for a dead sailor's family and deliberated upon the advantage of the benefit in retaining naval men. The naval man's ability to maintain a family upon meagre wages was jeopardised further by the dangerous nature of his work. Widows were only awarded a lump sum gratuity if their husbands were killed in active service during wartime, which meant that a naval widow and her children would be impoverished if her husband had died from accident or illness. Prince Alfred, Duke of Edinburgh and Commander-in-Chief at Devonport, chaired an 1886 committee on pension reform and criticised the system for putting sailors' families at risk and damaging the 'respectability attaching to the position of men who have served in the Royal Navy'.[164] Apart from extending its sympathy, the committee tried to decide whether a more comprehensive pension would be a cost-effective method of persuading men to enlist, or naval men to re-engage. After soliciting the opinions of naval men, the committee concluded that pensions did not induce men to join but did serve as an incentive for men to re-engage.[165] From interviews with career servicemen, the committee found that many men were married and valued the advancement of their professional career. These men had tried to organise death benefit societies but the provisions offered by these clubs offered little long-term security to the seaman's family.

The committee recommended pension reform in which a new scheme 'would confer a great benefit upon the men and their families and help to render the whole service more attractive'.[166] Ralph Hardy, an Admiralty official, had concluded that the provision of an Admiralty-funded pension scheme would be a wise strategy especially when considered in terms of the benefits it would offer the Royal Navy and the easy support that the reforms would receive from the public. Such pensions 'would certainly raise the tone of the service, induce a better class of woman to inter-marry with the seaman, and supply an additional steadying influence and aid to discipline'.[167] For Hardy, the provision of a pension helped to make the naval man a respectable suitor in the eyes of his community. From the committee's perspective, pensions helped to promote the navy as a respectable profession. In order to pay for the plan, the committee proposed that the Admiralty supplement men's voluntary allotments to their own pension. Despite the committee's approval, the proposal failed to receive parliamentary support because of allegedly prohibitive costs of the programme, given that the plan appeared to have little impact on initial recruiting.[168] Rather than state intervention, Parliament and Admiralty expected that private charities like the Royal Naval Fund or Lloyd's Patriotic Fund would continue to provide relief for naval families.

But the issue of pensions for naval families was not resolved by private benevolence. A general lower-deck reform movement, which began in the early 1900s, demanded greater compensation, extensive pension reform, and better conditions for naval men.[169] A parliamentary committee investigating pensions in the army and navy in 1902 again rejected the possibility of extending a widow's pension to servicemen who died while on duty. In 1904, naval reformers primarily from the petty-officer class submitted *A Naval Magna Carta*, described as a 'Loyal Appeal from the Lower Deck', to the Admiralty in which they argued for a variety of substantive reforms that focused on higher wages, promotions and better pensions.[170] Invoking patriotic sacrifice, men justified pension reform not for themselves but as fair compensation for their families. An anonymous stoker noted in a 1905 column from the *Bluejacket* that, 'Jack himself asks for no coddling; no lionising on one hand nor *matronising* on the other, *for himself*. While he floats or swims, his "tenders" (wife and kiddies, to wit) have no official existence . . . Is it much, then, if he asks for a grateful country to look after them when he is piped aloft'.[171]

Instead of legislating for an expensive pension system that covered naval widows and families, the Admiralty sought cheaper pension reforms to ease men's grievances. Stephen Reynolds, a lower-deck advocate who served as an editor for the *English Review* and a writer for the *Daily Chronicle*, commented that reform was unlikely since the Admiralty was 'notoriously clever at moving without progressing, at altering things without changing them'.[172] During manpower shortages of 1907, the Admiralty began easing pension restrictions in order to enable pensioners, many of whom were in their 40s, to work in the navy and still collect their pensions. In the First World War, pensioners were called up to work as office clerks in order to free younger men for service. Only the crushing need for more recruits in the First World War forced the Admiralty to acquiesce to long-standing lower-deck demands for family pensions and for increases in pension rates. As the War Office had done with soldier's wives, the Admiralty extended pension benefits to naval wives at the beginning of 1915. The effect of the government's acknowledged responsibility to war widows actually led to a rise in military and naval marriages.[173]

By the summer of 1917, fleet-wide discontent was on the rise. Embittered by the inadequacy of pay, a feeling intensified by inflation and evidence that civilian workers and hostilities-only men enjoyed better rates and benefits, lower-deck societies once again signed an appeal for better pay and allowances. In response, the War Cabinet created a Committee on Soldiers' and Sailors' Pay, with the support of the General Federation of Trade Unions and Ben Tillett, who had served in the navy before his instrumental work to unionise dockers and transport workers.[174] By September, the Admiralty and Cabinet granted concessions that included increasing an able seaman's pay by $3d$ after three years, improving the messing allowance, and providing an allowance for keeping up a man's kit. Significantly, the Admiralty conceded the first increase in basic pension rates in more than seventy-five years, from $10d$ per day to $11d$ per day – still a paltry sum – and enabled men to receive their pension after they had achieved their twenty years' service. Debates about pension reforms from the 1880s revealed that the Admiralty acknowledged the centrality of naval men's families to their livelihood, but it would take a war and swelling lower-deck discontent to push the Admiralty and Parliament to embrace extensive pension reform that protected naval families from hardship.

Promotion

Achieving a promotion also offered men 'desirous of getting on' the opportunity to earn higher wages. For seamen, advancement held prospects of higher wages and better pensions; for the Admiralty, institutionalised hierarchies helped retain qualified disciplined men with the lure of promotion and freed the Admiralty from the obligation of providing real pay increases for all. Once an ordinary seaman passed the test for able seaman, it was theoretically possible to advance through the ranks from leading seaman, to petty officer, then chief petty officer, followed by warrant officer, until finally reaching the highest rank of chief warrant officer.

The rank of chief warrant officer was realistically the best a non-commissioned man could expect. Although newer ship designs had blurred the spatial distinctions between quarter deck and lower deck, these terms remained meaningful in describing the impenetrable class system within the navy. In fact, only four men from the lower deck had achieved commissioned rank in the nineteenth century.[175] In 1853, the Admiralty allowed warrant officers to be promoted to the commissioned rank of a lieutenant in cases of gallantry but this clause was rarely applied. Thomas Lyne, who eventually rose to the rank of Rear Admiral, was the only naval man promoted to a lieutenant's rank in the Edwardian navy for his service in the Boer War.[176] Although newer fields like signalling and telegraphy had gained in prestige within the navy, surprisingly these branches initially offered proportionally fewer opportunities than the seaman's branch for promotion to the rank of warrant officer. Once again, the Admiralty inadvertently promoted the professionalisation of the service as it specialised the training of non-commissioned ratings in the late-Victorian and Edwardian period. Career servicemen increasingly saw themselves as professionals afloat, raising their own expectations of reforms and promotions.

When Henry Capper led a campaign of warrant officers in the 1890s to convince the Admiralty to open entry to an officer's commission to the lower deck, he met the mother of one of his commanding officers who informed him: 'I have the greatest sympathy with you personally in your desire to rise, but you have chosen the wrong service. The navy belongs to us, and if you were to win the commissions you ask for it would be at the expense of our sons and nephews whose birthright it is'.[177] Naval officers had been drawn primarily from naval families from the southern coast during the nineteenth century.

Fisher's reforms as Second Sea Lord were far-reaching – intending to improve the quality of the officer class by opening the officer's wardroom to a broader spectrum from the middle classes. In part because of the strong resentment of the traditional officer's class, Fisher was reluctant to open the wardroom fully to the lower deck and, instead, concentrated on recruiting middle-class boys from public schools and universities. As a symbol of his commitment to a meritocratic navy, and in response to lower-deck petitions, in 1903, Fisher promoted a hundred chief warrant officers, including Capper, from various branches to the rank of lieutenant.[178] These isolated appointments did little to open up the wardroom to the lower deck since these men were already nearing retirement. In essence, these lieutenancies were honorary appointments, rewarding men for years of good service.

Although Fisher made honorary lieutenants out of many warrant officers, he was unable to devise a plan for open entry that would be acceptable to both Admiralty and Parliament.[179] In 1905, there was a parliamentary suggestion to open the naval wardroom by awarding scholarships to qualified, but poor, candidates who were not otherwise able to afford the fees to enter the naval college. The *Naval and Military Record* had unequivocally warned against recruiting from the 'Democracy', cautioning, 'We should view with grave apprehension any attempt to officer the fleet at all largely with men of humble birth'.[180]

It was not until 1912 that Winston Churchill, as First Lord, continued Fisher's efforts and created a programme whereby qualified warrant and petty officers could be promoted to the rank of lieutenant. Fisher advised Churchill to support lower-deck commissions and to 'fight *like hell* against increasing entry of cadets. The remedy is to promote more Bluejackets and Marines from Warrant Officers . . . N.B. you will have fearful opposition but you will have a Mutiny at the Nore if you don't handle the Lower Deck grievances'.[181] Churchill's initial scheme, which was also informed by suggestions from Lionel Yexley, was too radical for most Admiralty Sea Lords. Parliament passed a modified plan in 1912, which introduced an intermediate rank of 'Mate' that enabled the transition of the petty officer to lieutenant. Given the time allotted to achieve certain ranks, such a system still made it all but impossible for an ambitious naval man, within his twenty years in the service, to rise to a rank higher than Commander. Mates who had achieved the rank of lieutenant formed an isolated class within the wardroom, shunned by traditional officers because they were ex-mates and still fundamentally 'rankers'. Since entry from the lower deck to an officer's commission was now open but limited by its design, the scheme did not jeopardise the paths to promotion for traditional naval officers, and so received the backing of the Admiralty. Fisher later complained about the effectiveness of the programme: 'Is there a single Post-Captain who has risen from the ranks? When they make a sailor a lieutenant, they stow him away in some small vessel so that he shan't mess with the blue bloods! King Edward said I was a Socialist! So I am! Because like the French Revolution riches now come before merit'.[182] The experience of war had transformed the programme. In 1914, only forty-four mates were in the programme, but by the end of the war, 544 naval ratings and marines had advanced to lieutenancies. As Anthony Carew has noted, the stagnation of promotions during the inter-war period revealed the extent to which the scheme had depended upon the pressures of war and the will of the Admiralty.[183]

In the sixty-five years that passed between the introduction of continuous service and the establishment of general conscription during the war, the navy had grown nearly tenfold – from 46,000 in 1853 to 450,000 in 1918. The introduction of continuous service in 1853 contributed to the creation of a permanent standing navy ready for wartime mobilisation. In the decades that followed, particularly during the 1880s, diplomatic tensions and naval scares led to massive naval budgets and increasing pressures to man ships with qualified men. With the Admiralty's heavy investment in new ship construction after the first Naval Defence Act of 1889, the navy constantly faced the need for more technically competent ratings. In order to recruit thousands of volunteers, the Admiralty needed to provide better incentives to recruit and retain men. The most effective inducement was increasing monetary compensation, whether in terms of supplementary pay, pensions, or promotions. But it would take until the Edwardian period and the experience of the First World War for the Admiralty to undertake real reforms in these areas. Aside from monetary benefits, the Admiralty also enlarged the supply of potential recruits by enlisting boys on a large scale and organising schools to educate and train boys for naval service. New technologies demanded new training of men in branches of gunnery, engineering, telegraphy and signalling. The cumulative effect of these reforms would be to professionalise the ranks of the navy, a development that would provide a new foundation from which to envision naval manhood in Victorian and Edwardian Britain.

Notes

1 A ship's commission was not fixed to a certain period but rather reflected the period in which a ship was put into active service with its full complement of officers and men. A commission ended when the ship completed its tour of duty and returned home.

2 Despite the Admiralty's conservative approach to personnel issues, there is increasing evidence to suggest that the Admiralty embraced technological innovation in *materiel*. See Andrew Lambert, 'Responding to the Nineteenth Century: the Royal Navy and the Introduction of the Screw Propeller', *History of Technology*, 1999.

3 Muriel Chamberlain, *'Pax Britannica'? British Foreign Policy, 1789–1914* (London: Longman, 1988).

4 Michael Lewis, *Navy in Transition: 1814–1864: A Social History* (London: Hodder & Stoughton, 1965), 69; Eric Grove, *The Royal Navy Since 1815: A New Short History* (Basingstoke: Palgrave Macmillan, 2005), 1; W. L. Clowes, *Royal Navy: A History*, vol. VI (London: Chatham Publishing, 1997), 190.

5 Chamberlain, *'Pax Britannica'*, 9.

6 Paul Kennedy, *Rise and Fall of British Naval Mastery* (London: Allen Lane, 1976), 171. For more on this period, see also C. J. Bartlett, *Great Britain and Sea Power, 1815–1853* (Oxford: Clarendon Press, 1963).

7 Grove, *Royal Navy Since 1815*, 27.

8 Andrew Lambert, *The Crimean War: British Grand Strategy, 1853–56* (Manchester: Manchester University Press, 1990).

9 Grove, *Royal Navy Since 1815*, 41; Andrew Lambert, *Warrior: The World's First Ironclad, Then and Now* (Annapolis, Maryland: Naval Institute Press, 1987).

10 Grove, *Royal Navy Since 1815*, 51.

11 Public Record Office, Kew (hereafter PRO), ADM 1/7076, 'Remarks on the First Lord's questions with Regard to the Ninth Report of the Manning Committee, 1901–1902', 4 November 1891.

12 David Brown, 'Wood, Sail, and Cannonballs to Steel, Steam, and Shells, 1815–1895', in *The Oxford Illustrated History of the Royal Navy*, ed. J. R. Hill (Oxford: Oxford University Press, 1995), 215–16; Jon Sumida, *In Defence of Naval Supremacy: Finance, Technology and British Naval Policy, 1889–1914* (London: Routledge, 1993), 10–18.

13 John Wells, *The Royal Navy: An Illustrated Social History, 1870–1982* (Dover, NH: Alan Sutton, 1994), 270.

14 Kennedy, *Rise and Fall*, 173. See also Karen Dale Logan, 'The Admiralty: Reforms and Reorganization, 1868–1892'. Unpublished dissertation, University of Oxford, 1976.

15 Chamberlain, *'Pax Britannica'*, 115.

16 *Pall Mall Gazette*, 15 September 1884.

17 William E. Gladstone, *The Gladstone Diaries with Cabinet Minutes and Prime-Ministerial Correspondence*, ed. H. C. G. Matthew, vol. 13 (Oxford: Clarendon Press, 1982), 372.

18 The Estimates for the navy, army and civil service were each subject to individual votes in Parliament. Like the other budgets, Naval Estimates were formulated in late autumn and revised by the Treasury before being submitted to Parliament in March.

19 Martin Pugh, *State and Society: British Political and Social History, 1870–1992* (London: Edward Arnold, 1994), 94.

20 Kennedy, *Rise and Fall*, 232; Bernard Semmel, *Liberalism and Naval Strategy: Ideology, Interest, and Sea Power during the Pax Britannica* (Boston: Allen & Unwin, 1986), 88.

21 Semmel, *Liberalism and Naval Strategy*, 88.

22 Arthur J. Marder, *The Anatomy of British Sea Power* ([1940] New York: Octagon Books, 1976), 16.

23 *London Quarterly Review*, January 1896, quoted in Marder, *The Anatomy of British Sea Power*, 15.

24 Wells, *The Royal Navy*, 38.

25 Marder, *Anatomy of British Sea Power*, 143; W. Mark Hamilton, *The Nation and the Navy: Methods and Organization of British Navalist Propaganda, 1889–1914* (New York: Garland Publishing, 1986), 17.

26 Pugh, *State and Society*, 96.

27 Gladstone, *The Gladstone Diaries*, vol. 13, 364.

28 Hamilton, *Nation and the Navy*, 71, 314–15; Semmel, *Liberalism and Naval Strategy*, 61; Marder, *Anatomy of British Sea Power*, 484–5. Few in Parliament or in the press listened to the anti-naval dissent voiced by Irish Nationalists and anti-imperialist Liberals belonging to the Peace Society, who complained that higher estimates and frenzied military production did not ensure peace or even stave off war but rather exacerbated diplomatic and international tensions.

29 Hamilton, *Nation and the Navy*, 71–3.

30 Albert E. Lilley, Chief Stoker, 000750/08, Oral History Recordings: Lower Deck, 1910–1922, Department of Sound Records, Imperial War Museum.

31 Marder, *Anatomy of British Sea Power*, 9. As a consequence, the Admiralty invited sympathetic naval correspondents and writers, like Rudyard Kipling and Frank T. Bullen, to tour commissioned naval ships or to join in naval manoeuvres in hopes of securing a good review in the press.

32 *Times*, 6 February 1891, 10.

33 'The Royal Naval Exhibition, 1891: Official Report of the Executive and Sub-Committee' (London, 1892), 14–15; PRO, TS 18/130.

34 *Times*, 6 February 1891, 10.

35 *Times*, 2 May 1891, 9.

36 *Times*, 4 May 1891, 8.

37 *Times*, 21 August 1891, 4.

38 *Times*, 12 October 1891, 3; Marder, *Anatomy of British Sea Power*, 45.

39 Jan Rüger, 'Nation, Empire and Navy: Identity politics in the United Kingdom 1887–1914', *Past & Present* 185 (2004), 159–87; Rüger, ' "The last word in outward splendour": the cult of the Navy and the imperial age', in *The Navy and the Nation: The Influence of the Navy on Modern Australia*, ed. David Stevens and John Reeve (Crows Nest, Australia: Allen & Unwin, 2005); Rüger, *The Great Naval Game: Britain and Germany in the Age of Empire* (Cambridge: Cambridge University Press, 2007).

40 Bernard Porter, *The Lion's Share: A Short History of British Imperialism, 1850–1970* (London: Longman, 1975), 123.

41 T. R. Threlfall, 'Labour and the Navy', *Nineteenth Century and After* 75 (March 1914), 688, quoted in Kenneth L. Moll, 'Politics, Power, and Panic: Britain's 1909 Dreadnought "Gap" ', *Military Affairs* 29: 3 (Autumn 1965), 136.

42 Rüger, 'Nation, Empire and Navy', 165.

43 Rüger, 'Nation, Empire and Navy', 167.

44 Alfred West, *Life in Our Navy and Our Army: A Synopsis of the Life-Work of Alfred West* (Portsmouth: Wessex Press, 1912), frontispiece.

45   H. V. Emy, 'The Impact of Financial Policy on English Party Politics before 1914', *Historical Journal* 15: 1 (March 1972), 114.

46   Aaron L. Friedberg, *The Weary Titan: Britain and the Experience of Relative Decline, 1895–1905* (Princeton: Princeton University Press, 1988), 89; Nicholas Lambert, 'British Naval Policy, 1913–1914: Financial Limitation and Strategic Revolution', *Journal of Modern History* 67: 3 (Sept. 1995), 597.

47   Marder, *Anatomy of British Sea Power*, 486. France and Russia had spent £5,000,000 less than Britain in 1900, and had spent £16,000,000 less in 1904.

48   Kennedy, *Rise and Fall*, 218–19.

49   Peter Kemp (ed.), *The Papers of Admiral Sir John Fisher*, vol. 1 (London: Navy Records Society, 1960), 17.

50   Friedberg, *Weary Titan*, 192.

51   G. R. Searle, *The Quest for National Efficiency: A Study in British Politics and Political Thought, 1899–1914* (London: Ashfield Press, 1971), 54–80.

52   Kennedy, *Rise and Fall*, 218.

53   Friedberg, *Weary Titan*, 175–8.

54   Arthur J. Marder, *From the Dreadnought to Scapa Flow: The Royal Navy in the Fisher Era, 1904–1919*, vol. 1 (London: Oxford University Press, 1961), 26–7; Marder, *Anatomy of British Sea Power*, 487; Nicholas A. Lambert, *Sir John Fisher's Naval Revolution* (Columbia: University of South Carolina Press, 1999), 97–109.

55   Wells, *The Royal Navy*, 76.

56   Kennedy, *Rise and Fall*, 222.

57   James Goldrick, 'The Battleship Fleet: The Test of War, 1895–1919', in *The Oxford Illustrated History of the Royal Navy*, ed. J. R. Hill (Oxford: Oxford University Press, 1995), 283.

58   Nicholas Lambert, 'British Naval Policy, 1913–1914: Financial Limitation and Strategic Revolution', *Journal of Modern History* 67: 3 (Sept. 1995), 598.

59   Marder, *Anatomy of British Sea Power*, 538.

60   Marder, *Anatomy of British Sea Power*, 540; Goldrick, 'The Battleship Fleet', 283.

61   Martin Pugh, *The Making of Modern British Politics, 1867–1939*, 2nd edn (Oxford: Blackwell, 1993), 119; Emy, 'Impact of Financial Policy', 120.

62   *Hansard's Parliamentary Debates*, 4th ser., vol. 130 (29 February 1904), col. 1302; Hamilton, *Nation and the Navy*, 330. Campbell-Bannerman commented that 'a tendency to increase expenditure was more likely to meet with approval in respect of the Navy than in respect of almost any other department of the public service'.

63   Marder, *Dreadnought to Scapa Flow*, vol. 1, 126–7. Under Campbell-Bannerman's administration, even mild reductions in naval spending resulted in negative publicity in the press, which portrayed the Liberals as 'anti-Navy'.

64   Chamberlain, 'Pax Britannica', 171; Kenneth L. Moll, 'Politics, Power, and Panic: Britain's 1909 Dreadnought "Gap"', *Military Affairs* 29: 3 (Autumn 1965),

65   Grove, *The Royal Navy*, 106.

66   Goldrick, 'The Battleship Fleet', 300. There were also naval engagements like those at Coronel off the west coast of South America, in the Dardanelles, and at Jutland.

67   PRO, ADM 167/57 quoted in Grove, *Royal Navy*, 143.

68   Arthur Herman, *To Rule the Waves: How the British Navy Shaped the Modern World* (New York: HarperCollins, 2004), 427.

69   Lewis, *Navy in Transition*, 185.

70   John Winton, *Hurrah for the Life of a Sailor* (London: Michael Joseph, 1977), 104.

71   Lewis, *Navy in Transition*, 185.

72   Lewis, *Navy in Transition*, 187–8.

73   Lewis, *Navy in Transition*, 186.

74   H. Noel Williams, *Life and Letters of Sir Charles Napier* (London, 1917), 257, quoted in Lewis, *Navy in Transition*, 186; Andrew Lambert, *The Crimean War:*

British Grand Strategy, 1853–56 (Manchester: Manchester University Press, 1990).

75 Semmel, *Liberalism and Naval Strategy*, 56.

76 Eugene Rasor, *Reform in the Royal Navy: A Social History of the Lower Deck* (Hamden, Conn.: Archon Books, 1976), 31.

77 Frank C. Bowen, *History of the Royal Naval Reserve* (London: Lloyd's, 1926).

78 Theodore Thring, *A Treatise on the Criminal Law of the Navy* (London: V. & R. Stevens and Sons, 1861).

79 Rasor, *Reform in the Royal Navy*, 71. Fines for leave-breaking increased in 1875 when men lost a day's pay for every six hours absent from their shipboard duties.

80 Despite these reforms, the captain still wielded a tremendous amount of summary authority, including the power to disrate enlisted men without a court martial. Thorough reform to shipboard discipline came in 1912 under the leadership of Winston Churchill as First Lord of the Admiralty. See Anthony Carew, *The Lower Deck of the Royal Navy, 1900–1939* (Manchester: Manchester University Press, 1981), 43–7.

81 Rasor, *Reform in the Royal Navy*, 116. For more on the relationship between flogging reform discourse and the construction of British identity, see Isaac Land, 'Customs of the Sea: Flogging, Empire, and the "True British Seaman", 1770–1870', *Interventions* 3(2), 169–85.

82 *The Times*, 29 July 1871.

83 Winton, *Hurrah for the Life of the Sailor*, 182.

84 Rasor, *Reform in the Royal Navy*, 115; Thring, *A Treatise on the Criminal Law of the Navy*, 115.

85 Initially directing sentences of at least three years for penal servitude, the Naval Discipline Act was amended in 1865 to require not less than five years' imprisonment. See Rasor, *Reform in the Royal Navy*, 117; Thring, *A Treatise on the Criminal Law of the Navy* (1877), 235.

86 A. D. Harvey, 'Prosecutions for sodomy in England at the beginning of the nineteenth century', *Historical Journal* 21, 4 (December 1978), 941.

87 Arthur Gilbert, 'Buggery and the British Navy', *Journal of Social History* 10 (Autumn 1976), 72–98.

88 Car. II, An. 13. Stat. I, 1661, 'An Act for the Establishing Articles and Orders for the regulateing and better Government of His Majesties Navies Ships of Warr & Forces by Sea', in *Statutes of the Realm*, ed. John Raithby, vol. 5: 1628–80 (1819), 311–14.

89 Gilbert, 'Buggery and the Royal Navy', 85.

90 Scholarship about the history of homosexuality in the maritime world has received scant attention when compared to the impressive work produced about the history of homosexuality in Victorian Britain. For the maritime world, see B. R. Burg, *Sodomy and the Pirate Tradition: English Sea Rovers in the Seventeenth-Century Caribbean* (New York: New York University Press, 1983); Hans Turley, *Rum, Sodomy, and the Lash* (New York: New York University Press, 1999); Arthur N. Gilbert, 'The *Africaine* courts-martial: A study of buggery and the Royal Navy', 1: 1, *Journal of Homosexuality* (1974), 111–22; Arthur N. Gilbert, 'Buggery and the British Navy, 1700–1861', 10: 1, *Journal of Social History* (Autumn 1976), 72–98. Christopher McKee deftly integrates the subject into his larger social history of naval sailors in the early twentieth century. See C. McKee, *Sober Men and True: Sailor Lives in the Royal Navy, 1900–1945* (Cambridge: Harvard University Press, 2002), 192–204. For historical scholarship on homosexuality in Victorian and Edwardian Britain, see Jeffrey Weeks, *Coming Out: Homosexual Politics in Britain, from the Nineteenth Century to the Present* (London: Quartet Books, 1977); H. G. Cocks, *Nameless Offences: Homosexual Desire in the Nineteenth Century* (London: I. B. Tauris, 2003); Sean Brady, *Masculinity and Male Homosexuality in Britain, 1861–1913* (Houndmills, Basingstoke: Palgrave Macmillan, 2005); Matt Cook, *London and the Culture of Homosexuality, 1885–1914* (Cambridge:

Cambridge University Press, 2003); Matt Houlbrook, 'Soldier Heroes and Rent Boys: Homosex, Masculinities, and Britishness in the Brigade of Guards, circa 1900–1960', *Journal of British Studies* 43, no. 3 (July 2003), 351–88.

91 George Chauncey cautions against resorting to 'hetero-homosexual binarism', noting that 'men's identities and reputations simply did not depend on a sexuality defined by the anatomical sex of their sexual partners'. See George Chauncey, *Gay New York: Gender, Urban Culture and the Making of the Gay Male World, 1890–1940* (New York: Basic Books, 1994), 97.

92 Walter N. Basford, Able Seaman, 000669/19, Oral History Recordings: Lower Deck, 1910–1922, Department of Sound Records, Imperial War Museum. For more recollections by British sailors about homosexual encounters in the navy, see McKee, *Sober Men and True*, 192–204.

93 Albert A. Heron, Leading Seaman, 000681/20, Oral History Recordings: Lower Deck, 1910–1922, Department of Sound Records, Imperial War Museum.

94 Cocks, *Nameless Offences*, 114–54.

95 John Tosh, *Manliness and Masculinities in Nineteenth-Century Britain: Essays on Gender, Family, and Empire* (Harlow, England: Pearson Longman, 2005), 43.

96 PRO, ADM 1/7608. In addition, a closer look at Admiralty records reveals that at least two cases involving charges of 'gross indecency' occurred in this period. See PRO, ADM 12/1324 'Court Martial Trials', 28.3; PRO ADM 1/7537.

97 McKee, *Sober Men and True*, 194.

98 Brady, *Masculinity and Male*, 41–3. In 1896, Parliament failed to pass the Publication of Indecent Evidence Bill to make it criminal for a newspaper to publish details of cases involving homosexual acts. During the debate, Lord Rosebery noted that the press already exercised caution in its coverage.

99 PRO, ADM 1/7537, ADM 1/7608, ADM 1/7755, ADM 156/9.

100 Rasor, *Reform in the Royal Navy*, 98. For an example, see PRO, ADM 12/1324, 1898.

101 Gilbert, 'Buggery and the British Navy', 81.

102 Gilbert, 'Buggery and the British Navy', 83. Gilbert notes that in 1762 two naval ratings who received an 'in part prov'd' verdict were each awarded a thousand lashes. In a reappraisal of the transformative reach of the 1885 Labouchere amendment, H. G. Cocks notes that by the eighteenth century all homosexual acts became liable to prosecution as an 'assault with intent to commit sodomy', adhering to a common law principle that an intent to commit a crime was in itself criminal. See H. G. Cocks, 'Trials of character: the use of character evidence in Victorian sodomy trials', in *Domestic and International Trials, 1700–2000*, ed. R. A. Melikan, vol. 2 (Manchester: Manchester University Press, 2003), 38.

103 Gilbert, '*Africaine* Courts-Martial', 122.

104 Gilbert, 'Buggery and the British Navy', 84.

105 PRO, ADM 116/1060, Letter from Medical Director-General to Board of Admiralty, May 1908; PRO, ADM 7/910, 'Nore Confidential Memorandum', 20 July 1910; Arthur Gilbert, 'Buggery and the British Navy: 1700–1861', 72–98. In one court-martial case from 1913, a stoker testified that he had overheard the defendant, an able seaman charged with sodomy, admit to acquiring gonorrhoea from having 'a lump of ass of a boy'. When asked whether such a comment was unusual to make, the stoker admitted that 'it was a sort of a remark made in the head night after night'. See PRO, ADM 156/9, 1913. Early twentieth-century sailors have spoken about the widespread presence and frequent homosexual nature of these 'winger' relations where older sailors took boys under their wing 'to teach them the ropes'. For examples, see the interviews of Albert Heron and James Cox, Oral History Recordings: Lower Deck, 1910–1922, Department of Sound Records, Imperial War Museum. Also see C. McKee, *Sober Men and True*, 198–201.

106 PRO, ADM 105/104, Secret Circular Letter, N.L. 5773, 18 December 1913.

107 Rasor, *Reform in the Royal Navy*, 91.

108 PRO, ADM 1/6418, 'Contagious Diseases Act'. See also Judith Walkowitz, *Prostitution and Victorian Society: Women, Class, and the State* (Cambridge:

Cambridge University Press, 1980); Philippa Levine, *Prostitution, Race and Politics: Policing Venereal Disease in the British Empire* (New York: Routledge, 2003).

109 Linda Colley, *Britons: Forging the Nation 1707–1837* (New Haven: Yale University Press, 1992), 91–2.

110 Rasor, *Reform in the Royal Navy*, 35.

111 Lewis, *Navy in Transition*, 185.

112 PRO, ADM 1/6680, 'Pay, Position and Prospects of Seamen and Boys of the Royal Navy', June 1883.

113 PRO, ADM 1/6680, 'Pay, Position and Prospects'.

114 PRO, ADM 1/6680, 'Pay, Position and Prospects'.

115 PRO, ADM 1/6680, 'Pay, Position and Prospects'.

116 Baynham, *Men from the Dreadnoughts*, 56–82; McKee, *Sober Men*, 26–34.

117 Sam Noble, *Sam Noble, Able Seaman: 'Tween Decks in the Seventies* (New York: Frederick Stokes, 1926), 5. Noble admitted time was a cure-all because if he had met his sergeant eight years after his enlistment, he would have embraced him in appreciation.

118 *Bluejacket*, August 1900, 550.

119 PRO, ADM 1/6272, 'Remarks on the Manning of the Navy and Reserves of Seamen, July 1872', Captain of HMS *Impregnable*, Devonport training ship, to Rear Admiral John W. Tarleton, 6 February 1873.

120 PRO, ADM 1/6272, 'Remarks on the Manning'.

121 PRO, ADM 1/6588, 'Recruiting for the Navy', November 1881.

122 PRO, ADM 1/6629, 'Report of the Committee appointed by the Lord Commissioners of the Admiralty to inquire into Pensions of Seamen and Marines', March 1882. By the end of the nineteenth century, there were fewer prospects for boys trained as apprentices aboard mercantile training ships as ship owners increasingly preferred cheaper foreign labour. See Laura Tabili, *'We ask for British Justice': Workers and Racial Difference in Late Imperial Britain* (Ithaca: Cornell University Press, 1994).

123 Jon Sumida, 'British Naval Administration and Policy in the Age of Fisher', *Journal of Military History* 54 (January 1990), 9; Rasor, *Reform in the Royal Navy*; 166, fn. 67; Lewis, *Navy in Transition*, 64–5.

124 Wells, *The Royal Navy*, 272–3.

125 Sumida, 'British Naval Administration', 1–26.

126 Marder, *Anatomy of British Sea Power*, 540. Although qualifications for entry had been lowered during this period in order to recruit greater numbers, age and height requirements were raised in 1904 for both non-commissioned and commissioned ranks indicating that the pressure to inflate manning levels had subsided.

127 PRO, ADM 7, Admiralty Circular, March 1903.

128 Wells, *The Royal Navy*, 63; David Phillipson, *Band of Brothers* (Phoenix Mill, Gloucestershire: Sutton Publishing, 1996), 40; Henry Baynham, *Men from the Dreadnoughts* (London: Hutchinson, 1976), 58.

129 Carew, *The Lower Deck*, 63–7.

130 Sumida, 'British Naval Administration', 10.

131 PRO, ADM 1/7522, 'Manning of the War Fleet of 1905–06', 6 June 1901; Sumida, 'British Naval Administration', 11.

132 PRO, ADM 7/909, 'Pay of the Royal Navy and Royal Marines', 19 December 1912, Circular Letter, No. 43; Sumida, 'British Naval Administration', 11.

133 Fisher quoted in Erik J. Dahl, 'From Coal to Oil', *Joint Force Quarterly* (Winter 2000–1), 52.

134 Wells, *The Royal Navy*, 63.

135 PRO, ADM 1/7895; Carew, *The Lower Deck*, 64–7.

136 PRO, ADM 1/8330, June 1913.

137 Patrick Riley, *Memories of a Bluejacket, 1872–1918* (London: Sampson Low, Marston & Co., 1927), 3. After seeing a naval recruiting poster that listed the height requirement for boy entries, Riley recalled how in October 1872 he raced home to measure himself and convince his family to let him join the navy.

138 Ursula Stuart Mason, *Britannia's Daughters: The Story of the WRNS* (London: Leo Cooper, 1992), 179; Wells, *The Royal Navy*, 117, 216, 257; Commandant M. H. Fletcher, *The WRNS: A History of the Women's Royal Naval Service* (Annapolis: Naval Institute Press, 1989), 13. Advertisements appeared in national papers, and the Admiralty sought to recruit qualified female applicants over eighteen who were unmarried. Preparation included gymnastic exercises, martial training, revolver instructions and naval history lessons. After initial instruction, Wrens were sent for specialty training as cooks, stewards, writers, telephonists, telegraphists, coders, drivers, porters in victualling stores, sailmakers, turners, fitters and storekeepers. Since its establishment was considered a wartime exigency, the WRNS were decommissioned in 1918. It was reintroduced by the Admiralty in 1938 and became a Permanent Service in 1949, although it remained a separate division within the Navy. In 1977, the WRNS was brought under the Naval Discipline Act; service women now enjoyed the same opportunities, and were subject to the same discipline, as their male colleagues.

139 PRO, ADM 7/908, 'Circular Letter: Discipline', November 1912. A seaman's good conduct badge, 'a reward for sobriety, activity, and attention' could be stripped summarily for any offence that compromised good behaviour. In 1912, a conviction of drunkenness by a civil power could also warrant removal of a badge. The purpose of such 'checks upon the behaviour of naval ratings ashore are to continue in order to uphold the honour of the naval uniform, which would almost certainly suffer in the event of any considerable increase in the number of offences committed by men on leave'.

140 Wells, *The Royal Navy*, 88. Pay increases are difficult to measure for many reasons, not least of which is that it was paid in lunar months of 28 days until 1852 when twelve monthly payments were authorised. See Lewis, *Navy in Transition*, 214.

141 Rasor, *Reform in the Royal Navy*, 105, 166.

142 PRO, ADM 7/892, 'Memorandum No. 5: Naval Savings Banks', November 1867; PRO, ADM 7/893, 'Circular No. 3: Payment of Full Wages to Seamen and Others who do not Allot: and retention of reduced amounts from Men making Allotments', 2 February 1872; PRO, ADM 7/895, 'Circular No. 18: Naval Savings Banks', 25 November 1878; PRO, ADM 7/896, 'Circular No. 70: Naval Savings Banks', 9 April 1881.

143 PRO, ADM 1/6233, 'Advertising for Boys', 11 March 1872. Good Conduct medals had been introduced in 1849 as a way to improve discipline by rewarding well-behaved seamen with benefits in pay and leave.

144 Rasor, *Reform in the Royal Navy*, 107.

145 PRO, ADM 1/6629, Captain George Tryon, 'Report of the Committee appointed by the Lord Commissioners of the Admiralty to inquire into Pensions of Seamen and Marines', March 1882.

146 PRO, ADM 1/6629, A. C. Key, 'Report of the Committee', March 1882.

147 E. J. Hobsbawm, *Industry and Empire: From 1750 to the Present Day* (London: Penguin Books, 1990), 162.

148 Henry Pelling, *A History of British Trade Unionism* (London: Macmillan, 1976), 131; Carew, *The Lower Deck*, 54. Pelling estimated that the cost of living rose by around 5 per cent between 1902 and 1908 and by another nine per cent between 1909 and 1913.

149 Carew, *The Lower Deck*, 53.

150 *Bluejacket*, December 1904, 318–19 and March 1907, 57–8. In 1904, a group of non-commissioned men began submitting *A Naval Magna Carta*, described as a 'Loyal Appeal from the Lower Deck', to the Admiralty in which they argued for a variety of substantive reforms like increases of pay and pensions. See also Carew, *The Lower Deck*, 62–80.

151 Eric Hobsbawm, *The Age of Empire, 1875–1914* (New York: Vintage Books, 1989), 48–9.

152 Wells, *The Royal Navy*, 88.

153 PRO, ADM 7/909, 'Pay of the Royal Navy and Royal Marines', Circular Letter, No. 43, 19 December 1912.
154 Carew, *The Lower Deck*, 53–61. For literature on the bread-winning wage in maritime communities, see Valerie Burton, 'The Myth of Bachelor Jack: Masculinity, Patriarchy and Seafaring Labour', in *Jack Tar in History: Essays in the History of Maritime Life and Labour*, ed. Colin Howell and Richard J. Twomey (Fredericton, New Brunswick: Acadiensis Press, 1991), 179–98.
155 Carew, *The Lower Deck*, 57.
156 Wells, *The Royal Navy*, 77.
157 *Hansard's Parliamentary Debates*, 5th ser., vol. 48 (12 February 1913), col. 973; Carew, *The Lower Deck*, 58.
158 Wells, *The Royal Navy*, 88; Carew, *The Lower Deck*, xix; *The Fleet*, September 1912, 591.
159 PRO, ADM 116/1661.
160 Carew, *The Lower Deck*, 73.
161 Lewis, *The Navy in Transition*, 229.
162 Gladstone, *The Gladstone Diaries*, vol. 8, 79.
163 PRO, ADM 1/6816, 'Report of the Committee 3 February 1886, Introductory letter', 6 February 1886.
164 PRO, ADM 1/6816, 'Report of the Committee', 6 February 1886.
165 PRO, ADM 1/6816, 'Report of the Committee', 6 February 1886.
166 PRO, ADM 1/6816, 'Report of the Committee', 6 February 1886.
167 PRO, ADM 1/6816, 'Report of the Committee', 6 February 1886.
168 PRO, ADM 1/6816, 'Report of the Committee', 6 February 1886.
169 Carew, *The Lower Deck*, 1–16.
170 Carew, *The Lower Deck*, 11–14.
171 *Bluejacket*, March 1905, 67.
172 Stephen Reynolds, *The Lower Deck, the Navy, and the Nation* (London: J.M. Dent and Sons, 1912), 99.
173 John Gillis, *For Better, For Worse: British Marriages, 1600 to the Present* (New York: Oxford University Press, 1985), 237.
174 Carew, *The Lower Deck*, 74.
175 Baynham, *Men from the Dreadnoughts*, 127–8; Winton, 'Life and Education', 274. Of that number, only one, John Kingcome, had achieved flag rank as a result of service in the Napoleonic Wars.
176 Thomas J. Spence Lyne, *Something of a Sailor: From Sailor Boy to Admiral* (London: Jarrolds, 1940). In an unusual case, Lyne, who had entered the navy in 1885, was promoted for gallantry in the field, during the Boer War, and received his lieutenancy in King Edward's Coronation List. See John Winton, 'Life and Education in a Technically Evolving Navy, 1815–1925', in *Oxford Illustrated History of the Royal Navy*, ed. J. R. Hill and Bryan Ranft (Oxford: Oxford University Press, 1995), 274.
177 Henry D. Capper, Lieutenant-Commander, *Aft – from the Hawsehole: Sixty-two Years of Sailors' Evolution* (London: Faber & Gwyer, 1927), 55, 106, 130.
178 Harry Pursey, 'From Petitions to Reviews: the Presentation of Lower-Deck Grievances', *Brassey's Naval Annual* (1937), 100; Wells, *The Royal Navy*, 87.
179 Wells, *The Royal Navy*, 87.
180 *Naval and Military Record*, 22 June 1910, quoted in Marder, *Dreadnought to Scapa Flow*, vol. 1, 31.
181 Carew, *The Lower Deck*, 50.
182 Marder, *Dreadnought to Scapa Flow*, vol. 1, 267–8.
183 Carew, *The Lower Deck*, 52; Wells, *The Royal Navy*, 87.

CHAPTER TWO

For the good of the boys in blue: philanthropy, Agnes Weston and contested manhood

As the Admiralty reformed the navy and its men, private naval chari- ties sought to administer additional relief, often in spiritual form, to naval personnel. Although maritime missions had enjoyed a long history of providing aid to sailors, Victorian maritime philanthropy was distinctive for a number of reasons. First, new structural distinc- tions between the navy and merchant marine led to the formation of new charities, which catered to specific services. The growth of these new maritime missions, often administered by women, took place during an age marked by philanthropic impulse, evangelical zeal and a cult of domesticity. While Christian outreach to wayward sailors characterised early naval charity, by the mid- to late nineteenth century naval philanthropy developed into an elaborate network of services that provided for both the physical and spiritual relief of the sailor and his family. In particular, philanthropists, like Agnes Weston, high- lighted the importance of home, family and nation in their outreach to naval men, whether in temperance campaigns, port accommoda- tion, spiritual ministrations, or disaster relief. What is interesting is how dependent her temperance campaign was upon the imagery of naval manhood in publicising its charitable efforts. Her ministrations either castigated naval men for their profligate vices or celebrated them for their domestic virtues. While reforming naval manhood was central to her mission, her consistent allusions to reprobate naval manhood helped to cultivate older stereotypes of the Jolly Jack Tar. As a consequence, her portrayals of naval manhood often earned her the contempt of naval men, who argued that her depictions slandered their reputation and that their profession was not in need of charity but only redress by Admiralty reforms.

This discourse points to the centrality of home in defining nation and empire, whether for female philanthropists who organised their charities or for the naval men who defended their manhood.[1] As Frank

Prochaska has suggested, 'the home, the very fountain of the nation's life, was the most invigorating image in the philanthropic world and was commonly raised to the metaphor'.[2] As a metaphor, the idea of 'home' offered security and stability to naval men whose work took them far from their real homes. In their memoirs, sailors spoke of the comforts of home and family and how the longing desire to be near their wives, children and mothers kept up their spirits during long stretches at sea.[3]

Since the womanly ideal envisioned women as the domestic guardians of home and hearth, the philanthropic metaphor of 'home' enabled the participation of middle-class women who could put their domestic skills to use as well as 'their much heralded characteristics of kindness and compassion'.[4] A woman's philanthropic pursuits confirmed her virtue, fulfilled her Christian duty, appealed to her religious sensibilities, as well as offered a change of pace to the banality of domestic life. It was not only an outlet for middle-class wives but also an acceptable occupation for unmarried middle-class women whose choices for employment were limited. Middle-class women were active in a variety of different charitable and moral pursuits that included the anti-slave trade movement, the social purity campaign and the temperance movement.

Agnes Weston

Agnes Weston, although unmarried and childless, offered herself not only as the sailor's friend but also 'like a mother' to naval ratings. Weston believed that the object of her port accommodations was 'to provide a happy home for him, and lead into a sober, clean, godly life'.[5] Nicknamed 'Mother of the Navy', Weston did not initiate the idea of naval temperance or naval rests, yet she holds a prominent place in the history of missionary work for seamen.[6] From 1868 until her death in 1918, Weston devoted her life to caring for the spiritual and moral welfare of her 'boys' whether it was through her sailors' homes in Portsmouth and Plymouth, her Naval Temperance and Christian Unions, or her publications, sent monthly to ships across the fleet.

While Victorian philanthropy was an acceptable outlet for women's moral influence, it was rare to find a woman in such authority within Victorian philanthropic organisations.[7] And, it was certainly more unusual that Weston attained such status through her service to an all-male navy.[8] Weston was able to manoeuvre in a man's world because she had promised that she 'would speak to the lads just as if she were their mother'.[9] One religious journal, drawing on the stereotypes of sailors, commented on the potential dangers of her task, 'In spite of twenty years' work among the uncouth Jack Tars, Miss Weston is still a woman, and displays the native delicacy of her sex'.[10] By carefully crafting a maternalist nurturing image as 'mother' of the navy, Agnes Weston enjoyed the autonomy to carry out her mission.

Following in the tradition of earlier maritime missions, Weston's efforts worked to better both the physical and spiritual condition of the sailor. Influenced by a larger evangelical Christian temperance movement that considered prohibition vital to the spiritual reclamation of sinners, she placed naval temperance at the centre of her outreach. Her missionary work combined practical reform, which stressed temperance, thrift, and family responsibility with spiritual reform, which stressed religious conversion and earnest Christianity. Although Weston herself belonged to the Church of England, she boasted of the 'broad and unsectarian basis' of her institutions and organisations.[11] Her objective was 'to bring personal influence to bear upon every seamen and marine in the Service'.[12] Weston's missionary work with sailors began when she was twenty-eight as written correspondence to naval men overseas. By the early 1870s, she had established the Royal Naval Temperance Society and the Royal Naval Christian Union and had set up branches of each aboard ships to help steer sailors towards the proper Christian and temperate path. Within around fifteen years, Weston could boast almost 200 temperance branches and 10,000 pledged abstainers.[13]

Although Weston became famous with British public for her efforts to reform the navy morally, she was never able to gain widespread support among naval men for her teetotalism. While naval men admired Weston because her rests provided inexpensive, clean and safe housing for sailors in port, by the twentieth century, many scorned her attempts to convert the fleet to teetotalism and Christianity. By the early twentieth century, naval men attacked her benevolence, arguing that it reduced them to children who required constant guidance and protection rather than valorising them as defenders of the empire, responsible husbands and dutiful fathers. Although naval seamen had few avenues for self-representation, naval men did criticise Weston's work in their published letters to the lower-deck paper, the *Bluejacket*.

Naval philanthropy

Naval philanthropy was not just a specific expression of the maritime mission; it was also, like the general maritime mission, an outgrowth of the Victorian preoccupation with philanthropy.[14] One cannot understand the charitable work of Agnes Weston, a prominent naval philanthropist, during the late nineteenth century without locating it in a larger framework of Victorian piety and philanthropy.[15] For Weston, who grew up in Bath and had no familial naval connections, her commitment to temperance and Christianity preceded her devotion to helping seamen. As Victorian philanthropy embraced a wide variety of projects and programmes, naval philanthropy developed into an elaborate network of services catering to naval men and their families. While Christian ministrations to individual sailors characterised the early missions, by the late nineteenth century naval philanthropy provided both physical and spiritual relief to the seaman and his family. In addition to providing disaster relief to the families of naval men, naval charities performed a number of different functions like organising temperance clubs for naval men, establishing teetotal sailors' homes in naval ports, and providing naval wives with mothers' meetings. By the turn of the century, charities also provided retiring naval men with training for civilian jobs. What was distinctive about naval philanthropy was the range of relief projects intended to help naval men and their families.

Such wide-ranging philanthropic efforts articulated a moral response to the social and economic problems within Victorian society, yet these charitable enterprises often perpetuated social injustices by offering palliatives and not solutions. As Anne Summers has argued, middle-class philanthropists 'reaffirmed that poverty was not a structural or economic problem of society, but a moral one'.[16] Since 'pauperism' did not reveal structural decay but rather reflected personal moral failure, poverty could then be alleviated, it was assumed, through the moral reform of individuals. If the answer was in the 'personal reformation' of the poor, most philanthropists agreed that the government intervention in social problems only obstructed moral progress.[17]

Just as philanthropists focused on reforming the individual rather than the state, naval philanthropists focused on reforming the sailor rather than the navy. As well as occasionally lobbying the Admiralty to provide men with higher wages to enable them to maintain a family, naval philanthropists continued to see the debased position of the naval family in terms of the naval man's own moral failings, highlighted by his reputation for drunkenness, licentiousness and lack of self-control. Naval philanthropy thus focused on improving both the physical and spiritual character of the sailor by promoting virtues of self-discipline, respectability, self-examination and obedience.

Evangelicalism provided the crucial link in establishing the connections between Christianity, morality and philanthropy.[18] Beginning in the late eighteenth century, evangelicals, who belonged to the Church of England, called for a religious reawakening to reform what they perceived as a morally corrupt nation. In fact, the evangelical concern at the end of the eighteenth century with the moral decline of Britain shaped their interest in abolishing the slave trade and in initiating a national campaign of manners and morals.[19] Through public campaigns of speeches, sermons, and essays, the influential Clapham Sect intended to create public support for their morality campaign and hoped to institute moral change by legislation affecting the content of literature, the style of dress, and public entertainments.[20]

According to evangelicals, Britain's future at the turn of the nineteenth century depended upon the nation's religious reawakening. Moral regeneration was only possible from within, through an individual's faith in God. Evangelicalism's emphasis on moral redemption and spiritual reclamation had consequences for the perceived sinner and for philanthropy. The possibility of moral redemption for the sinner was granted through God's grace. As a result, the sinner was not doomed to a life of sin but rather the possibility of God's grace held open the door to salvation. The emphasis on individual salvation positioned self-examination and self-discipline as central to the realisation of God's grace.[21] Once converted, the individual thus had a moral responsibility to rescue others from damnation. Through vivid evocations of heaven and hell, evangelicals encouraged philanthropy to redeem the hordes of sinners who threatened to destroy Britain's moral foundations.[22] These spiritual beliefs redefined charity from a project of Christian compassion and responsibility to a project of conversion. In terms of naval philanthropy, missionaries at the end of the eighteenth century became active in naval and maritime communities because they recognised that the reputedly deviant Jack Tar now had a soul that was worthy of being saved.

Historically, religion and the sea have had close connections and maritime missions capitalised on this relationship.[23] Missioners reminded their subscribers and seamen about the symbolic importance of the seafaring community to Christianity, that Jesus himself was a fisherman and St Paul was the first sailor missionary. Like other evangelicals who stressed spiritual reform as a vital necessity to the reclamation of sinners, maritime missionaries believed that salvation was the best hope for sailors. The words of one clergyman in the early nineteenth century highlighted the moral imperative of saving sailors' souls by urging his congregation to action:

> what guilty neglect and vicious treatment could have led to all the depravity of the maritime population? Christians of all denominations! Do you desire a new sphere for your benevolent exertions? Let us work till every sailor becomes a Christian missionary and every seaport a Tyre whose merchandise shall be holiness to the Lord and every ship a floating church.[24]

As early Victorian philanthropy was driven by a 'thirst for souls', so too naval charities, like the Naval and Military Bible Society, the Naval Correspondence Mission, and the British and Foreign Sailors Society, were also impelled to save the sailor.[25]

Aside from a sense of spiritual responsibility, by the late nineteenth century, men and women involved themselves in naval charity and missions for many other reasons. Middle-class residents in port towns had special interests in encouraging naval temperance or in the moral rescue of prostitutes since temperance and reclamation were considered practical measures to clean up the streets.[26] While local factors and spiritual motivation may explain the dedication of individual workers or of key donors in naval ports, they do not necessarily explain why naval temperance and naval charity garnered national attention and popular support throughout Great Britain. In their requests for support, naval charities appealed to the public's patriotism and jingoistic fears. Like evangelicals who argued that Britain's political condition would wither without moral regeneration, Victorian naval missionaries argued that Britain's empire would be lost without the spiritual redemption and temperance of naval men. In 1888, invoking social Darwinist rhetoric, Weston claimed that if morality and temperance did not spread throughout the fleet, 'the "survival of the fittest" will no doubt be the outcome of all this . . . and some other nation better, purer, and more temperate, will take her place'.[27] To donate money to naval temperance or to a sailors' home was one way that contributors could believe that they contributed to the maintenance of naval supremacy and to the nation's defence.

To assess the motivations of these philanthropists is a bit of conjecture, but surely as Brian Harrison hints, it was not done solely out of a sense of altruism.[28] Bourgeois hegemony was partially solidified and confirmed within society through the various philanthropic agencies that ministered to the lower classes and thus worked to 'control' the poor.[29] In particular, the historian's temptation to cast temperance as merely a middle-class movement intent on guiding working-class behaviour is alluring but, unfortunately, does not account for the wide spectrum of temperance activism.[30] Temperance had its roots in evangelicalism and non-conformity and was initially a movement with popular appeal and working-class leadership.[31] But with the emergence of large national temperance organisations like the National Temperance League by the late nineteenth century, middle-class leadership eventually governed the direction of the national temperance movement.[32]

This was similarly the case in the development of naval temperance. The autonomy of independent teetotal societies waned with the official establishment of the Royal Naval Temperance Society. The direction and trusteeship of the society had been first selected from naval officers, rather than non-commissioned men, and the choice of Agnes Weston to manage the organisation was decided by the National Temperance League rather than by naval teetotalers.

Unlike earlier appeals made directly to the naval man, naval philanthropic societies in the late nineteenth century embraced a much wider mission that cared for the spiritual and social welfare not only of the naval man but also his family. In addition to Christian missions and temperance organisations, there were related programmes that provided disaster relief and orphanages to naval families. Emphasising doctrines of domesticity and self-reliance, benevolent associations, from mothers' meetings, needlepoint guilds, to social clubs were even established in the late nineteenth century by the wives of naval officers to encourage mutual friendships between themselves and the wives of non-commissioned men. Philanthropic societies established sailors' homes or rests to provide inexpensive accommodation for naval men in port. Often, these homes were Christian establishments but some, like the Union Jack Club in London, were established by civilian non-denominational organisations.[33]

The provision of sailors' rests, the promotion of temperance, the organisation of mothers' meetings, and the education of naval orphans were all part of an elaborate network of philanthropic activity that, in different ways, sought to instil Christianity, domesticity and respectability into the lives of the sailor and his family. Charitable institutions justified their mission as Christian responsibility and attempted to impress upon naval men their own class-based definitions of the virtues of self-restraint and respectability as well as imperial attributes of self-sacrifice, duty and patriotism. Efforts to spread temperance among naval men intended to steer them away from pubs and to train them not only as good Christians but also as attentive sober soldiers.

Although older organisations like the Royal Naval Benevolent Society, which catered to orphaned children of naval officers, and the Naval Scripture Society, which focused on Bible reading in the navy, continued during the later century, what was most remarkable about this period of naval philanthropy was the creation of new organisations devoted to helping naval families of non-commissioned men. New societies like the Soldiers' and Sailors' Family Association (SSFA), the Royal Naval Friendly Union of Sailors' Wives, and Agnes Weston's sailors' rests reflected the intense interest of philanthropy in domestic concerns and the growing reality that non-commissioned men maintained families.

In times of disaster

While non-maritime philanthropists catering to those ashore responded to cycles of depression and unemployment, philanthropists catering to naval men afloat responded to the rhythms of sea and war. Shipwrecks and disasters at sea were extraordinary moments that propelled communities and philanthropists to come to the aid of sailors' families. Some types of charity were specific to the navy, like disaster relief – aid that came pouring in from across the nation whenever a ship was lost at sea. Although mid-century naval reforms had improved conditions for naval men, seafaring presented its own dangers and uncertainties for the sailor that jeopardised his career and the economic well-being of his family. The Admiralty provided little or no compensation to their men and families after shipwrecks, collisions, or accidents. As a consequence, ship disasters at sea left naval families unprotected. In addition, stoppages of pay, which occurred during bouts of sickness, pushed naval families to near poverty, the workhouse, or the parish doorstep. Naval philanthropy could fill the void left by the Admiralty. In times of shipwreck, private organisations, like the Royal Patriotic Fund, the SSFA and Agnes Weston's sailors' rests organised national campaigns and raised money from the British public to alleviate the suffering of naval families. In the case of a naval disaster, fundraising organisations relied on the patriotism of the British public to contribute to relief efforts. For example, receipts raised from public attendance at the Royal Naval Exhibition of 1891 contributed to the establishment of the Royal Naval Fund in 1893, which aimed to provide assistance to the widows, orphans and dependent relatives of deceased seamen and marines. While a patchwork of organisations arranged relief efforts for naval disasters during the late Victorian and Edwardian periods, the First World War finally compelled the Admiralty to provide comprehensive insurance and benefits for naval men and their families.

Established in 1885 in the wake of the Egyptian campaign, the SSFA was first organised to provide relief for the military families of soldiers and sailors serving in Egypt. Soon, the SSFA developed into a general support organisation that provided disaster relief to families, training to destitute wives, an employment network to discharged men, and medical attention to military communities.[34] It was an organisation that endeavored, in the words of Admiral Cyprian Bridge, 'to help those who help themselves' by promoting standards of morality, self-help, self-respect and individual responsibility to the non-commissioned men and families to whom it catered.[35] Its services intended to provide some comfort to sailors and soldiers who were to feel secure when they were away that their wives were not left 'to the mercies of the unknown'. Vice-Admiral William R. Kennedy, another SSFA supporter, argued that the circumstances of naval disasters had no equal in the army and necessitated extraordinary and prompt action. In the case of peacetime naval disasters, quick action was necessary to help 'the poor widows and orphans who have lost their breadwinners . . . It is poor consolation for the widow to be told that her case is being taken into consideration, and that she will receive some benefit six months hence'.[36]

The loss of the HMS *Serpent* off the coast of Camariñas in November 1890 highlights how ship disasters mobilised naval philanthropic organisations and brought the lives of drowned sailors and their families to the attention of the nation. An error of navigation led the *Serpent* to wreck over the rocky shoals off the Spanish coast in November 1890. With only three survivors, the loss of the *Serpent* took the lives of around 170 men, most of whom hailed from Plymouth. Weston's Sailors' Rest in conjunction with the SSFA organised a national campaign to raise public money for the Disaster Relief Fund and to allocate the money to the most deserving families.[37] In fact, such charities were highly successful in stirring national compassion and generosity for the victims' families. They published appeals in regional newspapers across the nation stressing the sacrifice of the sailors and the urgency of donations to help out their families in need. One Admiral, supportive of the SSFA, had even suggested that naval officers travel around the country seeking donations.[38] The fund claimed that 'every penny subscribed would be used for the individuals for whom it was intended'.[39] In particular, the SSFA emphasised 'that sobriety and good conduct should govern all assistance'.[40] Established to compensate for the Admiralty's meagre gratuities to some of the victims' families, the *Serpent* Relief Fund raised £13,000.

The fundraising strategies of charities like the *Serpent* Relief Fund relied upon connecting the memory of the drowned naval men with their roles as fathers and husbands. In her campaign to solicit donations to the *Serpent* Relief Fund, Weston appealed to her subscribers and to the seamen who read her monthly Christian and temperance periodical for naval men, *Ashore and Afloat*. She devoted the cover of January's issue to an engraving of the *Serpent* foundering in the storm with sailors bobbing on the waves, grasping for sinking masts and the gunwales of smaller boats. Within the pages of *Ashore and Afloat* were also illustrations intended to depict the drowned sailor's widow and family grieving over her loss. In making her appeal to the public, Weston emphasised that the naval men who drowned had left behind devastated and impoverished families. In the following poem featured in *Ashore and Afloat*, the message for the reader is clear – to donate to the *Serpent* Fund and alleviate the financial woes of the families of the drowned men:

> Alas! for the brave,
> The brave that are no more;
> All sunk beneath the wave,
> Off Caraminas shore.
>
> No more the luckless 'Serpent',
> Will plough the ocean main;
> She and her gallant seamen,
> Will ne'er be seen again.
>
> Oh! Ye that God hath given,
> Wealth and golden store;
> Have pity on the fatherless.
> And Heaven will give you more.
>
> See the weeping mother,
> Her weeping babes caress;
> May the Father of the Fatherless
> Relieve their great distress.[41]

It was not unusual for nineteenth-century shipwrecks to serve as the subject of poetry and ballads to mourn the dead and to dramatise the existential struggle between man and nature. While Gerald Manley Hopkins's 'Loss of the Eurydice', commemorating the loss of the boy's training ship off the coast of the Isle of Wight in 1878, served as a larger metaphor about national loss and God's salvation – this utilitarian poem about the *Serpent* was an intimate portrayal of domestic loss where the deaths of fathers and husbands hurled families into precarious despair. As the poem alludes to God's mercy on those left behind, the poem appealed to the reader's Christian compassion to come to the aid of distressed naval families.

Rather than lobby the government to reform naval conditions that would have provided insurance to families for sailors lost at sea, naval philanthropists focused upon charity as a private individual responsibility and used the opportunity provided by crises to approach sailors to contribute to their own behalf. In her appeals for the *Serpent* fund, Weston even suggested that naval men donate half a day's pay. It was not unusual for naval men to contribute to naval charity. Upon the death of a messmate, naval men might 'pass around the hat', to collect money and auction off the deceased man's belongings, sending all proceeds to his family.[42] In the early 1900s, philanthropists established a Royal Naval Provident Fund that relied on money raised from the lower deck to fund relief to naval families in times of disaster. National schemes dependent on lower-deck subscriptions had failed in the past mostly because naval men were sceptical about the legitimacy and efficiency of the charity. They preferred to raise funds from mess collections on board their own ship in times of crisis rather than making a personal monthly contribution from their wages to a fund in which naval men had no voice.

Lionel Yexley, the outspoken advocate for lower-deck affairs, also hesitated to support a national voluntary fund like the Provident Fund because it justified inaction by the state in reforming pension schemes for naval men. According to Yexley, the successful creation of the Provident Fund 'would form a very effectual excuse for the State not doing its obvious duty' and would 'dry up those springs of lower deck charity known as "passing the hat"' when a shipmate died while in service.[43] Yexley asserted: 'Has the nation the right to neglect the duty towards the dependents of those who pay the "price of Admiralty"?' Likewise, *The Times* commented that the provision of the Provident Fund needed to be the responsibility of the Admiralty rather than the lower deck.[44]

By the early twentieth century, lower-deck petitions to the Admiralty demanded widow's pensions. Naval men sought government recognition that the state, rather than private charities, would be responsible for the fate of naval men and their families. Although the SSFA had been able to provide over a £1 million after the Boer War to relieve military and navy widows, the First World War overwhelmed the resources of private charity.[45] When the Naval and Military War Pensions Bill was passed in 1915, the new legislation made much of the work of the SSFA and the various other relief funds redundant.

Naval temperance

While ship disasters brought the navy and charitable work to public attention in moments of crisis, the naval temperance movement was a decades-long campaign that kept public attention focused on the problem of drink in the navy.[46] The movement took place during the late nineteenth century, just as a campaign for naval expansion and efficiency, in terms of both materiel and personnel, was underway. As we have seen, despite the introduction of a permanent standing navy with the adoption of continuous service in the 1850s, the Admiralty was still confronting a manning problem two decades later. In response to inadequate manning levels and public pressure, the Admiralty began to introduce personnel reforms in an effort to recruit and retain more men. While these reforms led to improved living conditions for seamen through financial inducements, regularised discipline, a better diet and more recreation time, they also sought to transform large numbers of recruits into a uniform well-trained and well-disciplined military force. In addition, the British naval man was also more literate and better educated by the late Victorian period as a result of reforms such as the Education Act of 1870.[47] Personnel changes and social reforms, in addition to new technical skills required to maintain the sophisticated naval materiel of an iron man-of-war, contributed to the better trained and treated British bluejacket of the late nineteenth century.

Public imagery of the naval seaman, however, did not reflect these new realities, and popular representations of naval men during this period continued to depict the brave but bawdy sailor. The most lasting popular representation of the merchant or naval man was that of the drunken sailor. One popular sea ballad 'The Homeward Bound' recalled the sailors' drunken sprees ashore,

> And when we arrive in Malabar,
> Or any port not quite so far,
> The purser he will tip us the chink,
> And then like fishes we will drink.[48]

To the British public, the naval man's reputation as 'drunken sailor' was perhaps confirmed by his assumed attachment to grog and by the notoriety of his debauchery when on leave in port towns.[49]

Afloat, it appeared that the Admiralty gave tacit approval for drunkenness through the daily issue of the rum ration. Rum had been issued daily to the ship's crew since 1687 when it was issued as an alternative to fetid water.[50] But by 1740 an admiral's concern over 'the swinish vice of drunkenness' had led to the dilution of rum with water, the concoction known better as 'grog', after the admiral's nickname of 'Old Grogram'.[51] Temperance activists were dismayed by Queen Victoria's apparent fondness for naval grog when she tried it during an inspection of the British fleet in 1842.[52]

Although the daily ration of grog had rooted itself as a firm naval tradition, by mid-nineteenth century, the Admiralty had gradually reduced the rum ration by further watering down grog in an attempt to decrease incidents of drunkenness on board, and any accompanying social problems.[53] In addition, water consumption had increased with improved methods of storing water in iron casks for longer periods on board ship. The Admiralty encouraged naval temperance, not so much for its virtuousness, but to ensure that disciplined sober bodies were attentive to their duties. Naval discipline and the maintenance of efficiency afloat, rather than religious motivation, were the main incentives for Admiralty reforms that promoted sobriety. The

Admiralty also offered monetary compensation of 1¼d per ration for teetotalers and introduced tea, cocoa, coffee and sugar as alternate rations.[54] Although drunkenness aboard ship was relatively uncommon, the Admiralty hoped that halving the ration, stopping the evening issue of rum, punishing excessive drunkenness and offering monetary compensation to teetotalers would foster naval discipline and efficiency.[55] In a more forceful attempt to end drunkenness, in 1863, the Admiralty made excessive drunkenness a punishable offence. The Admiralty's liberalisation of its leave policy combined with its clear punishments for transgressions connected to drunkenness and leave-breaking was rewarded by fewer offences connected to drunken sprees ashore.[56] By the early twentieth century, the Admiralty had organised annual lectures throughout the fleet and in port stations on the 'evils of intemperance'.[57] The Admiralty may have considered drunkenness a disciplinary problem and inconsistent with the demands of a modern navy, but it never seriously considered abolishing liquor.

The naval temperance movement developed alongside a national campaign for temperance. As alcohol consumption in Britain and liquor licences rose by the mid-nineteenth century, a teetotal campaign gained national attention in its battle against the liquor trade and its efforts to win over teetotalers.[58] Evangelical Christians portrayed drinking as a moral, social and national problem that required total prohibition as the only solution to the destruction caused by the demon drink.[59] Although temperance had once implied moderation in drinking, by the mid-century temperance now implied total prohibition. Yet, while a national temperance movement garnered widespread popular support by mid-century, naval temperance by the 1860s was of concern only to a few officers and men.

When afloat, much depended on the initiative of the commanding officer or the popular support of its crew. The hagiography of the early naval temperance movement included the promise of Admiral Sir William King-Hall in the 1850s that he would join the ranks of abstainers once those naval men habitually on punishment lists for drunkenness signed the temperance pledge. The HMS *Reindeer* was the site of the first temperance society, established in 1868 under the direction of Admiral James Sullivan.[60] Teetotalers on board a ship naturally sought the company of others, and the initiative of a few teetotalers led to the formation of naval branches of the International Order of the Good Templars, a pseudo-masonic mutual help society that was especially active in England in the 1870s.[61] But apart from the sporadic efforts of a few temperance activists, a movement to spread temperance throughout the Royal Navy did not begin until the last third of the nineteenth century.

Localised efforts by a few naval abstainers to encourage temperance, and the Admiralty's attempts to ensure discipline by diluting grog or by offering men cocoa, may have achieved some minor success but were not enough to spark a fleet-wide temperance movement. Only under the wing of the national temperance movement was an aggressive naval teetotal campaign launched. With the guidance and financial support of the National Temperance League, the Royal Naval Temperance Society (RNTS) was formed in 1873 with the grand object of creating a sober Christian navy.[62] The national temperance campaign targeted the navy because its reputation for drunkenness served as a good rallying cry for the temperance crusade.[63] Admiral Sir William King-Hall, an ardent teetotaler, was appointed president while Agnes Weston was assigned to the main role of superintending this society. She accepted the position because as 'a total abstainer myself, I knew very well that the sailor's spiritual interests were closely bound up with the temperance question'.[64]

The promotion of abstinence, rather than moderation, by the RNTS reflected the redefinition of temperance within the national movement where it became synonymous with teetotalism and total prohibition during the second half of the nineteenth century. Although the RNTS was sponsored by the larger National Temperance League, naval temperance campaigns were distinct from national prohibition movements. Naval temperance faced particular challenges because of the institutionalised status of alcohol within the navy. Yet like the leaders of the national temperance movement, naval temperance advocates, like Weston, used a variety of different arguments to win the sailor to temperance, all of which grounded temperance as the foundation of ideal manhood and cast drunkenness as the threat to one's masculine social status. Was temperance the attribute that saved souls, strengthened families, or won wars? Within the scope of Weston's mission, it did not really matter how the naval teetotaler was converted. Once temperance was secured, salvation was at least possible.

As a consequence, temperance was a prominent feature in all of Weston's projects, from her afternoon teas with naval boys, her mothers' meetings with sailors' wives, or her purchase and closure of dockyard pubs. Like national temperance activists who blamed alcohol for a host of social problems including poor health, crime, poverty, violence and family problems, Weston believed that getting rid of the scourge of drunkenness was a necessary prerequisite to dealing with other social problems.[65] For maritime missionaries and temperance activists, however, drinking was not merely a disciplinary and social problem – it was sinful and inexorably led to the sailor's moral ruin. Despite the structural personnel conditions that faced the British naval man in the late Victorian navy, temperance advocates like Weston continued to argue that drink was responsible for the sailor's distress.

Apart from recruiting individual men to temperance, Weston and the Naval Temperance Society pushed for an increase in the monetary allotment for forgoing the ration and lobbied for the complete abolition of the rum ration. Temperance advocates pressed the Admiralty for increases in the monetary compensation given to teetotalers, arguing that the meager 1¼d allowance hardly induced men to forsake their grog. Their main goal was the abolition of the rum ration, which had initiated many naval men into the dangerous ritual of drinking. According to the poem the 'Indignant Templar Tar', published in Weston's temperance periodical *Ashore and Afloat,*

> Tis drink, and drink alone, that lays the British Navy low,
> If you would raise our British tars, not need for you to flog;
> Remove temptation from their path – in one word, banish grog.[66]

But grog was not banished in Weston's lifetime. And although she pressed the Admiralty to increase compensation for sailors not taking the ration, it was not until 1919 that the allowance was increased to 3d a day. Considered a traditional right of the naval man, grog was not finally ended as a ration until 1970.

Weston's sailors' rests and the temperance pledge

While the RNTS was the official naval temperance organisation, Weston's sailors' rests acted as the headquarters for her temperance movement. The sailors' rests, which were homes for naval seamen ashore, were organised on temperance and Christian principles and established in the main naval ports of Devonport in 1876 and Portsmouth in 1882.[67] The purpose of the rests was to 'to assure the men of personal friendship, and to seek to bring them, by the power of God's spirit, into living union with the Lord Jesus Christ'.[68]

Eager to note that naval men supported her work, Weston stressed that the impetus to start a sailors' home in one of the home ports came from the naval men with whom she had corresponded. She remembered a Sunday gathering in Devonport for naval men, when one sailor pleaded for her help: 'What we want is a place here, close to the dockyard gates – a nice little place where we could be safe when we paid off from the land sharks and alligators, where there would be no drink; we talked about it before we paid off and we said, "Wonder whether Miss Weston will be outside the dockyard gates to keep us from going wrong"'.[69]

Weston intended that her rests would be safe havens for sailors away from the temptations, which surrounded naval men when ashore. By first getting the sailor off the street and away from drink and 'lewd women', Weston could then work upon the religious and spiritual well-being of the sailor 'where he can be kept free from all that could harm him'.[70] As temperance homes, her rests featured coffee canteens, which Weston attested 'have been found, where tried, to do so much for the men physically and morally'.[71] Although no alcohol was permitted inside the buildings, Weston's policy was to welcome even the most drunken sailors in hopes that they would eventually realise God's grace and take the pledge. Her goal was not merely to provide beds at a low cost, but also to provide 'a real harbour of refuge' where drunken bluejackets could be sent at all hours of the night for a sobering night's sleep.[72] They were generally popular places to stay, although their popularity most likely did not reflect a growing adherence to temperance principles among the men of the lower deck but rather the seamen's appreciation for inexpensive clean lodgings.[73]

The rests also accommodated meetings for the Royal Naval Temperance Society. As a concerned 'mother', Weston instructed her 'boys' to keep away from the demon drink. As with the British national temperance campaign, Weston's group was obsessed with pledges and converting men to the teetotaler flock. The temperance pledge taken by naval men was similar to the pledge offered by other temperance groups with one exception – the naval man pledged to forgo his daily grog. An elaborately ornamental certificate that noted that with the seaman's 'word and honour; God helping me to abstain from all intoxicating drinks and from taking up rum as a ration', the naval temperance pledge card cast the abstaining sailor as a heroic warrior.[74] By signing the temperance pledge, the naval man, like the legendary St George, chivalrously battled against his own personal demon. With such emotional, religious and militant imagery and such significance placed on the ritual of abstinence, taking the pledge represented the symbolic conversion of the sinning drinker becoming the virtuous teetotaler. One temperance historian has compared the moment of signing the pledge to the rite of baptism.[75] By bettering men's bodies, Weston had hoped to save their souls.

As a colourful addition to any man's ditty box, the card also served as a physical reminder every time the box was opened of the sailor's promise to stay clear of drink. Weston's success in garnering pledges was most noticeable among the boys in the training ships. From the beginning of her work with sailors, Weston visited boys in training ships and invited them for afternoon teas at her rests. It was on these occasions that she recruited boys to take the teetotal pledge. By the turn of the century, thousands of boys had taken the pledge, which in practice meant little since the Admiralty disallowed liquor to boy ratings. Still, Weston realised that this was an opportunity to inspire a future generation of sober Christian naval men.[76]

Weston's writings and publications were also an integral component of her temperance campaign. Her missionary work followed sailors to sea with the free delivery of her 'Blue Backs', her monthly letters to naval men, and her monthly temperance periodical, *Ashore and Afloat*.[77] Through her various publications, Weston was able to use different strategies to recruit both the naval man to temperance and the subscriber to support her cause financially.

Clearly, Weston was primarily interested in the spiritual regeneration of the sailor but she was more than willing to use social, political and naval arguments to appeal to both naval men and potential subscribers. As a result, her strategies for recruiting both sailor and subscriber to the temperance cause invoked their devotion to family, God and nation. Even the temperance pledge invoked the rhetoric of Christian militarism by proclaiming that forgoing one's grog was both 'For the Glory of God and the Good of the Service'. And through allegorical temperance stories, ballads and naval yarns, which highlighted proper and improper behavior for naval men, Weston hoped to impart moral instruction to naval seamen by contrasting the virtues of the naval abstainer with the vices of the drunken sailor. For Weston, only a naval abstainer could fulfil his duties as husband, father, Christian, and British sailor. By implication and denunciation, those men who took their grog were invariably drunken sailors who not only impoverished their family but also were poor fathers, poor Christians and poor patriots. But the outlook for these drifting souls was not so bleak because Weston believed that naval men were like children – despite being easily led astray, they could be shown the right path through proper guidance and sobriety. These representations, reproduced repeatedly in her publications, aimed not only to instruct sailors in moral lives, but also to gain admiration and financial support from subscribers for her missionary efforts. The conflicting depictions of drunken and temperate seamen were thus equally important in the conversion of both sailor and subscriber.

Weston appealed to the naval man's self-respect and patriotism as a British bluejacket in order to win him over to temperance. In Weston's literature, naval seamen were often portrayed as patriotic, manly and dutiful, 'ready at any time to sacrifice their lives for their country'.[78] In her pamphlet, 'A True Blue! What is he?' the bluejacket 'taken at his best' was 'a very fine fellow. Bright, cheery, and sunny faced, picturesque and stalwart, he stands true to his old friends as he stands to his country. Brave to a fault, he is ready to do or dare anything – the greater the danger the more eager he is to face it'.[79] Naval seamen were kind and generous to the fault of being too trusting. Although Jack in her estimation was noble and kind-hearted, he was as 'easily led to the right and to the wrong'. For Weston, the traditional grog ration encouraged drinking and, with it, delinquency. She wrote that, 'Drink has always been the seamen's snare – the cause . . . of nearly all the crime in the Service.'[80] Aside from punishments, drinking disgraced the naval man's noble character. She felt compelled to help these brave men to live honourably because 'to see the fine, manly, stalwart form of a man-o'-war's man reeling up the street, all his manliness gone, and the kindly, pleasant-spoken fellow turned either into a drivelling idiot or a rough swearing bully, is a spectacle sad enough to make men and angels weep'.[81] It was drunkenness that potentially robbed the sailor of his manhood and transformed the stalwart British bluejacket into his degenerate state.

Whereas drunkenness represented deviancy, weakness and a loss of masculinity, temperance for Weston symbolised strength, duty and manliness. 'Far from its being the sign of a weak mind', temperance showed 'the greatest strength of character – for the bravest man is ever the humblest, and the wisest always feels that he knows the least'.[82] Weston's abstainers realised that they could not be 'brave and faithful' naval men without giving up drink and 'leading a Christian life'.[83] All of these images imparted the message that military success, which depended upon bravery and duty, could only be attained through constant sobriety.

For Weston, the health of both nation and navy depended upon the moral and physical health of the British bluejacket. In the 1880s, Weston also took advantage of increasing naval estimates and contemporary naval scares to argue that temperance was a logical national policy if the British public valued their navy and their nation:

> with the increase of men and machinery, and everything else in our ships, and all the intricacies of modern welfare, if our bluejackets and marines are not, at the least, sober men, I would tremble for the safety of these great ships, worth their mills of money, and for the safety of my country too.[84]

In the pamphlet *England Home and Duty*, Weston remarked that, 'All know that a "sober navy is a national insurance" '.[85] Such a strategy of categorising temperance as naval efficiency targeted both the professional seaman and the concerned patriotic subscriber. In the early twentieth century, one naval official echoed Weston's demands for a Christian temperate fleet when speaking at the Portsmouth rest, 'without men of high moral stamp, our modern intricate ships can never be manned or manoeuvred. True, moral men we must have; Christian men are best of all'.[86] In describing the requirements to become a torpedo gunner in the pamphlet *A Handful of Yarns*, Weston highlighted the technological imperative for naval temperance. The gunner would have 'downright good brains, well-exercised, and kept bright and clear from drink. You don't make a torpedo gunner out of a drunkard. A man must be calm, cool, best of all if he trusts in God, and must do his duty at whatever risk'.[87] In this way, Weston widened the appeal for naval temperance by portraying temperance as a necessity for the highly trained, dutiful bluejacket in the modern Royal Navy. In a pamphlet especially directed at subscribers and invoking navalist rhetoric, Weston proclaimed the patriotic imperative of her naval charity,

> The great Navy of England, is under God the best asset that the nation has, and the supremacy of the seas is our vital point. To keep that Navy efficient as to ships, guns, and men, is the duty of every patriotic Briton, and . . . even from a selfish point of view we should try to make Jack's life as bright and happy as possible.[88]

After all, as she pointed out in another pamphlet, 'our naval seamen protect our commerce, act as police all over the world, and guard our hearths and homes. They are ready at any time to sacrifice their lives for their country, as they have shown again and again'.[89] Since these 'deservedly popular' men 'would shed the last drop of their blood, if need be, for the defence of their country', it was imperative for the British public to help naval men in need.[90]

Weston also encouraged temperance among sailors through an appeal to their own personal salvation. Like other religious prohibitionists of this period, Weston cast drunkenness as a sin, which impeded the sailor's road to salvation. She attested that 'the deep religious life of seamen is a true and abiding fact, and when, with all the energy of their characters, they turn from a sinful to a Christian life, they are as potent for good as they were for evil'.[91] And like the sinner who found forgiveness in Christ, the drunkard could also be reclaimed. She often shared stories of sailors, who after leading a life of drink and near death would confess to Weston that they wished their lives to be different, bless her for her work, and finally ask for God's mercy. These tales of redemption cautioned her naval readership to give up alcohol and also informed subscribers of her worthy mission. During a visit to a naval hospital in the late 1870s, Weston described her conversation with a naval patient dying from consumption. They discussed Weston's efforts to purchase the three Devonport pubs, which she had intended to convert into a Sailors' Rest. As Weston described it:

> With his skeleton finger he beckoned me to his bedside, and between his gasps he whispered in my ear, 'Have you got the "Dock Gates Inn"?' 'Not yet', I said, 'but I believe we shall; we are praying for it'. 'And so am I', he said earnestly, laying his bony hand on my arm; 'I am praying to God night and day on my bed, to give you that place; there I learned to drink, and the drink has brought me here'. Poor fellow, like a sinking boat he was going down; whether he was resting for salvation on Christ was not very clear, but his one desire was that the public house that had worked his ruin, might be done away with.[92]

This image of the ruined sailor who in his final hour embraced Weston's temperance work became an allegory of redemption. For naval men who wanted to avert such a fate, the choice was clear: to sign the temperance pledge. For subscribers, the message was also equally apparent: to pledge money to ensure that those pubs were closed down for good.

Similarly, *Ashore and Afloat* presented temperance as a key step to spiritual regeneration. In the temperance ballad 'A Forecastle Yarn' the 'sailor' revealed that,

> Tho' he had been in darkness once, and fallen as others low,
> And tho' he'd steeped his life in sin, and drowned each thought in drink,
> God, in His love, had saved his soul and caused his heart to think.

Not only did the sailor become a better Christian, he also became a teetotaler who urged others 'to cast the cursed drink away'.[93] In order to overcome the overwhelming temptation to drink, the naval abstainer needed to realise the 'absolute necessity of looking to God for strength to keep such a resolution'.[94]

Temperance, home and family

Weston also implored the naval man to give up drinking for the sake of his family. She appealed to naval men to understand that drunkenness threatened to undermine their masculine social status as husbands and fathers. One of her chief worries was that a sailor's drunken sprees in port helped to impoverish his family who depended on his wage. In her publications, she employed the images of both temperate and intemperate sailors to proclaim the advantages of a sober life and to warn of drinking's disastrous effects (see figure 2.1). The poem 'Jack's Come Home from Sea', published in *Ashore and Afloat* in 1893, features teetotaler Jack, a caring and thrifty husband, who comes home with wages to buy his wife 'some wholesome things' and puts

2.1 'A Home without the Drink', *Ashore and Afloat*, XXV, No. 5, May 1901.

the extra money into the bank. Temperance and respectability are linked because it is Jack's abstinence from liquor that enables him to be a responsible husband whose first priority is his family's welfare. If others are to learn from his success, he advises, 'Don't let the ale-house tempt you in,/ But throw the glass away'.[95] Sobriety was the foundation for the maintenance of a content, stable and healthy naval home.

Her publications also warned the sailor of the consequences of a life of drinking. The February 1901 issue of *Ashore and Afloat* featured a caricature of a drunken sailor entitled 'A Sad Hobby', in which the sailor is depicted holding in one hand the reins of what first appears to be a hobby horse but upon closer inspection is really a keg of liquor and, in the other hand, an empty liquor bottle (see figure 2.2). Unlike most of the romanticised illustrations featured in her paper, the 1901 cartoon had a particularly primitive design. In the corner is his wife grieving at the bare kitchen table, holding a baby, as her young daughter tugs at her dress. By cautioning naval readers to the dangers of a life of drink, she hoped the allegorical illustration would prompt them to turn to teetotalism for the good of their families. By invoking men's domestic responsibilities as husbands and fathers, Weston strategically appealed to sailors to become temperate to uphold their masculine social status.

Much to Weston's surprise, instead of pledging themselves to temperance, ratings wrote to the lower-deck newspaper the *Bluejacket* to voice strong objections to Weston's portrayal of naval men. Between March and September 1901, the *Bluejacket*, under the editorship of Lionel Yexley, published letters from ratings angry about the illustration of 'A Sad Hobby', defending their manhood, resentful of Weston's depiction of them as drunkards.[96] In the months before 'A Sad Hobby' was published the *Bluejacket* had featured articles that disparaged sailors' rests like Weston's for their paternalistic proselytising campaigns. Yexley, who had served in the navy and coastguard for over twenty years, spent as much time criticising Weston's efforts as he did lobbying for reform from the Admiralty. The appearance of 'A Sad Hobby' provided Yexley with the opportunity to stoke lower-deck resentment of Weston's efforts by encouraging ratings to write to the paper to challenge Westons' allegations.

Naval seamen resented the cartoon for many reasons. First, was the implication that all naval men were drunkards. One seaman argued that the caricature disgraced naval men with its assumption that the navy was rife with drunken vagrants.[97] Not only did the sketch picture the sailor as a drunkard but it also emasculated him by portraying him as a dishonourable husband and irresponsible father. In the March

A Sad Hobby.

2.2 'A Sad Hobby', *Ashore and Afloat*, XXV, No. 2, February 1901.

issue of the *Bluejacket*, a serviceman from the HMS *Caesar* rejected the cartoon's message and condemned Weston's accusations.

> I have never seen the married man yet who could go so far as to forget himself and family in the way this pictures him ... I can hardly conceive that she who poses as a sailor's friend should try to poison the minds of the British public by holding to ridicule the branch of the Empire who so lately have shown their value.[98]

In June, a petty officer explained why sailors were outraged, 'There is no qualifying phrase; the British bluejacket is pourtrayed [*sic*] as a drunken, dissolute scoundrel, who is willing to bring mother, wife, and children to the verge of beggary so that he may give full gratification to his unholy lust for drink.'[99] A seaman from the HMS *Prosephone* contended that he and his crew were 'utterly disgusted with it'. Aside from the illustration's personal attack on the sailor's character, it sent the wrong message to potential recruits, 'Young men and boys, who live in inland towns, would surely hesitate from joining such a Service. Such a thing, in my opinion, is degrading the King's uniform ...'[100] Sailors were enraged because the caricature threatened their newly acquired status as naval professionals by dishonouring and humiliating their roles in the navy and within the family.

Sailors not only wrote to Yexley but also sent letters to Weston. Although none of their letters were published in *Ashore and Afloat*, Weston's reply to a naval seaman was published in the *Bluejacket*. There she defended the cartoon by explaining that:

> the picture is intended as an object lesson, and is a perfect representation of scenes that I am sure that you must see every time general leave is given ... I myself have relieved hundreds of such cases and grieved I am to see so many sad homes ... but if he will give up the drink ... he will quickly rise and his home become happy and bright.[101]

For Weston, the disappointing truth was that the navy was full of men whose drunken sprees ashore jeopardised men's abilities to carry out their familial duties and stripped men of their manliness. Her hopes that the illustration would succeed in spreading temperance were dashed, as sailors' letters revealed that they objected to the condescending style of the cartoon, the temperance periodical, and Weston's naval mission.

By May, the cartoon prompted naval men to reconsider the merits of naval philanthropy. Although many, including Yexley, praised Weston's good intentions, they argued that the cartoon undermined Weston's work on behalf of the sailors. Yexley and naval seamen contended that Weston domesticated naval seamen by treating them like children with her tract literature and constant preaching. Yexley wrote that:

> We have protested over and over again about this addressing of present day fleetmen in words more fitted for infant school children than grown up men. The day of tracts . . . whose words are those of a mother address-ing very young children, are gone . . . Everybody is too obviously trying to nurse a sailor to please him. They want to be talked to and treated to a higher quality of appeal to their intelligences; to be treated more like men.[102]

Although it was perhaps 'instinctual' for the 'Mother of the Navy' to protect her boys, Yexley and others argued that naval men were no longer the boy ratings who had once frequented her afternoon teas. According to them, the problem with her naval charity was that she failed to distinguish between the needs of boys and men.

The illustration also offered the opportunity for naval men to remark on their own social advances as a naval professional class. In their responses, seamen worked to define their own masculine identities in contrast to Weston's (and society's) representations of them. One seaman claimed that Agnes Weston had failed to recognise that the modern bluejacket of the twentieth century 'was a very different man' from the bluejacket of the 1870s.[103] Another sailor claimed that before he read Weston's published reply, he 'always pictured her a noble woman trying to do good to our navy, . . . but if she persists in holding an opinion about the picture as she does, she will prove herself to be narrow minded and prejudiced, and will do an irreparable injury to the cause which she has undertaken for the British Navy'.[104] According to naval men, the sailors' progress by the early twentieth century resulted not from naval charity but from educational improvements, Admiralty reforms, and the self-conscious professional advances of naval men. In their responses to the cartoon, naval servicemen had the opportunity to defend their manhood against mythic popular imagery of sailors. One writer argued that naval seamen were,

> not the ramping, roaring, godless individuals that some people appear to imagine and that great changes have taken place in this and all other respects since the time 'Captain Marryat' was serving in the 'Royal Navee'. That there is serving in the Navy at present a thoughtful, deep thinking, intelligent class of men, that have the welfare of the Service and of their Country at heart.[105]

By the end of this letter-writing frenzy, seamen had loudly voiced their consternation. Naval seamen represented themselves as an intelligent professional body of men who resented attempts to dishonour their character by accusations, however crudely designed, which impugned their roles as husbands, fathers and seamen.[106]

As can be gauged by such invective, Weston's success in her temperance campaign was limited. Yet Weston claimed to have thousands of naval teetotalers belonging to the Royal Naval Temperance Society. Her claims to have 20,000 abstainers by 1908 may be impressive but it represents the cumulative total of pledges received by the RNTS since its formation in 1873. In addition, there is some difficulty in gauging these numbers in that they represent pledge-takers rather than verifiable abstainers. Committed abstainers who would have earned temperance medals for faithful membership represented only a fraction of pledge-takers.[107] Even if the movement to recruit earnest naval teetotalers failed, temperance remained an integral part of Weston's overall moral mission to ameliorate the naval man's physical and spiritual condition.

To determine Weston's moral influence on naval men would be a more difficult task. She was well-admired by appreciative servicemen and the British public for establishing her rests, which had provided inexpensive, clean and safe room and board for all sailors. Her philanthropic work was certainly popular with subscribers who pledged over one million pounds on behalf of naval men between the 1870s and the First World War. Such money contributed to her building projects, publications and organisations, as well as providing temporary relief for impoverished sailors' widows and children. In a period when philanthropies competed for patronage, Weston could boast the patronage of royalty, aristocracy and Admiralty. To her delight, her sailors' rests acquired the title 'Royal' after the Naval Exhibition of 1891. Royal appreciation of her lifelong work on behalf of the naval man's welfare was demonstrated by her appointment as Dame of the British Empire just one year before her death in October 1918. Groups like the Navy League commended her efforts, 'Nor can it be forgotten, in the face, ... of such an enterprise as that of Miss Weston, that the increased comfort, respectability and sobriety of our seafaring population result largely from the initiative and devoted work of a woman and her sister-helpers'.[108] In addition, the Admiralty, realising that her private philanthropy contributed to the stability and efficiency of the service, gave its tacit assent to her work and allowed Weston and her fellow missioners to board ships and speak to the crews about temperance.

Although the Admiralty did not provide financial support to her mission, its representatives attended and spoke at the frequent ceremonies at her rests.[109] Commodore A. A. C. Galloway, the superintendent of the Portsmouth naval barracks, also a teetotaler, even permitted

Weston and Wintz to organise a temperance canteen within the barracks in mid-1907.[110] Set up in the wake of the Stokers' Riots, which had occurred in the barracks in November 1906 and had been blamed by some on drunken unruly stokers, the temperance canteen was intended to promote a healthy and quiet diversion for the men. But its unpopularity with naval men led to its quick demise. Although men appreciated the many services offered by the rests, Weston's naval temperance continued to arouse bitter criticism by naval men who no longer cared to be 'mothered'.

Throughout her fifty years in service to the navy, Agnes Weston remained committed to spreading temperance and Christianity throughout the fleet. Like other temperance activists, she believed that temperance offered the possibilities for converting the sinner to the Christian faith. Yet in order to attract naval men to take the pledge and to gain the financial support of subscribers, Weston had to employ a variety of different arguments, in addition to religious ones, to win over the flock. Her difficulties were not in her tactics, such as arguing for temperance on the grounds of naval efficiency, but in her portrayal of the problem. Throughout the years, Agnes Weston relied upon older traditional imagery of the disreputable drunken sailor to portray the urgency of missionary work among naval seamen and warrant the continued support for her charities. Yet naval men, the Royal Navy, and British society had actually changed in those fifty years. The Admiralty had pursued a policy to reduce drunkenness on board ship in order to discipline bodies rather than to save souls; and naval men rejected her temperance efforts because they disparaged their claims to respectable manhood. They did not disagree with Weston's premise that drunkenness threatened the maintenance of their masculine social status; they disagreed with her portrayal of drunken sailors. Laws like the Inebriate Act of 1899, which were small victories for the national temperance movement, had made excessive public drunkenness a civil felony. By the turn of the century, drunkenness, rather than drink, was agreed to be the problem. Like the national British temperance movement, which was collapsing by the early twentieth century, Agnes Weston's movement to create a navy of teetotalers had also met with defeat because of its refusal to moderate its views on prohibition.

Notes

1   Anne Summers, 'A Home from Home –Women's Philanthropic Work in the Nineteenth Century', in *Fit Work for Women*, ed. Sandra Burman (New York: St Martin's Press, 1979), 33–63; Leonore Davidoff and Catherine Hall, *Family*

Fortunes: Men and Women of the English Middle Class, 1780–1850 (London: Hutchinson, 1987); John Tosh, *A Man's Place: Masculinity and the Middle-Class Home in Victorian England* (New Haven: Yale University Press, 1999).

2 Frank Prochaska, 'Philanthropy', in *The Cambridge Social History of Britain, 1750–1950*, vol. 3, ed. F. M. L. Thompson, (Cambridge: Cambridge University Press, 1993), 360–1.

3 John Bechervaise, *Thirty-Six Years of a Seafaring Life* (Portsea: W. Woodward, 1839), 13, 306. Samuel Noble, *Sam Noble, Able Seaman: 'Tween Decks in the 'Seventies* (New York: Frederick Stokes, 1926), 185, 264.

4 Prochaska, 'Philanthropy', 385. Prochaska estimates that over 500,000 women worked 'continuously and semi-professionally' as volunteers in philanthropic institutions by the end of the century.

5 Agnes Weston, *Signals of Distress!* (Portsmouth, 1905), 2.

6 Surprisingly, there has been little scholarship on Agnes Weston's life and what there is tends to rely on three sources. Sophia Wintz, Weston's companion and partner in naval philanthropy, wrote Weston's first biography, *Our Blue Jackets: Miss Weston's Life and Work Among our Sailors* (London: Hodder & Stoughton, 1890). Weston wrote her own autobiography, *My Life Among the Bluejackets* (London: Nisbet, 1911), which traced the success of her life's work among seamen. The most recent biography of Weston is Doris Gulliver, *Dame Agnes Weston* (London: Phillimore, 1971) – a helpful though sentimental portrait. The difficulty in providing a balanced account of Agnes Weston's life and achievements is that much of her own personal writings were lost in the bombings of Portsmouth and Devonport during the Second World War.

7 Martha Vicinus, *A Widening Sphere: Changing Roles of Victorian Women* (Bloomington: Indiana University Press, 1977); Vicinus, ed., *Suffer and Be Still, Women in the Victorian Age* (Bloomington: Indiana University Press, 1973); Kathleen D. McCarthy, ed., *Lady Bountiful Revisited: Women, Philanthropy, and Power* (New Brunswick: Rutgers University Press, 1990).

8 Jane Lewis, *Women in England, 1870–1950: Sexual Divisions and Social Change* (Sussex: Wheatsheaf Books, 1984), 93. Apart from Florence Nightingale, Mary Seacole, and Sarah Robinson, few Victorian women distinguished themselves in their service to the British military. Sarah Robinson, who had set up the Soldiers' Institute in Portsmouth, encouraged Weston to carry on similar work with naval men. See Sarah Robinson, *'My Book': A Personal Narrative* (London: S. W. Partridge and Co., 1914). Contemporary didactic literature heralded their good work. See Jennie Chappell, *Noble Work by Noble Women* (London: S. W. Partridge, 1910).

9 Weston, *Temperance Work in the Royal Navy* (London: Hodder & Stoughton, 1879), 8.

10 Excerpt from the *Rock* about Weston's speech at Exeter Hall, quoted in *Ashore and Afloat*, July 1887, 66.

11 Weston, *Temperance Work*, 11.

12 Weston, *Safe Moorings* (London: Hazell, Watson and Viney, n.d.), 4.

13 *Ashore and Afloat*, April 1887, 39; *Onward: Subscription List, 1908–1909* (Portsmouth, 1909), 4; *From One Generation to Another, Balance Sheets and Subscription Lists, 1912–1913* (Portsmouth, 1913), 25; *What the Wild Waves are saying* (Portsmouth, 1914?), 6; *Ashore and Afloat* (March 1917), 47. Naval teetotalers were estimated to be 10,000 in 1887; 20,000 in 1908; 25,000 in 1912; 27,000 in 1914; and around 47,000 in 1917. Rather than report an annual total of pledges, her numbers represented a cumulative total of boys and men who had pledged to abstain from alcohol from the formation of her rests. Although the numbers of pledge-takers may have increased, the proportion of Weston's abstainers to total manning levels actually reflects a decrease in the percentage of naval men signing the pledge. A better, though painstaking, gauge for measuring temperance in the fleet would be to calculate Admiralty records of the number of men who annually abstained from their grog ration.

14 In this chapter, philanthropy is defined broadly to encompass what Brian Harrison has defined as 'any organisation devoting money, time, thought, or energy to relieving the miseries of the poor, the neglected, or the oppressed'. Brian Harrison, 'Philanthropy and the Victorians', *Victorian Studies* 9, no. 4 (June 1966), 356.

15 David Owen, *English Philanthropy* (Cambridge: Harvard University Press, 1964); Harrison, 'Philanthropy and the Victorians', 353–74 and *Peaceable Kingdom: Stability and Change in Modern Britain* (Oxford: Oxford University Press, 1982); F. K. Prochaska *Women and Philanthropy in Nineteenth Century England* (Oxford: Oxford University Press, 1980), *The Voluntary Impulse* (London: Faber & Faber, 1988), and 'Philanthropy'; Alan J. Kidd, 'Philanthropy and the "social history paradigm"', *Social History* 21, no. 2 (May 1996), 180–92.

16 Anne Summers, 'A Home from Home', 52.

17 F. K. Prochaska, 'Philanthropy', 389.

18 For more on evangelicalism, see J. Christopher Soper, *Evangelical Christianity* (New York: New York University Press, 1994); John Wolffe, 'Evangelicalism in mid-nineteenth-century England', in *Patriotism: The Making and Unmaking of British National Identity*, ed. Raphael Samuel, vol. 1 (London: Routledge, 1989), 188–202; Ian Bradley, *The Call to Seriousness: The Evangelical Impact on the Victorians* (1976); J. D. Walsh, 'Origins of the Evangelical Revival', in *Essays in Modern English Church History*, ed. G. V. Bennett and J. D. Walsh (1966); F. K. Brown, *Fathers of the Victorians* (Cambridge: Cambridge University Press, 1961).

19 Adam Hochschild, *Bury the Chains: Prophets and Rebels in the Fight to Free an Empire's Slaves* (Boston: Houghton Mifflin, 2005); Boyd Hilton, *The Age of Atonement: the Influence of Evangelicalism on Social and Economic Thought, 1785–1865* (Oxford: Clarendon Press, 1991); David Brion Davis, *The Problem of Slavery in the Age of Revolution, 1770–1823* (Ithaca, NY: Cornell University Press, 1975); Roger Anstey, *The Atlantic Slave Trade and British Abolition* (Atlantic Highlands, NJ: Humanities Press, 1975).

20 Catherine Hall, 'The Early Formation of Victorian Domestic Ideology', in *Fit Work for Women*, 16.

21 Hall, 'Early Formation of Victorian Domestic Ideology', 17. Despite the role of self-inquiry, to qualify as a good Christian meant to be passive and obedient. Also see Brian Harrison, *Drink and the Victorians: The Temperance Question in England: 1815–1872* (London: Faber & Faber, 1971) where he concludes that the spiritual understanding of temperance was actually a moment of liberation for individual Christians who worked towards achieving their own salvation through abstinence, thus undermining religious doctrines of God's authority.

22 Prochaska, 'Philanthropy', 379; James Obelkevich, 'Religion', in *The Cambridge Social History of Britain, 1750–1950*, vol. 3, 322.

23 Roald Kverndal, *Seamen's Missions* (Pasadena: William Carey Library, 1986); Peter Anson, *The Church and the Sailor* (London: John Gifford Limited, 1948); and Harry R. Skallerup, *Books Afloat and Ashore: A History of Books, Libraries, and Reading among Seamen during the Age of Sail* (Hamden, Conn: Archon Books, 1974).

24 Arthur Marsh and Victoria Ryan, *The Seamen: A History of the National Union of Seamen, 1887–1987* (Oxford: Malthouse Press, 1988), 5.

25 Harrison, 'Philanthropy and the Victorians', 359.

26 Donna T. Andrew, *Philanthropy and Police: London Charity in the Eighteenth Century* (Princeton: Princeton University Press, 1989); Judith R. Walkowitz, *Prostitution and Victorian Society* (Cambridge: Cambridge University Press, 1980). After the repeal of the Contagious Diseases Acts in 1886, many of the repealers continued to be active in the social purity crusade to reclaim prostitutes from what crusaders perceived was their moral ruin.

27 *Ashore and Afloat*, April 1888, 32. Anna Davin, 'Imperialism and Motherhood'. *History Workshop* 5 (Spring 1978): 9–66.

28 Harrison, 'Philanthropy and the Victorians', 357.

29 F. M. L. Thompson, 'Social Control in Victorian Britain', *Economic History Review* 34, no. 2 (1981), 189–208; Gareth Stedman Jones, 'Class Expression versus Social Control? A Critique of Recent Trends in the Social History of "leisure"', in *Languages of Class* (Cambridge: Cambridge University Press, 1989); A. P. Donajgrodzki, ed., *Social Control in Nineteenth Century Britain* (London: Croom Helm, 1977).

30 Victor Bailey, '"In Darkest England and the way out": The Salvation Army, Social Reform and the Labour Movement, 1885–1910', *International Review of Social History* 29, no. 2 (Part 2, 1984), 133–71; David M. Fahey, *Temperance and Racism* (Lexington, KY: University of Kentucky Press, 1996); Jennifer Hart, 'Religion and Social Control in the Mid-Nineteenth Century', in *Social Control in Nineteenth Century Britain*, 108–37; Gerald Wayne Olsen, 'From Parish to Palace: Working-Class Influences on Anglican Temperance Movements, 1835–1914', *Journal of Ecclesiastical History* 40, no. 2 (April 1989), 239–52.

31 Harrison, *Drink*, 378. Harrison argues that working-class, rather than middle-class, activism shaped the early temperance movement.

32 Soper, *Evangelical Christianity*, 93.

33 Alston Kennerley, 'Seamen's Missions and Sailors' Homes: Spiritual and Social Welfare Provision for Seafarers in British Ports in the Nineteenth Century, with some reference to the South West', in *Studies in British Privateering, Trading Enterprise and Seamen's Welfare, 1775–1900*, ed. Stephen Fisher (Exeter: University of Exeter, 1987).

34 Colonel Sir James Gildea, *Historical Record of the Work of The Soldiers' and Sailors' Families Association from 1885 to 1916* (London: Eyre and Spottiswoode, 1916), 7.

35 Gildea, *Historical Record*, 133.

36 Gildea, *Historical Record*, 65.

37 *Ashore and Afloat*, July 1891, 70.

38 Gildea, *Historical Record*, 31.

39 *Ashore and Afloat*, July 1891, 70.

40 Gildea, *Historical Record*, 78.

41 *Ashore and Afloat*, January 1891.

42 Marcus Rediker, *Between the Devil and the Deep Blue Sea* (Cambridge: Cambridge University Press, 1987), 198.

43 Lionel Yexley, 'A National Need', *The Fleet*, June 1908, 167.

44 *The Times*, 4 May 1908. Cited in *The Fleet*, June 1908, 167.

45 Gildea, *Historical Record*, 107. During the South African War, the SSFA had distributed over £1,205,877 to 198,438 families.

46 Some of this material was previously published in '"You don't make a torpedo gunner out of a drunkard": Agnes Weston, Temperance, and the British Navy', *Northern Mariner/Le Marin du nord*, IX, 1 (January 1999), 1–22. I thank the editors for permission to reuse this material here.

47 Gillian Sutherland, 'Education', in *The Cambridge Social History of Britain, 1750–1950*, edited by F. M. L. Thompson (Cambridge: Cambridge University Press, 1993), III, 142.

48 Reverend G. Goodenough, R. N., *The Handy Man Afloat and Ashore* (London: T. Fisher Unwin, 1901), 79.

49 Henry D. Capper, Lieutenant-Commander, *Aft–from the Hawsehole: Sixty-Two Years of Sailors' Evolution.* (London: Faber & Gwyer, 1927), xi. See Judith Fingard, *Jack in Port* (Toronto: University of Toronto Press, 1982) and Sarah Palmer, 'Seamen Ashore in Late Nineteenth Century London: Protection from the Crimps', in *Seamen in Society*, ed. Paul Adams (Bucharest: Proceedings of the Conference of the International Commission of Maritime History, 1980), III, 55–67.

50 Peter Kemp, ed., *Oxford Companion to Ships and the Sea* (Oxford: Oxford University Press, 1994). See entry for 'grog', 357. Rum was introduced after the

conquest of Jamaica in 1655 as a liquid alternative, along with beer, to fetid water.

51 Eugene Rasor, *Reform in the Royal Navy* (Hamden, Conn.: Archon Books, 1976), 82; Winton, *Hurrah*, 24; Lewis, *Navy in Transition*, 271. Until 1825, ratings received two gills (one-half pint) of grog, which was divided into two allotments served at midday and evening. Until 1825, a grog ration was constituted of .25 pint of rum with an equal amount of water. In 1825, the grog ration was reduced to one gill per day. In 1831, the beer ration was abolished.

52 Gulliver, *Weston*, 28.

53 Michael Lewis, *Navy in Transition* (London: Hodder & Stoughton, 1965), 269; Rasor, *Reform*, 83. The rum ration was halved in 1850 to a half gill, or one-eighth of a pint, and the evening issue was cancelled. In 1870, the rum ration was reduced even further by diluting the ratio of grog with three parts water to one part rum.

54 Public Record Office, Kew (hereafter PRO), ADM 7/938, Public Record Office, Kew, 'Circular No. 105: Spirit Ration and Substitutes for it', 19 November 1881. In 1881, the grog ration was discontinued for officers of the wardroom.

55 Wells, *The Royal Navy*, 29; Admiral Lord Charles Beresford, *The Memoirs of Admiral Lord Charles Beresford*, 3rd edn, 2 vols. (London: Methuen and Co, 1914), 17–18, 567.

56 PRO, ADM 7/908, 'Circular Letter: Discipline', November 1912.

57 PRO, ADM 116/1060, Letter from Medical Director-General to Board of Admiralty, 6 May 1908; PRO, ADM 7/910, 'Nore Confidential Memorandum No. 3: Lectures on Personal hygiene', 20 July 1910.

58 Harrison, *Drink*, chapter three; Soper, *Evangelical Christianity*, 63.

59 Harrison, *Drink*, 182; Soper, *Evangelical Christianity*, 67.

60 Agnes Weston, *Temperance Work* (London: Hodder & Stoughton, 1879).

61 Capper, *Aft–from the Hawsehole*, 24. See also David M. Fahey, *Temperance and Racism: John Bull, Johnny Reb, and the Good Templars* (Lexington, KY: University of Kentucky Press, 1996). One benefit of the Templars was that they bridged social gaps by allowing social relationships between abstaining sailors afloat and civilian teetotallers of often higher social rank ashore.

62 Wintz, *Our Blue Jackets*, 57. At a meeting in Devonport on 28 April 1873, the National Temperance League took control of the Royal Naval Temperance Society (RNTS).

63 The naval seaman was also easily recognisable due to the introduction of a naval uniform in the 1850s.

64 Weston, *Temperance Work*, 9.

65 Soper, *Evangelical Christianity*, 65.

66 *Ashore and Afloat* (November 1890), 102. Reprinted from *Good Templar's Watchword*.

67 Wintz, *Our Blue Jackets*, chapter five. Smaller rests would also be established in Chatham, Keyham, Sheerness, and Portland as opportunity and demand arose.

68 Weston, *Personal Work among Our Blue Jackets Ashore and Afloat, From 1879–1880: Annual Report of Sailors' Rest and Institute* (Devonport: A.H. Swiss Printers, 1880), 4.

69 Weston, *Shaking out a Reef* (London: Hazell, Watson and Viney, 1895), 8.

70 Weston, *Signals of Distress!* (1905), 2.

71 Weston, *Temperance Work*, v.

72 Weston, *Safe Moorings*, 7.

73 Naval men remembered Weston's rests more fondly than her religious mission. In addition, the rests also provided needed accommodation in overcrowded port towns especially before the introduction of the barrack system in the early-twentieth century. Capper, *Aft–from the Hawsehole*, 42; *Oral History Recordings: Lower Deck, 1910–1922*, Department of Sound Records, Imperial War Museum; Christopher McKee, *Sober Men and True: Sailor Lives in the Royal Navy, 1900–1945* (Cambridge: Harvard University Press, 2002), 5, 166.

74 Leonard Tozer, RN, RNTS membership card, 1913, 45/88 (25) 6.16, Royal Naval Museum, Portsmouth England.
75 Lilian Shiman, *Crusade against Drink in Victorian England* (London: Macmillan, 1986), 19; Soper, *Evangelical Christianity*, 70.
76 Weston, *Jottings from my Log* (Portsmouth, 1889), 22–3. See also *Temperance Work*. In their reminiscences, some retired naval men fondly remembered the afternoon teas at her rests when they were boy ratings. See *Oral History Recordings: Lower Deck, 1910–1922*, Department of Sound Records, Imperial War Museum.
77 Weston's temperance periodical was first called *Naval Brigade News* but was changed to *Miss Weston's Ashore and Afloat* in 1887. Sophia Wintz was responsible for the editorship of both papers, which were sent both to sailors, their families, and subscribers.
78 Weston, *Shaking out a Reef*, 34.
79 Weston, *A True Blue! What is he?* (Portsmouth: Royal Sailors' Rests, 1904), 3.
80 Weston, *Temperance Work*, 3.
81 Wintz, *Our Bluejackets*, 56.
82 Weston, *Temperance Work*, 27.
83 Weston, *Shaking out a Reef*, 43.
84 *Ashore and Afloat*, June 1887, 53.
85 Weston, *England Home and Duty* (NP, 1910), 13.
86 Weston *Shaking out a Reef*, 34.
87 Agnes Weston, *A Handful of Yarns* (London: S. W. Partridge & Co., 1898), 1.
88 Weston, *One Flag, One Fleet, One Throne* (1902), 5.
89 Weston, *Shaking out a Reef*, 34.
90 Weston, *One Flag, One Fleet, One Throne*, 5.
91 Weston, *Safe Moorings*, 4.
92 Weston, *Shaking out a Reef*, 24–6.
93 *Naval Brigade News*, January 1886, 6.
94 Weston, *Temperance Work*, 27.
95 C. H. Moore, HMS *Hecla*, 'Jack's come home from Sea', *Ashore and Afloat*, February 1893, 16.
96 The *Bluejacket* protected the confidentiality of naval men by allowing them to air their grievances anonymously. Admiralty regulations regarding speech and combination of naval personnel had made it especially difficult for men to organise and lobby for reform. See Anthony Carew, *The Lower Deck of the Royal Navy 1900–1939* (Manchester: Manchester University Press, 1981), 5.
97 *Bluejacket*, April 1901, 85.
98 *Bluejacket*, March 1901, 58.
99 *Bluejacket*, June 1901, 122.
100 *Bluejacket*, April 1901, 84.
101 *Bluejacket*, April 1901, 85.
102 *Bluejacket*, May 1901, 101.
103 *Bluejacket*, July 1901, 147.
104 *Bluejacket*, July 1901, 147.
105 *Bluejacket*, February 1902, 321.
106 After Yexley left the editorship of the *Bluejacket* in 1904 to start a new naval paper the *Fleet*, Thomas Holman, a temperance man and Weston supporter, undertook the editorship of the *Bluejacket*, and ended the diatribes against Weston.
107 *Onward: Subscription List, 1908–1909* (Portsmouth, 1909), 4; From *One Generation to Another, Balance Sheets and Subscription Lists, 1912–1913*, 25. The RNTS awarded nearly 1,400 medals for faithful membership in 1912 when membership claims stood at around 25,000 men. Given that Weston claimed to have 20,000 pledge takers in 1908, it is reasonable to assume that she had an active membership of 5,000 boys and men. There were also possibly some naval men who gave up their grog or were teetotalers without feeling the compulsion to belong to a temperance club.

108 Miss Woodruffe, 'Ladies Page', in *Navy League Journal*, November 1897, 6.
109 Her admirers in the navy included the King-Hall family, Admiral Edmund Fremantle, Admiral Charles Beresford, and Admiral John Jellicoe.
110 Weston, *My Life among the Bluejackets*, 285; Lionel Yexley, *Charity and the Navy* (London: the Fleet Ltd, 1911), 34.

CHAPTER THREE

From powder monkey to admiral: social mobility, heroism and naval manhood

The naval temperance movement was not singular in revealing the clear class dimensions in the portrayal of naval manhood. A significant component in constructing gendered identities in their lived and hegemonic forms, class influenced most distinctly the complexion of gender and manliness in Victorian Britain and empire.[1] Analysing the class implications of representing naval manhood serves as a useful way to understand the domestic formation of imperial manhood. Such a study cannot treat class in isolation. Popular constructions of imperial manhood in Victorian Britain relied as much upon idealisations of class as upon empire, race or home. As Anne McClintock has argued, gender and class 'are not distinct realms of experience ... Rather, they come into existence *in and through* relations to each other – if in contradictory and conflictual ways'.[2] Popular representations of naval manhood in the mid- to late Victorian period highlight this relationship. As the navy served to symbolise both nation and empire, depictions of naval manhood came to embody Victorian manly ideals, which valued masculine attachments to family, home and empire.

Yet, Victorian manliness, though widely visible in popular culture, represented and reflected the interests of the upper and middle classes. In mid-Victorian society, respectable manliness was marked by an adherence to duty, from which all other moral virtues like discipline, rationality and purity emanated. Defined as an in-born quality that would reveal itself in time and in circumstance, mid-Victorian manliness was not within the reach of all boys and men, just those within the upper and middle classes. Although class standing was the barrier to 'true' manhood in mid-Victorian Britain, popular culture encouraged men and, particularly, boys both to emulate their social betters and to be content with their station. Instructing boys to be dutiful was a lesson in self-abnegation, in controlling tendencies to profligacy and sloth.[3] If true manliness was seemingly out of the grasp of most men, how did the common sailor come to represent imperial manhood?

The answer is complicated and the reconstruction of naval manhood in late Victorian Britain reflected and reinforced the slow democratisation of manhood, albeit defined and limited by the frame of politics and empire in the mid- to late nineteenth century. As international competition for markets and territories intensified ideologies of national difference, electoral reforms in 1867 and 1884 redefined who belonged within the nation.[4] Democratisation and imperial competition represented internal and external challenges that threatened traditional centres of domestic and imperial control. The achievement of manhood was often portrayed through the setting of military and imperial adventures. In addition, by the 1870s, increasing concerns with the health of the national body emerged as to whether the 'stock' of the nation could withstand the challenges of military and economic competition of other nations.[5] Conservatives like Benjamin Disraeli were able to transform patriotism from its radical democratic roots into a belief system that emphasised the unity of the British (often represented as English) race over subordinate competing regional, religious and class identities. Although historians have debated the nature of working-class patriotism, there can be no doubt regarding the propagandistic impulse of the late nineteenth-century state and press to promulgate a patriotic British and imperial identity.[6] The late nineteenth century was full of imperial pageantry from the crowning of Victoria as Empress of India in 1878 to the coronation jubilees and the imperial exhibitions.

New popular portrayals of naval men that appeared within and alongside this imperial pageantry began to celebrate a democratised model of British imperial manhood, albeit produced by state authorities and within elite circles. In particular, patriotic rhetoric that promoted the exploits of the navy and its men, served as a bond between patriotism from Georgian and early Victorian political radicalism to its manifestations in the age of new imperialism. Popular portrayals of naval men in mid-to late Victorian Britain could at once remind Britons of the navy's historic legacy in securing both freedom and empire and the compatibility between them. Such celebratory depictions concealed the problematic roles that impressment and corporal discipline played in achieving those ends.[7] The irony was that British naval men did not win the tangible rewards of citizenship awarded to many of their fellow working men in the 1867 and 1884 Reform Acts.[8] And, yet, naval men would find themselves championed within popular culture as the defenders of Britain's empire.

[100]

Duty, self-help, and manhood

Within late nineteenth-century British society, family, home and empire were all rhetorically conceived as outgrowths of the nation. Duty, the naval watchword made famous by Nelson, joined navy, home, nation and empire into one common bond. Popular representations of naval men appeared in the late Victorian period in a wide variety of mass media from the press, advertisements and fiction, which posited them as the stalwart defenders of civic virtues whether at home or across the empire. Although older stereotypes of the bawdy tar no doubt flourished, refashioned images of naval men in imperial Britain emerged as models of manhood ashore and afloat who were able to carry out their responsibilities as husbands and fathers all the while safeguarding the empire. These late Victorian portrayals of naval manhood, produced in popular, public, and political discourse contributed to a cross-class ideal of manliness in which all men were expected to defend the interests of family, home and empire.

The ideal of Victorian manliness was highlighted most famously in Thomas Hughes' *Tom Brown's School Days*, which informed its young middle-class readership that 'the crown of all manliness, of all Christian manliness, is purity'.[9] Although the stereotypic image of the naval man as Jolly Jack Tar, whose boundless passions and lack of discipline made him an unlikely model for such manliness, to Victorian writers like Hughes, the Royal Navy and its men seemed particularly suitable vessels in which to embody the virtues of muscular Christianity. The phrase 'muscular Christianity' first appeared in the 1850s to describe the tenets of Charles Kingsley and Thomas Hughes' writings. The doctrine of muscular Christianity rejected displays of effeminate piety and promulgated a rugged manliness that embraced good health, physical strength and Christian ethics.[10] Muscular Christianity was particularly well-suited to justify empire. According to Hughes, it was in the navy where 'a man's body is given him to be trained and brought into subjection, and then used for the protection of the weak, and advancement of all righteous causes and the subduing of the earth, which God has given to the children of men'.[11] Since the navy was a male preserve, it became, like the Army, a good model for imparting such manly virtues. For example, Gordon Stables, a former naval surgeon and a popular boys' fiction writer, advised his readership on the meaning of duty in 'On Special Service: a Naval Story', a serialised story that appeared in the *Boy's Own Paper* in 1884: 'the bravest men are those who can see the danger of a situation they may be called upon to face, but who face it nevertheless'.[12]

Naval stories for boys imparted the importance of duty, self-denial and hard work, which together helped produce manly Christian heroes. Nelson's message at Trafalgar to his men that they do their duty for England was a lesson learned by all English children when they entered the classroom.[13] The first issue of another boys' story paper, *Comrades*, from 1898, featured a story called 'A True British Sailor-Boy'. The cover from the magazine showed a 12-year-old boy hugging the mast of a sinking ship as waves lapped at his feet. The caption below the illustration read, ' "I did not desert you!" was all he said'.[14] The true British boy did his duty even if it meant the sacrifice of his own life for his country. According to the boys' story paper, *Boys of England*, this manliness was 'the cause of England's moral as well as physical supremacy over the other nations of the earth'.[15]

In particular, new representations of naval men were preoccupied with class distinctions that elided realities of class tensions and represented manliness as an inborn virtue. Popular representations from literature, advertising, games and theatre portrayed the navy, which was in reality layered in rigid social hierarchies, as an institution that rewarded hard work and good character with steady advancement through the ranks. By seamlessly resolving questions about class and masculinity within the seemingly safe confines of the ship, these stories ignored the real class obstacles of Victorian society and presented their boy readers with the illusion of a unified egalitarian Britain. But even in these stories, promotion and advancement aboard ship depended upon clever plots, which maintained the social order at the expense of true social democracy.

The interaction between duty, nation and individual advancement within Victorian maritime literature reflected the ascendancy of the ideology of self-improvement, best articulated in Samuel Smiles' enormously successful *Self-Help*, based on lectures he had given to young working men in Leeds and first published in 1859.[16] Self-improvement, as elucidated by Smiles, was not simply a guide to individual advancement; rather it was a bourgeois ideology that would encompass both the enrichment of individual and nation through its emphasis on hard work, duty and thrift. According to Smiles, 'the spirit of self-help is the root of all genuine growth in the individual; and, exhibited in the lives of many, it constitutes the true source of national vigour and strength'.[17] In fact, self-help was British in character providing the 'true measure of our power as a nation'.[18] If self-help was British, it was also masculine in nature. All of Smiles' anecdotal biographical models in *Self-Help* were men. The masculine enterprise of self-help with its 'spirit of industry' 'laid the fountains and built up the industrial greatness of the empire'.[19] For Smiles, 'truthfulness, integrity, and goodness' formed the 'essence of manly character' and embodied 'human nature in its best form'.[20] Inspired by the possession of good character, every man would strive for it and 'his idea of manhood, in proportion as it is elevated, will steady and animate his motive'.[21]

Although Smiles had written celebratory biographies of men who had achieved tremendous financial success as a result of inventions or business ventures, Smiles' vision of manhood was to be measured by character, not monetary wealth. When Smiles first spoke before Leeds workers in the 1840s, he explained that the doctrine of self-help was not,

> to be regarded merely as a means of gaining a higher position in society than that which you now hold ... The education of the working-classes is to be regarded, in its highest aspect, not as a means of raising up a few clever and talented men into a higher rank of life, but of raising the entire condition of the working class. The grand object aimed at should be to make the great mass of people virtuous, intelligent, well-informed, and well-conducted.[22]

While Smiles' vision of self-help intended to uplift the working classes, his scheme did not aim to provide a path for working men to advance materially and socially to the standard of the middle classes. Rather than democratise society, the language of self-improvement endeavoured to produce better behaved classes. But for those who read Smiles' books about great inventors, like *The Life of George Stephenson* (1857), or his books about virtues, like *Character* (1871), *Thrift* (1875), and *Duty* (1887), the message was probably interpreted in a different way – anyone could rise to the top of the social ladder through perseverance, good conduct and individual enterprise.

Smiles' conception of the social order reflected a bourgeois definition of manhood and a gendered conception of class. Reform of the working class, with its consequent benefit to both nation and empire, depended first upon transforming working men. Although Smiles considered that the working classes were naturally undisciplined and given to profligate spending, he also believed that through discipline, working men could rise above their natural tendencies.[23] In this way, he celebrated working men 'who have successfully battled with and overcome the adverse circumstances of life ... [rising] from out of the lowest depth of poverty'.[24]

Writing in the wake of the Crimean War Smiles, like other social critics, saw the benefits of military discipline in moulding a new class of working men. As a consequence of working men who 'were the people at large compelled to pass through the discipline of the army, the country would be stronger, the people would be soberer, and thrift would become much more habitual than it is at present'.[25] Smiles' celebration of the martial virtues of manliness was increasingly a commonplace in Victorian Britain. To Smiles, the 'heroism' of the common 'private' and 'men in the ranks' not only contributed to Britain's military success, it highlighted the working man's ability to better himself.[26] In *Duty*, Smiles' later companion to *Self-Help*, he contended that the sea 'nursed the most valorous of men' who learned 'courage', 'duty', 'patience' and 'responsibility'.[27] To characterise the standard for manliness, Smiles quoted from the description of an annual award that the queen gave to an exceptional marine boy, noting that the young sailor would display 'cheerful submission to superiors, self-respect and independence of character, kindness and protection to the weak, readiness to forgive offence, a desire to conciliate the differences of others, and, above all, fearless devotion to duty and unflinching truthfulness'. Smiles proclaimed that such values were not singular to the sailor but 'would produce an almost perfect moral character in every condition of life'.[28]

Although it is difficult to gauge Smiles' direct influence on popular literature in the second half of the nineteenth century, the doctrine of self-improvement and the virtues of military service permeated children's, and particularly boys' literature in mid-to late Victorian Britain.[29] Children's military stories of the late Victorian period provided didactic models of good conduct for their young readers whose contact to and understanding of the navy was limited mostly to reading.[30] The naval and imperial adventures of popular children's writer William Henry Giles (W. H. G.) Kingston, for example, mixed Smiles' ideas of self-improvement with evangelical morality, revealing that self-advancement was possible for boys who trusted in God rather than submitted to selfish indulgence.[31] Kingston was both a prolific and popular writer, publishing one hundred books between 1850 and 1880. And there was a large audience for his writings. In an 1884 survey of 2000 English schoolchildren, regarding their reading habits, Kingston ranked as the boys' second favourite author next to Charles Dickens.[32]

As well as being a popular writer of boys' fiction, Kingston established the Society for Missions to Seamen in 1856 and organised the Rifle Volunteers in 1859, and was active in the Colonisation Society and the Society for the Promotion of Christian Knowledge (SPCK). Often commissioned by these groups, Kingston wrote stories that aimed to steer his readers towards good behaviour and reflected his devotion to patriotism, Christianity and things maritime. In stories like *Peter the Whaler*, *Mark Seaworth* and *Old Jack*, Kingston wrote about the adventures and dangers faced by fishermen, merchant sailors and naval men that awakened them to their Christian responsibilities. These maritime adventures were didactic outlets for Kingston to inspire his readers to be better Christians. Although Kingston drew from a tradition of maritime fiction, he departed from the rough character of the navy depicted in Frederick Marryat's books from the early nineteenth century and portrayed the navy as a virtuous institution, even claiming in one story that 'religion flourished' in the Royal Navy 'more than among most communities on shore'.[33]

Whether didactic literature or boys' story papers, the subjects of most mid-Victorian children's adventures primarily came from the middle and upper classes. While the adventures may have served as vehicles to test a character's mettle or to chart his moral development, the rewards and challenges nearly always came to boys of the right social standing. Kelly Boyd has argued that adventures in boys' story paper functioned 'to crystallise the link between masculinity and class status' where mid-Victorian manliness was presented as an inborn quality that only needed time to reveal itself.[34] While common seamen served as useful backdrops in Kingston's stories, he seldom centred entire stories around ordinary non-commissioned naval men. Most of Kingston's maritime stories focused on beneficent naval officers and young officers-in-the-making. For example, in *Three Midshipmen* (1873), he charted the adventures of three dutiful and brave midshipmen who rise in their naval careers to become admirals.[35] Kingston's naval officers were exemplary models for midshipmen to emulate and seamen to obey. However, in *True Blue* (1862), he chose an ordinary seaman, named Billy, as his hero.[36] Born afloat on a man-of-war in the Caribbean as Britain battled France during the American Revolutionary War, Billy was soon orphaned after his mother died in childbirth, and his father, 'Will Freeborn', died during the 'Battle of the Saintes' off Guadaloupe. Brought up by sailors and their wives aboard ship, Billy was christened in Jamaica with the name 'Billy True Blue' because he was born at sea and destined for a life as a sailor. Although the story was set in the Napoleonic period, its themes reflected Victorian preoccupation with self-improvement, duty and Christianity.

What is interesting here is that Kingston chose a different ending for *True Blue* from that of *Three Midshipmen*. While the conduct of the midshipmen facilitated their rise to admiral rank, Billy's good character and behaviour that lived up to his namesake of 'True Blue' posed a problem for Kingston. After Billy demonstrated his heroism in battle in the Caribbean during the Napoleonic Wars, saving the fleet from French defeat, Billy's naval superiors repeatedly offered Billy a promotion to an officer's commission but nothing could 'rouse True Blue's ambition'. Modestly attributing his actions to duty, Billy deliberately chose to remain on the lower deck, accepted promotion to boatswain (a warrant officer in charge of ship's rigging and sails), and told his mates, 'I would rather be boatswain of such a crew as you are, than Captain'. Kingston cast this choice as a moral decision to accept the humility and simplicity of non-commissioned life. By the end of the story, he returned to Portsmouth welcomed by his friends and family and married his sweetheart. As Kingston noted at the novel's end, 'up and down the harbour pulled the bridal squadron, and the crews of every ship, as they passed, took up the cheer and welcomed the bridegroom, for True Blue and his deeds were now well known throughout the British fleet. He had not aimed high, in one sense of the word, and yet he had in another sense always aimed high and nobly – *to do his duty*'.[37] Ashore his duty was to his wife, his children and his many grandsons whom he advised,

> lads be content with your lot. Do your duty in whatever station you are placed, on the quarter-deck or fo'castle, in the tops aloft or at the guns on the main or lower deck, and leave the rest to God. Depend on it, if you obey His standing orders, if you steer your course by the chart and compass He has provided for you, and fight your ship manfully, He will give you the victory.[38]

In *True Blue*, Kingston echoed the rhetoric of self-help that self-improvement had little in common with attaining social status. Billy's choice had offered him contentment in his lifetime with an admirable vocation and a loving family, and his moral behaviour, Kingston implied, would lead to eternal happiness in his next world. By remaining true to his station, his nation and his family, Billy served as a model of proper Christian manliness to Kingston's boy readers and demonstrated the integrity of common sailors.

By the late Victorian period, the virtues of self-improvement became distant from earnest Christian rhetoric and developed into an ideology more firmly attached to material progress. Victorian critic and historian James Anthony Froude admitted that self-improvement amounted to a social obligation, 'To push on, to climb vigorously on the slippery steps of the social ladder, to raise ourselves one step or more out of the rank of life in which we were born, is now converted into a duty'.[39] G. A. Henty, the popular boys' writer, highlighted the importance of self-improvement and the opportunities that awaited the ambitious boy in his novel *Sturdy and Strong, or How George Andrews Made His Way*,

> Whatever may be said as to distinction of classes in England, it is certain that in no country in the world is the upward path more open to those who brace themselves to climb it than in our own. The proportion of

those who remain absolutely stationary is comparatively small. We are all living on a hill-side, and we must either go up or down. It is easier to descend than to ascend; but he who fixes his eyes upwards, nerves himself for the climb, and determines with all his might and power to win his way towards the top, is sure to find himself at the end of his day at a far higher level than when he started upon his journey. It may be said, and sometimes foolishly is said, that luck is everything; but in nineteen cases out of twenty what is called luck is simply a combination of opportunity, and of the readiness and quickness to turn that opportunity to advantage. The voyager must take every advantage of wind, tide, and current, if he would make a favourable journey; and for success in life it is necessary not only to be earnest, steadfast, and true, but to have the faculty of turning every opportunity to the best advantage; just as a climber utilises every tuft of grass, every little shrub, every projecting rock, as a hold for his hands or feet . . . If similar qualities and similar determination are yours, you need not despair of similar success in life.[40]

Henty's books repeatedly stressed that material success resulted from possessing good character, demonstrating perseverance, and taking advantage of every opportunity. While Kingston's writings intended to inspire boys to become dutiful Christian men, Henty's stories sought to model paths for boys to succeed in this life. Despite Henty's optimism, however, class barriers were all but impenetrable.

The language of improvement and the impermeability of class

The navy often served as the backdrop for stories of social advancement. In addition to inculcating Christian manliness, within popular representations, the navy was depicted as a meritocratic institution that rewarded any seaman who displayed good character and exceptional talent. For example, the title of Kingston's later story, *From Powder Monkey to Admiral*, originally published in 1879 in the first issues of *The Boy's Own Paper*, charted the perseverance and success of a common boy in Nelson's navy.[41] Games also instructed children in the doctrine of self-improvement, teaching them the importance of duty and responsibility. Adapted from a 'chutes and ladders' type of game, 'From Sailor Boy to Admiral' was a popular board game from the 1880s that promoted the sailor boy who possessed good conduct and worked hard (see figure 3.1).[42]

Boys who played these games or read these stories would have been misled into believing that similar opportunities still existed. Within the Victorian navy, the non-commissioned naval man faced innumerable barriers to being promoted to the officer's class of the

3.1 A children's board game, 'From Sailor-Boy to Admiral'.

quarterdeck. Although mobility occurred within Nelson's navy where promotion was awarded in battle, it proved increasingly elusive within the late Victorian and Edwardian navy. Until the Napoleonic Wars, it was possible for common seamen, who were not gentlemen by birth, to be promoted to commissioned officers on the quarterdeck.[43]

[108]

However, from the end of the Napoleonic Wars, an oversupply of naval officers in the Royal Navy meant that promotion from lower deck to quarterdeck was effectively closed off, making it virtually impossible for non-commissioned men to receive a commission.[44] Trying to depict the Victorian navy as a site of social mobility was a difficult task since the best that a non-commissioned seaman could hope for would be promotion to warrant officer. The predominance of boys' adventure stories about the romance and daring of the Royal Navy during the Napoleonic Wars rather than the navy's later Victorian imperial exploits enabled the proliferation of promotion stories.

Within naval adventures written for boys, a young naval hero could not make the leap from lower deck to quarterdeck on virtuosity or merit alone. Instead, boys' naval stories like Henty's *Do Your Duty* (1900) and 'Jem Hopeful; or, the Ladder of Life', a serialised story from *Boys of the British Empire*, mark the similar journey of a humble boy hero, often orphaned or adopted, who proves his manhood at sea.[45] His entry to an officer's commissioned rank is only possible when he discovers his lost birthright as a gentleman or is adopted by a beneficent ship's captain. Although these adventures chart the steady success of the dutiful but common boy, a close examination of the literature reveals that boys' literature was still ambivalent about embracing a fully meritocratic society. In fact, it is difficult to conclude that the navy, as imagined by these stories, was really a proponent of meritocracy and self-advancement. Rather, boys' naval adventures upheld class distinction and validated the importance of birthright even as they purported to be about self-improvement.

In his rare naval adventure *Do Your Duty*, Henty, whose books mainly featured the fictionalised daring of boys during famous British and imperial military campaigns, followed the adventures and heroism of a common English boy in Nelson's navy during the Napoleonic Wars.[46] The main character, Harry Langley, is a boy whose heroic actions save England from defeat. Evoking Nelson's message at the battle at Trafalgar, which asked for each man 'to do his duty' for England, Henty's story emphasises that boys have the ability to do great things if they are dutiful. In particular, Henty, through the voice of Harry's adopted father Peter Langley, a naval pensioner, encourages Harry and his readership 'to do his duty to his country' and to serve in the navy where 'there's a great difficulty in finding hands'.[47] After Harry's actions single-handedly save the British fleet from a possible French attack, Admiral Nelson personally meets the young boy and compliments him, 'You showed great bravery and did your duty nobly'.[48]

The message of *Do Your Duty* may be clear – young boys should be dutiful and patriotic, but the context and meaning of Harry's life is far more ambiguous. Although Harry has passed the test of manhood when he helps defeat the French, it is a test destined to be won by a chosen few. Harry's uncertain parentage encourages the reader to think that manhood's lessons are within the reach of the lowliest orphan, given the nurturing support of family and nation. Although the Langley family live on Peter's meagre pension, Harry's adopted father hires a schoolmaster to teach him, and this education distinguishes Harry from his peers. The plot moves quickly after Harry's kidnapping in Portsmouth by French pirates, his chance rescue by the Royal Navy, and his ensuing naval service. In possession of the pirates' logbook, Harry is able to provide the naval captain with important information about French battle plans. As a reward for Harry's heroism, the captain appoints Harry to a midshipman's berth. Within minutes of his appointment, 'Harry was rigged out in full midshipman's dress, and being a very good-looking and gentlemanly lad, his appearance favourably impressed his new messmates, who had at first been disposed to resent the intrusion among themselves of a youngster whose appearance was at least the reverse of reputable'.[49] Harry's new clothing serve as a tangible marker of his social and moral progress, facilitating his passage and acceptance onto the quarterdeck.

The navy and the war were vital to Harry's attainment of manhood. At the battle of Copenhagen in 1801, Harry's actions prove crucial to British victory, meriting the praise of Admiral Nelson, but the victory is bittersweet since Harry is seriously wounded in the fighting and later loses his leg. His short career in the navy and his steady rise up the ranks appear to be in peril until Harry learns of his real birthright while recuperating in the naval hospital at Portsmouth. Through a series of implausible coincidences, he discovers that his real parents died in a shipwreck from which Peter Langley had rescued Harry. From a visiting naval captain, Harry learns about his esteemed parentage and the existence of an uncle on his father's side. Once informed of Harry's condition, the uncle adopted Harry as his heir. So Harry, although an invalid, becomes a true gentleman after all.

In addition, the Board of Admiralty along with Nelson invites Harry to London to commend him for his brief service to the navy. As reward, the Admiralty promotes him to lieutenant and places him on the full-pay list for the rest of his life. In fact, Harry is promoted up the ranks every three years until he reaches the rank of post-captain. Henty quickly surveys Harry's life, which includes a gentleman's career in Parliament, the leisure of yachting, and the fulfilment of a marriage and family. Looking back upon Harry's life, Henty concluded that Harry,

> to the end of his life declared that, after all, the luckiest point in his career was the cutting off of his leg by the last shot fired by the Danish batteries, for that, had this not happened, he should never had known who he was, would never have met the wife whom he dearly loved, and would have passed his life as a miserable bachelor.[50]

By doing his duty, Harry had sacrificed his body for the nation but was rewarded tenfold in return. In charting Harry's entry into manhood, Henty contends that sacrifice, particularly wartime sacrifice, was crucial for Harry's development – not because it simply helped prepare him for the challenges of manhood but because it revealed that the foundations of his true manliness lay in his birthright.

Harry's steady success in life, achieved through sacrifice, affirmed a vision that promoted patriotic individualism while upholding the class system. *Do Your Duty* was hardly unique in boys' fiction in offering a trope of lost birthright.[51] Such stories reflected the extent to which Victorian Britain lived in paradox; the language of self-improvement imparted that social mobility was possible for those of good character while rigid social barriers mapped distinct class identities. If an elite class status was a crucial component in defining Victorian manly ideals, then the navy's lower deck was an unlikely source to model idealised manhood. Yet, as in *Do Your Duty*, the navy was a crucial site in fostering the attainment of imperial manhood. In fact, the navy's prominent place in the British imagination often meant that it served as a backdrop in adventure stories to sort out larger social concerns. Although there were few similarities between social structures within the navy and Britain, within these stories the navy came to symbolise British society.

Late Victorian boys' literature portrayed the navy oddly – an institution layered in its own rigid hierarchies – as a model meritocracy in which all boys could advance. The division of space aboard ship imparted geographies of social power. In the days of sail, officers lived on the quarterdeck, while seamen lived on the lower deck of the ship. Although newer ship designs had blurred the distinctions between quarterdeck and lower deck, the terms remained meaningful in describing the impenetrable class system within the navy. Naval hierarchies were distinguished by rank, which were readily apparent by glancing at uniforms and badges, and were continuously reinforced through ritualistic obedience to discipline. Yet, merit, duty and self-improvement were celebrated within popular maritime fiction as well as within non-fiction and advertisements about the navy. Within popular culture, the navy offered the lesson that steady advancement was the result of hard work, popularising the belief that merit would find its reward. In these naval adventures, questions of social mobility were discussed within the clearly defined boundaries of the ship, safely removed from the realities of everyday life for ordinary Britons.

Similar stories found their way into boys' story papers. A story entitled 'Jem Hopeful; or, the Ladder of Life', featured in the early 1880s in the boys' story paper, *Boys of the British Empire*. This was an anti-slaving naval adventure, set in the French Revolutionary and Napoleonic Wars, which focused on the reclamation and advancement of the young, orphaned Jem Hopeful. Jem's guardian was a naval seaman named Bill Hopewell who 'was a fine, manly fellow, his handsome face bronzed with the exposure to the different climates he had been inured to'.[52] Bill Hopewell had adopted Jem after Bill found him 'on the Common Hard, Portsmouth, where he was a-shivering with cold and starving with hunger. I saw the poor little fellow shivering like an animated bundle of rags'.[53] While Bill was away at sea, his sister's family looked after Jem who, by the age of fourteen, had experienced 'appalling signs of want and destitution upon him', and yet 'was finely formed'. Despite his unfortunate beginnings, Jem displayed good character because 'Dame Nature, in her bountiful goodness, had not deserted him'.[54]

An unlucky set of circumstances led Jem from his Portsmouth home onto the *Black Witch*, a disguised slaving ship, moored in Portsmouth. Once at sea and headed without cargo for Africa, the *Black Witch* encountered a storm, which tossed its sleek but delicate frame about and destroyed it to pieces. Jem was the sole survivor of this shipwreck, drifting on a makeshift raft that eventually tossed him onto a small deserted island where he awaited his rescue. After days without food and without a sign of another ship, Jem appeared near death. Luckily, the HMS *Spitfire*, a frigate, 'bearing the glorious standard of Old England', was cruising nearby in the vicinity of Loango to catch slaving ships 'that infested that part of the coast'. The frigate, 'one of the finest in the navy' was commanded by a Captain Goldstone, 'who was an ornament to his profession, and the country that gave him birth'. The officers and crew were likewise remarkable and 'vied with each other in the zealous performance of their duty'.[55] By chance, Bill Hopewell, Jem's guardian, was serving aboard the *Spitfire*. It was Hopewell who sighted the distress flag that Jem had hoisted, and rescued him from the island.

Once Jem recovered, Captain Goldstone appointed him to the rank of a boy seaman, a rank that was in accordance with his guardian's station on the ship. Jem quickly proved his value to the ship when he provided the captain with the log of the *Black Witch*, revealing the slaving ship's plans to meet up with slave traders. With *Black Witch*'s plans in hand, the captain intended to intercept the slavers. In the chase and fighting that followed, Jem exhibited both courage and modesty, attracting the captain's notice, as the *Spitfire* captured the *Black Witch*.[56]

The capture of the slavers provided the captain with the opportunity to appoint Jem to a midshipman's rank. And when an inquiry into Jem's parentage yielded no information, the captain decided to adopt him, announcing, 'He will for the future be known by the names of James Hopewell Goldstone, and it shall not be long before he shall be placed in a position that shall win him fame and glory'.[57] Jem helped the captain win victories against the Spanish and the French. On Jem's appointment to third-lieutenant, Captain Goldstone proclaimed, 'the gallant and good conduct you have evinced during your arduous career has gained you this, and I hope before I furl my sails for ever that I shall find you made post-captain'.[58]

Jem later served alongside Nelson at the Battle of the Nile in 1798 earning his promotion to first lieutenant and Nelson's admiration. Nelson commended Jem, 'Be it my task to see your valour rewarded. No wonder we won the battle when a stripling like you fought four ships, with all the skill and courage of a veteran. Return to your ship, and command her until further orders from me.'[59] After Jem's contribution to the victory at Trafalgar, Jem was promoted to Captain and visited his retired benefactor, Captain Goldstone. The story ended, 'yes, the cabin-boy, who has stood so often on the "Verge of the Gulf", has by honesty, truth, and courage, gained the distinction that all, by practising the golden rules of life, will ultimately gain'.[60] Yet, Jem's original guardian, Bill Hopewell, lived by these golden rules and was as honest and as fearless as Jem but Hopewell had never risen above the lower deck. The acknowledgement of Jem's character and achievements depended upon the patronage of Captain Goldstone.

As is clear, such stories like 'Jem Hopeful' or *Do Your Duty* were not only full of adventure, they also contained moral instruction. Through hard work, duty and perseverance, boy readers might believe that any man could succeed. By the late Victorian period, writers of boys' fiction no longer measured self-improvement by spiritual contentment, as felt by Billy in *True Blue*, but rather measured it by material rewards, like that experienced by Harry and Jem. In addition, Harry and Jem did not succeed by their own abilities. Harry succeeded only when his uncle adopted him as an heir, and Jem when Captain Goldstone adopted him. Although these stories appeared to be meritocratic allegories, they really reaffirmed impermeable class hierarchies of Victorian society.

Levelling the ranks on the HMS Pinafore

The reality of class hierarchies was more honestly, albeit satirically, addressed in W. S. Gilbert and Arthur Sullivan's popular burlesque opera *HMS Pinafore*, first produced in May 1878.[61] By satirising life in the Royal Navy, *Pinafore* was not an assault upon the class gradations that existed within British society; rather, the nautical opera comically attacked the hypocrisy of entrenched elitism that paraded itself as egalitarianism. The story revolves around the proscribed love between Ralph Rackstraw, a common sailor who is 'the smartest lad in all the fleet', and his captain's daughter, Josephine. Even when the two reveal their love for each other, it seems impossible that their love will be able to overcome the class divisions that separate them. Although both agree 'that differences in rank are unnatural', their different stations pose unavoidable obstacles that attempt to frustrate their future happiness together.[62]

As the site of the opera, the *Pinafore* served as a metaphor of the nation. By setting the comic opera within the safe but symbolic confines of a ship, absurdly named after a woman's apron, W. S. Gilbert, the lyricist of the creative team mocked the rigidity of social hierarchies within British society. As Jane Stedman has argued, *Pinafore* is a parody of 'equality' dramas, first launched in 1838 by Edward Bulwer-Lytton's popular *The Lady of Lyons*.[63] In such plays, the impossible love shared by two characters of different social stations is reconciled by the revelation of a stolen birthright or by social gains like the dramatic military promotion of Claude to Napoleonic marshal in *The Lady of Lyons*. In *Pinafore*, Gilbert mocks this form, exposing that one's social station, which accorded privilege and status, was merely accidental. Upon the visit of Sir Joseph Porter, KCB, to Corcoran's ship, the First Lord of the Admiralty reminded Captain Corcoran to respect his crew since only 'an accident of birth has placed you above them and them below you'.[64]

In fact, the opera was saturated with class references, which measured the distance that separated Ralph from Josephine, Josephine from Sir Joseph, and even Captain Corcoran from Buttercup.[65] Ralph Rackstraw was portrayed as 'the lowliest tar that sails the water', while his love Josephine was depicted as 'highly born'. Similarly, Captain Corcoran was described as 'rich and lofty', while Buttercup, the bumboat woman, was portrayed as 'poor and lowly'. When Ralph reveals to his comrades that he loves Josephine, the ship's boatswain is quick to pity Ralph's romantic optimism, 'Ah, my poor lad, you've climbed too high'. And when Josephine admits to her father that she loves Ralph, a common sailor, she speaks of 'the depth to which I have stooped'.[66]

Although the plot of *Pinafore* focused upon romance, the problems of class and social mobility permeated the story. When Ralph falls in love with Josephine, he threatens to disturb ship hierarchies and social mores.[67] But Ralph defends his right to marry above his station: 'For a man is but a man, whether he hoists his flag at the maintruck or his slacks on the main-deck'.[68] When Josephine tells her father that she loves Ralph Rackstraw, Captain Corcoran admits that he attaches 'but little value to rank or wealth, but the line must be drawn somewhere'. Corcoran explains to Josephine that her love for Rackstraw is a social impossibility: 'A man in that station may be brave and worthy, but at every step he would commit solecisms that society would never pardon'.[69] As Corcoran intimates, Rackstraw's manhood may have been laudable for his class, but his manhood was no match for the respectable manliness cultivated within proper society.

Sir Joseph Porter's visit to the *Pinafore* to woo Josephine into marriage further complicated and added to the absurdity of the comedy's unfathomable plot. Boasting that he was a self-made man, Sir Joseph professes that he was a 'radical democrat' who rose through the ranks as a lowly office clerk to become the 'ruler of the Queen's Navee'.[70] Sir Joseph may have proved that social mobility was possible. However, his arrogance tests the limits of egalitarianism when he argues that 'a British sailor is any man's equal' excepting his. His egalitarian pronouncements in front of the ship's crew merely act as encouragement for Ralph to proclaim his love to Josephine. Although Sir Joseph is unknowingly Ralph's rival for Josephine's affections, during most of the opera his actions unwittingly promote the union between Ralph and Josephine.

Even though Josephine loves Ralph and has decided to elope, she is disturbed by the social consequences of her actions. Alone, she weighs her decision, contrasting the middle-class world that she shares with her father the captain with the lower-class world she would inhabit with Ralph, the common sailor. After planning to run away with Ralph, Josephine wonders to herself about the social sacrifice that she is making. She considers her folly in trading,

> On the one hand, papa's luxurious home,
> Hung with ancestral armour and old brasses,
> Carved oak and tapestry from distant Rome,

> Rare 'blue and white', Venetian finger-glasses,
> Rich oriental rugs, luxurious sofa pillows

with,

> On the other, a dark and dingy room,
> In some back street with stuffy children crying,
> Where organs yell, and clacking housewives fume,
> And clothes are hanging out all day a-drying.
> With one cracked looking-glass to see your face in,
> And dinner served up in a pudding basin![71]

Josephine's confusion over which lot to choose is further muddled when she ponders her future. She imagines Ralph's work as,

> A simple sailor, lowly born,
> Unlettered and unknown,
> Who toils for bread from early morn
> Till half the night has flown!
> No golden rank can he impart –
> No wealth of house or land –
> No fortune save his trusty heart
> And honest brown right hand!
> And yet he is so wondrous fair
> That love for one so passing rare,
> So peerless in his manly beauty,
> Were little else than solemn duty!
> Oh, god of love, and god of reason, say,
> Which of you twain shall my poor heart obey![72]

Any uncertainty felt by Josephine was alleviated by her conversation with Sir Joseph Porter, who assured her that she need not be embarrassed by their own different social stations (he a knight, and she only a captain's daughter). Despite Sir Joseph's belief that he has convinced Josephine to marry him by explaining to her that 'love is a platform upon which all ranks meet', Josephine instead feels vindicated to love Ralph Rackstraw, her common sailor.[73]

Josephine and Ralph's plans to elope appear dashed when Dick Deadeye informs the captain of their intentions. While Corcoran's opposition to their engagement makes sense given the social mores, Deadeye's opposition to Ralph's plans is less so because as a fellow crew member he shares the same social class as Ralph. While Deadeye is the stock villain in the opera who thwarts the elopement of the two lovers, he is also the realist and pragmatist of the crew who realises the implications of disturbing social hierarchies. Reviled by everyone for his brutish manner and his ugly physique, Deadeye reminds the crew that 'captain's daughters don't marry blue jackets' and Ralph that 'she's your gallant captain's daughter,/ And you the meanest slave that crawls the water!'[74] He explains, 'When people have to obey other people's orders, equality's out of the question'.[75] Despite Deadeye's warnings, Ralph and Josephine commit themselves to elope that night.

In the opera, the love between Ralph and Josephine would have ended in tragedy if not for the manoeuvring of Buttercup, the bumboat woman who sells her wares to the ship's crew. Buttercup explains that, by accident, she switched two infants – one born to a patrician and the other to a 'low condition' in her care when she had been a 'baby farmer' in her earlier life.[76] By exchanging infants, Buttercup changed history so that Captain Corcoran and Ralph Rackstraw had really lived the life intended for the other. Soon after Buttercup's admission, the two appear with Corcoran dressed in a sailor's uniform and Ralph in a captain's uniform.[77] The opera revels in its absurdity since Ralph, who had been depicted as a young sailor has implausibly matured to Corcoran's age, and become old enough to be Josephine's father.[78] Since Corcoran is now a common sailor, Sir Joseph revokes his proposal to Josephine, now a sailor's daughter, contending that love may level ranks but 'it does not level them as much as that'.[79]

But the story's ending revealed that *Pinafore* was not advocating radical social reform; rather, *Pinafore* exposed the false egalitarian rhetoric of English society. The ending of *Pinafore* fits within acceptable social parameters. Ralph can marry Josephine because his birth proves that he is a gentleman. Although Josephine is no longer a gentlewoman by birth, Ralph, as a true democrat, overlooks her social descent. Captain Corcoran, an ordinary seaman, can now marry Buttercup and Porter decides to marry his own first cousin Hebe. The unbelievable ending, in which Ralph and Corcoran were switched at birth, paradoxically supported the maintenance of distinction and hierarchy. Gilbert did not intend to use the stage as a platform to sway the audience to radical political positions. In a children's edition of *HMS Pinafore*, Gilbert assessed Ralph's character that, 'Unhappily,' he said, 'he had got it into his silly head that a British man-of-war's man was a much finer fellow than he really is'.[80] Positions may have been reversed for Ralph and Corcoran, but social hierarchies still existed. While Gilbert's 'topsy-turveydom' is satiric, it is not politically subversive. *HMS Pinafore* was not meant as a radical manifesto for a democratic and idyllic society where 'love levels all ranks'.

In one moment, Gilbert seems to claim that Ralph's manhood is in part undeniable given his English heritage, as witnessed by the raucous reprise of 'He is an Englishman', sung by Ralph and the cast in which Ralph declares that, 'Above the dust to which you'd mould me/ In manhood's glorious pride to rise,/ I am an Englishman – behold me!' Yet, the consequences of Buttercup's secret reveal that Ralph's manhood and its rewards were secured by his birthright, not won by overcoming the scorn and derision of his humble beginnings. If the absurdity of the *Pinafore*'s ending abandoned any attempts on Gilbert's part, to be subversive, 'He is an Englishman' revealed his satiric genius in the jingoistic song, which was both able to pacify class tensions and to mock the patriotic pretensions of the audience by glorifying in national transcendence.

Although it is a parody, Gilbert's *Pinafore* highlights the Victorian obsession with class distinction. As this chapter has shown, class was an important component in shaping the contours of naval manhood. The depiction of naval manhood within popular culture changed over the course of the Victorian period as class relations shifted with the enfranchisement of working male householders, public education, and the growth of unionisation. While a study of popular depictions of naval manhood in the Victorian period reveals more about domestic than imperial Britain, it also reveals the significance of navy, war and empire in shaping British manhood. The process of democratising British society was slow and the effect on representing manhood was complex and often contrary. Naval adventure stories, which focused upon the attainment of manhood, envisioned the navy as a meritocratic model for British society, which rewarded individual merit and good character. This idealisation of the navy was an attempt to offer didactic lessons to readers about how to advance, or at least, behave within Victorian Britain. As the doctrine of self-help encouraged men to be dutiful and hard-working for their own merit rather than social status, mid-Victorian portrayals of naval manhood celebrated naval men as exemplars of their class who chose familial and spiritual contentment over material advancement. Later portrayals of naval manhood focused upon the material success of naval men whose good character enabled their advance through the ranks and on to the quarterdeck. Although these images seem to acknowledge the democratisation of naval manhood, the stories revealed the uncertainty of where true manliness resided. In these boys' stories, naval manliness was something imprinted by birth but revealed through time and circumstance rather than attained by anyone through mere experience. The democratisation of naval manhood would have to wait until the Edwardian era to offer true working-class heroes of empire.

Notes

1 John Tosh, *A Man's Place: Masculinity and the Middle-Class Home in Victorian England* (New Haven: Yale University Press, 1999); Anna Clark, *Struggle for the Breeches: Gender and the Making of the British Working Class* (Berkeley: University of California Press, 1997); Joanna Bourke, *Working-Class Cultures in Britain, 1890–1960: Gender, Class and Ethnicity* (London: Routledge, 1994); Sonya Rose, *Limited Livelihoods: Gender and Class in Nineteenth-Century England* (Berkeley: University of California Press, 1992); Keith McClelland, 'Masculinity and the "Representative Artisan" in Britain, 1850–1880', in *Manful Assertions*, ed. Michael Roper and John Tosh (London: Routledge, 1991), 74–91.
2 Anne McClintock, *Imperial Leather: Race, Gender and Sexuality in the Colonial Contest* (New York: Routledge, 1995), 5.
3 Norman Vance, *The Sinews of the Spirit: The Ideal of Christian Manliness in Victorian Literature and Religious Thought* (Cambridge: Cambridge University Press, 1985); Norman Vance, 'The Ideal of Manliness', in *The Victorian Public School: Studies in the Development of an Educational Institution*, ed. B. Simon and I. Bradley (Dublin: Gill and Macmillan, 1975); Donald Hall, ed., *Muscular Christianity: Embodying the Victorian Age* (Cambridge: Cambridge University Press, 1994).
4 Catherine Hall, Keith McClelland, Jane Rendall, eds, *Defining the Victorian Nation: Class, Race, Gender and the British Reform Act of 1867* (Cambridge: Cambridge University Press, 2000).
5 Pat Thane, 'The British Imperial State and the Construction of National Identities', in *Borderlines: Gender and Identities in War and Peace, 1870–1930*, ed. Billie Melman (New York: Routledge, 1998), 30.
6 John M. MacKenzie, *Propaganda and Empire* (Manchester: Manchester University Press, 1985); Gareth Stedman Jones, *Languages of Class* (Cambridge: Cambridge University Press, 1989); Raphael Samuel, ed., *Patriotism: The Making and Unmaking of British National Identity*, 3 vols (London: Routledge, 1989); Bernard Porter, *The Absent-Minded Imperialists: Empire, Society, and Culture in Britain* (Oxford: Oxford University Press, 2004), 194–226.
7 Hugh Cunningham, 'The Language of Patriotism', in *Patriotism: The Making and Unmaking of British National Identity*, ed. Raphael Samuel, vol. 1 (London: Routledge, 1989), 60; Isaac Land, 'Customs of the Sea: Flogging, Empire, and the "True British Seaman", 1770–1870', *Interventions* 3(2), 169–85.
8 José Harris, *Private Lives, Public Spirit: Britain, 1870–1914* (London: Penguin Books, 1994), 13–14. The 1918 Representation of the People Act would award suffrage to the remaining 40 per cent of working men (including naval men) still without the vote and to women over the age of 30.
9 Thomas Hughes, *Tom Brown at Oxford* ([1861] New York: H. M. Caldwell Co., 1899), 237.
10 David Newsome, *Godliness and Good Learning: Four Studies on a Victorian Ideal* (London: Cassell, 1961), 207; Vance, *The Sinews of the Spirit*; Donald Hall, *Muscular Christianity*.
11 Hughes, *Tom Brown at Oxford*, 112.
12 *Boy's Own Paper*, 4 October 1884, 458.
13 Stephen Heathorn, 'Representations of War and Martial Heroes in English Elementary School Reading and Rituals, 1885–1914', in *Children and War*, ed. James Marten (New York: New York University Press, 2002), 108–9.
14 *Comrades*, 17 January 1898; Cynthia Behrman, *Victorian Myths of the Sea* (Athens, Ohio: Ohio University Press, 1977), 63.
15 Quoted in Kevin Carpenter, comp., *Penny Dreadfuls and Comics* (London: Victoria and Albert Museum, 1983), 12.

16 Asa Briggs, 'Samuel Smiles and the Gospel of Work', in *Victorian People: A Reassessment of Persons and Themes, 1851–67* (Chicago: University of Chicago Press, 1972), 118. *Self-Help* proved to be enormously successful, selling 22,000 in the first year; 55,000 after five years, and 150,000 by 1889, and over a quarter of a million by 1905.

17 Samuel Smiles, *Self-Help*, revd edn (Chicago: Belford, Clarke and Co., 1886), 21.

18 Smiles, *Self-Help*, 25.

19 Smiles, *Self-Help*, 48.

20 Smiles, *Self-Help*, 419, 417.

21 Smiles, *Self-Help*, 420.

22 Briggs, *Victorian People*, 121.

23 Briggs, *Victorian People*, 123.

24 Quoted in Tim Travers, *Samuel Smiles and the Victorian Work Ethic* (New York: Garland Publishing, 1987), 173.

25 Briggs, *Victorian People*, 128.

26 Travers, *Samuel Smiles*, 173.

27 Samuel Smiles, *Duty: With Illustrations of Courage, Patience, and Endurance* (Chicago: Belford, Clarke, and Co., 1881), 146.

28 Smiles, *Duty*, 159.

29 J. S. Bratton, *Impact of Victorian Children's Fiction* (London: Croom Helm, 1981), 110–15, 148; Kirsten Drotner, *English Children and their Magazines, 1751–1945* (New Haven: Yale University Press, 1988), 77–97; Joseph Bristow, *Empire Boys: Adventures in a Man's World* (London: HarperCollins Academic, 1991), 32–3; John Springhall, 'Building character in the British boy: the attempt to extend Christian manliness to working-class adolescents, 1880–1914', in *Manliness and Morality*, ed. J. A. Mangan and James Walvin (New York: St Martin's Press, 1987), 52–74; Jeffrey Richards, 'With Henty to Africa', in *Imperialism and Juvenile Literature*, ed. Jeffrey Richards (Manchester: Manchester University Press, 1989), 72–106.

30 Boys' story papers were widely read in Victorian England. For example, the *Boys of England* enjoyed a peak weekly circulation of 250,000 but actual readership was much higher. Kevin Carpenter estimates that the actual readership was much larger since many children shared and traded magazines; contemporaries estimated that there were nine readers for every paper sold. Kelly Boyd notes that, in the Victorian period, the combined circulation of the top children's magazines reached at least a million readers. See Carpenter, *Penny Dreadfuls and Comics* and Kelly Boyd, 'Exemplars and Ingrates: Imperialism and the Boys' Story Paper, 1880–1930', *Historical Research* 67, no. 163 (June 1994), 143–55.

31 Bratton, *Impact of Victorian Children's Fiction*, 115.

32 Bratton, *Impact of Victorian Children's Fiction*, 115.

33 Bratton, *Impact of Victorian Children's Fiction*, 127; *Boy's Own Magazine*, February 1864, 123–4, quoted in Drotner, *English Children and their Magazines, 1751–1945*, 99.

34 Kelly Boyd, *Manliness and the Boys' Story Paper in Britain: A Cultural History, 1855–1940* (Houndmills, Basingstoke: Palgrave Macmillan, 2003), 47.

35 W.H.G. Kingston, *The Three Midshipmen* (London: Griffith and Farran, 1873).

36 W.H.G. Kingston, *True Blue; or, The Life and Adventures of a British Seaman of the Old School* (London: Griffith and Farran, 1862).

37 Kingston, *True Blue*, 439.

38 Kingston, *True Blue*, 440.

39 James Anthony Froude, 'England and Her Colonies', *Short Studies* (2), 208. Quoted in Walter Houghton, *Victorian Frame of Mind, 1830–1870* (New Haven: Yale University Press, 1957), 187.

40 G. A. Henty, *Sturdy and Strong or How George Andrews Made His Way* (London: Blackie and Son, 1900), iii–iv.

41 W. H. G. Kingston, 'From Powder Monkey to Admiral', *Boy's Own Paper*, February 16, 1879.

42 Mary Hilton, Morag Styles and Victor Watson, *Opening the Nursery Door: Reading, Writing, and Childhood* (New York: Routledge, 1997), 17; Drotner, *English Children and Their Magazines*, 83.

43 The careers of James Cook and William Bligh are well-known cases of achieving such distinction. But their example was not uncommon. N. A. M. Rodger estimates that almost 10 per cent of officers from the mid-eighteenth century were not gentlemen by birth. See N. A. M. Rodger, *The Wooden World: An Anatomy of the Georgian Navy* (Annapolis, Md.: Naval Institute Press, 1986), 266–8.

44 In addition, by the 1859, the HMS *Britannia* was being used as a separate training ship for naval cadets. This effectively made it structurally impossible for lower-deck men to obtain an officer's commission.

45 'Jem Hopeful; or, the Ladder of Life', in *Boys of the British Empire*, 28 November 1882.

46 Henty, *Do Your Duty* (London: Blackie and Son, 1900).

47 Henty, *Do Your Duty*, 14.

48 Henty, *Do Your Duty*, 68.

49 Henty, *Do Your Duty*, 75.

50 Henty, *Do Your Duty*, 112.

51 Kelly Boyd, *Manliness and the Boys' Story Paper*, 82–7.

52 'Jem Hopeful; or, the Ladder of Life', in *Boys of the British Empire*, 28 November 1882, 75.

53 'Jem Hopeful', 28 November 1882, 76.

54 'Jem Hopeful', 28 November 1882, 58.

55 'Jem Hopeful', 2 January 1883, 135.

56 'Jem Hopeful', 23 January 1883, 182.

57 'Jem Hopeful', 23 January 1883, 184.

58 'Jem Hopeful', 13 February 1883, 236.

59 'Jem Hopeful', 13 February 1883, 238.

60 'Jem Hopeful', 13 February 1883, 238.

61 *HMS Pinafore* was first performed at the Opéra Comique on 25 May 1878, running for 571 performances and proved to be Gilbert and Sullivan's 'first major success'. See W. S. Gilbert and Arthur Sullivan, *HMS Pinafore*, in *The Complete Annotated Gilbert & Sullivan*, ed. Ian Bradley (Oxford: Oxford University Press, 1996), 116; Gayden Wren, *A Most Ingenious Paradox: The Art of Gilbert and Sullivan* (Oxford: Oxford University Press, 2001); Jane W. Stedman, *W. S. Gilbert: A Classic Victorian and His Theatre* (Oxford: Oxford University Press, 1996).

62 Geoffrey Smith, *Savoy Operas* (New York: Universe Books, 1985), 55. Many of the actual characters like Ralph Rackstraw, Buttercup and Captain Corcoran were originally inspired by Gilbert in his *Bab Ballads*, published as separate pieces for *Fun* magazine in the 1860s and then published as *The Bab Ballads*. See W. S. Gilbert, *The Bab Ballads*, ed. James Ellis (Cambridge: Belknap Press of Harvard University Press, 1980).

63 Stedman, *W. S. Gilbert*, 162.

64 Gilbert and Sullivan, *HMS Pinafore*, in *The Complete Annotated Gilbert & Sullivan*, 113–85.

65 Charles Hayter, *Gilbert and Sullivan* (New York: St Martin's Press, 1987), 84. Hayter's work originally catalogued the references of vertical separation between the characters that follow.

66 Hayter, *Gilbert and Sullivan*, 84.

67 Bradley, *The Complete Annotated Gilbert & Sullivan*, 122.

68 Bradley, *The Complete Annotated Gilbert & Sullivan*, 125.

69 Bradley, *The Complete Annotated Gilbert & Sullivan*, 131.

70 Gilbert claimed that the resemblance between Sir Joseph Porter and W. H. Smith, Disraeli's First Lord of the Admiralty, was purely coincidental. Porter, who advises, 'stick close to your desks and never go to sea, And you all may be Rulers of the Queen's Navee!', appeared to have a lot in common with Smith, a Conservative MP from Westminster who had no naval experience, having made his fortune and

reputation establishing a chain of newsagents. Disraeli even referred to his First Lord as 'Pinafore Smith'. See Bradley, *The Complete Annotated Gilbert and Sullivan*, 134; Smith, *Savoy Operas*, 58; H. M. Walbrook, *Gilbert and Sullivan Opera* (London: F. V. White, 1922), 53.

71 Bradley, *The Complete Annotated Gilbert & Sullivan*, 161.

72 Bradley, *The Complete Annotated Gilbert & Sullivan*, 162–3. Bradley notes that the original unproduced libretto was quite different, 'And then his relations,/ Their mean and sordid lives,/ Their vulgar explanations and their oaths,/ His father's a mechanic, I dare say/ His soapy mother washing all the day,/ I do not mean herself, but dirty clothes'.

73 Bradley, *The Complete Annotated Gilbert & Sullivan*, 163.

74 Bradley, *The Complete Annotated Gilbert & Sullivan*, 124–5, 151. Gilbert had originally written 'foremast hands' but this was changed to 'blue jackets' before being finally returned to 'foremost hands' for the 1908 revival. The term refers to ship's crew who served 'before the mast', meaning all those who served below the rank of officer.

75 Bradley, *Complete Annotated Gilbert & Sullivan*, 120.

76 Bradley, *Complete Annotated Gilbert & Sullivan*, 115, 179.

77 Bradley, *Complete Annotated Gilbert & Sullivan*, 180. Bradley comments that in early performances when the former Captain and Ralph emerge as the other, the former Captain Corcoran shows his fall in station by adopting a common Cockney accent and dropping his 'h's.

78 Stedman, *W. S. Gilbert*, 160. Stedman notes that 'the age difference in which Ralph is simultaneously as old as the Captain and young enough to be his son-in-law parodies the variable age of Thaddeus in *The Bohemian Girl*, while Little Buttercup's confusion of infants, as Gilbert himself once pointed out, resembles Azucena's in *Il Trovatore*'.

79 Stedman, *W. S. Gilbert*, 181.

80 Quoted in Geoffrey Smith, *Savoy Operas* (New York: Universe Books, 1985), 59.

CHAPTER FOUR

Strong men for a strong navy: naval scares, imperial anxieties and naval manhood

Although Britain's national identity had long been defined by its position as an island nation, its relationship to the sea, and its reliance on the navy, British and imperial identities became even more sharply attached to Britain's naval heritage during the Age of Empire. The Royal Navy remained central to this new phase of imperial conquest that witnessed the expansion of the Empire by 2.5 million square miles between 1884 and 1896. Unlike earlier periods, European states increasingly challenged Britain's dominance over the seas and threatened its trading and imperial relationships abroad. Naval scares awakened the British public to the possibility that British naval supremacy might be illusory and fuelled British anxieties, particularly those of Conservatives and imperialists, about the instability of imperial control. Imperialists and navalists who advocated a strong navy defended British claims to the seas and argued that naval supremacy was crucial to ensuring the safety of Britain and its empire. The formation of the British Navy League in 1895 reflected public anxieties about the state of the navy and the stability of the Empire. In addition to portraying the sea as Britain's imperial highway and the navy as the bulwark of home and empire, navalist discourse propagated images of naval men as rugged but respectable models of imperial manhood.

The production of these images was not isolated to navalist literature. In fact, similar depictions of the British bluejacket circulated within advertisements and fiction of the period when the navy had achieve cult-like status.[1] The navy's heightened profile within society also provided naval men with opportunities to reject older portrayals of 'Jack Tar' and assert their own manhood as educated, responsible professionals, as they lobbied public, Parliament and the Admiralty to reform personnel conditions. Demands by lower-deck advocates for personnel reforms were couched in the rhetoric of manhood and justified by the exigencies of maintaining naval supremacy. Concurrently, a host of journalists and novelists like Arnold White, Rudyard Kipling, Frank Bullen, Archibald Hurd and Fred Jane – all dedicated navalists – justified greater naval spending by championing the lives of hard-working non-commissioned men. Both navalists and lower-deck advocates recognised that the persistent caricature of the irresponsible tar jeopardised the reputation of the navy and its men. In place of the caricature, navalists and lower-deck advocates constructed a new image of the sailor that celebrated the modern bluejacket for his professionalism, discipline, intellect and domesticity. The consequence was an indirect critique of older models of elite manliness and the continued democratisation of the British manly ideal. In a period of increasing challenges to British authority from within and without, the symbol of the British bluejacket could at once embody and safeguard the navy, the nation and the Empire.

For navalists and imperialists, the seas represented the unity of the British empire, and the navy served as the guardian of the seas and, thus, the defender of empire. To popular Victorian writers, the sea was the 'natural home of the Englishman', who looked upon 'upon the blue waters as his especial birthright'.[2] Spenser Wilkinson, the naval and military journalist who would help to establish the Navy League in 1895, explained that the sea was vital to the maintenance of the British empire because it was from the sea that the colonies, 'like ourselves, derive their nourishment and their strength'.[3] As a symbol of a national and imperial identity, the sea united the Empire, linking colonies to each other as well as to Britain. The navy served as the guardian of this inheritance. In the midst of the 1884–85 naval scare, poet laureate Alfred Lord Tennyson warned in his poem, 'The Fleet', that all that England valued would wither without the strength of a strong navy: 'The fleet of England is her all-in-all;/ Her fleet is in your hands,/ And in her fleet her fate'.[4] For Tennyson, the British Empire was an organic whole composed of 'One life, one flag, one fleet, one throne!'[5]

Navalists cited Alfred T. Mahan's 1889 work, *The Influence of Sea Power on History*, which asserted that sea power distinguished great nations, as a powerful argument for investing in a stronger navy that could defy any foreign challenges by French or Russian navies.[6] H. W. Wilson, naval columnist for the *Daily Mail* and a Navy League member, explained the goals of navalists:

> For our end is to strengthen that England which has made us what we are: to retain the inheritance of greatness which our fathers bequeathed to us: to confirm that proud national position without which many of us feel that life in this smoky island would be intolerable; and to do this by making the Navy strong. For by the Navy we stand or fall.[7]

Political and public arguments over naval supremacy revealed dis-
agreement over how the navy should be organised but none questioned
the importance of the navy to both nation and empire.[8]

Casting off Jack Tar

As British and imperial identities became even more sharply attached
to Britain's naval heritage, the reputation and popularity of naval men
at the close of the nineteenth century were intimately connected to
the growing presence and stature of the Royal Navy. Naval men came
to be represented as defenders not only of British interests abroad but
also of Britishness. One member of the Navy League declared that
British seamen were collectively 'a race that has been so instrumental
in building up this magnificent empire'.[9] One can even see this in
Gilbert and Sullivan's *HMS Pinafore* when the First Lord Sir Joseph
Porter, KCB, chides Captain Corcoran to 'Never forget that they [sailors]
are the bulwarks of England's greatness'. Gilbert and Sullivan's sincer-
ity may be in doubt, but they parodied an imperialist mood prevalent
within British society. The popularity of the navy and its men was also
evidenced in mass advertising around the turn of the century. Advertis-
ers took advantage of the naval man's popularity and used his patriotic
image to sell products like biscuits, cleaning products and cocoa. Celebrating the bluejacket's fealty to both nation and family, a Carr's
biscuit ad from 1901 featured a British sailor holding up his daughter
who is waving the Union Jack (see figure 4.1). In a 1902 Bovril advertisement, John Bull, as imperial father, provides sustenance to the
Empire as he serves cups of hot Bovril to his 'Kin' from across the
Empire and the globe (see figure 4.2).[10] Leading the imperial queue is a
sailor boy who personifies both England and Britain as he wears the
naval rig and prominently displays the Union Jack in one hand.

These depictions of the respectable patriotic British bluejacket circulated amid older imagery of the jolly 'Jack Tar'. Popular commentary
might have spoken of the indomitable spirit of the British sailor that
linked the Victorian sailor with his Georgian forebear, but increasingly
commentators in late nineteenth- and early twentieth-century Britain
noted the disjuncture between the two hearts of oak. Archibald Hurd,
the naval correspondent for the *Daily Telegraph*, dismissed any false
notions that naval men 'prance up and down the world's seas, eating,
drinking and making merry, chewing tobacco, drinking grog, and
telling lusty yarns smelling of the sea. Jack Tars do not languish in
genteel indolence until the call comes to fight for the flag ... it is
a fact that there are few men of his class who lead such downright
hard-working lives'.[11] British naval men also noted the dissonance

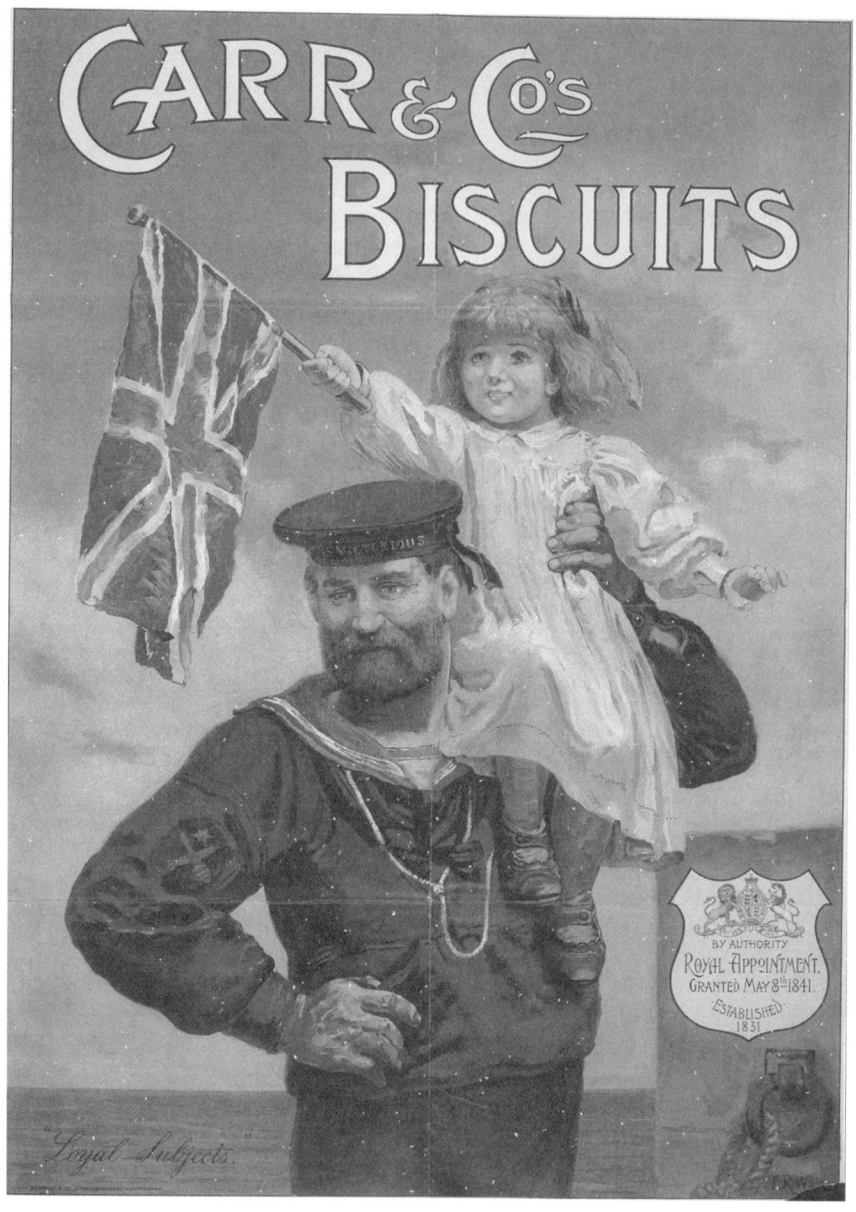

4.1 Carr & Co. biscuit advertisement, 1899.

4.2 The British sailor boy leads the way, Bovril advertisement, 1902.

between the character of Georgian and Victorian sailors. One sailor-correspondent writing to the naval men's service paper, the *Blue-jacket*, observed that there was 'more likeness between an elephant and an owl than between a bluejacket of to-day and one of Nelson's time'.[12] In fact, editors at the *Bluejacket* boasted that 'the modern bluejacket bears no resemblance whatever to the roystering rum-drinking sailor of Nelson's time, who, however brave he may have been, could certainly lay no claim to either a high moral or intellectual standard'.[13]

Thomas Holman, a naval seaman who wrote for the *Bluejacket* as 'Tom Seaman', belaboured the wretchedness of Georgian seamen who were comprised of pressed men, able-bodied seamen, as well as convicts, and 'beggars, street arabs, or riff raff earning a precarious living in the gutters'.[14] These seamen were a social menace ashore, courting classes that 'were the lowest of the low'.[15] Holman conceded that few had looked favourably on the British sailor's character, 'The respectable working man and all ranks above him looked upon our class of that day much as we do the lower type of costermonger now, only with much less favour and a feeling akin to fear and loathing.'[16] In contrast to Nelson's naval man who was recruited from the 'off-scourings of Society', the modern naval man had claims to respectability and citizenship because he now came 'from a fear-no-man, newspaper reading, grievance discussing, public-library-using, and injustice-resenting class'.[17]

By highlighting the rough character of the Georgian navy, writers from the naval ranks marked the professional transformation of the navy and, as such, demonstrated their attainment of masculine social status.[18] It was clear from naval memoirs, like those of retired Chief Gunner Henry Capper, that the respectable character of the modern naval man was 'indeed an evolution from the brawling, intemperate, and socially outcast sailor of my early days'.[19] By distancing themselves from their rough forerunners, naval writers of the late nineteenth and twentieth centuries constructed their manhood in relation to their moral stature, their professional advancement, and their familial responsibilities.

In terms of their professionalism, according to Stephen Reynolds, a journalist and lower-deck advocate, 'there is no class of men in the country – of full-blooded men, any how – which would know how to be steadier. Doubtless there were "hard causes" in the navy . . . but it doesn't do to be dissolute nowadays if a man wants to get on'.[20] As an ex-petty officer and leader of the lower-deck reform movement, Lionel Yexley attested that naval men 'as a class' were 'both sober, intelligent, and of a high moral standard'.[21] Naval manhood was not only gauged by professionalism, intellect and morality but by an attention to familial responsibilities and domestic life. Yexley noted, 'There is no other body of men in the world who are so attentive to the well-being of their dependants as bluejackets. Go on board any ship of war in the Dog Watches . . . and dozens will be seen, some with sewing machines

Photo. R. ELLIS, Malta.   Copyright.—HUDSON & KEAL.

MAKING AND MENDING CLOTHES ON THE LOWER DECK.

4.3 'Making and Mending Clothes on the Lower Deck', *Navy & Army
Illustrated*, 27 November 1896.

making clothes, others in quiet corners washing their ship-mates
clothes and all with a view of making money, not for a debauch, but
to send home to mother or wife'(figure 4.3).[22] While historians have
noted the tensions between homosociality and domesticity, as seen
here, the all-male shipboard environment did not necessarily preclude
domestic attachments – homosociality was domesticity.[23] By making
and mending clothes in their spare time, sailors' domesticity afloat
contributed to maintaining domesticity ashore. Although representations of the 'Jack Tar' persisted in the late nineteenth century, naval
men rejected these older portrayals of sailors because they threatened
contemporary sailors' own masculine identities as professionals and
fathers and undermined their claims for the better conditions expected
for men of their status.

Writing amid British navalist debates, naval writers like Yexley,
Capper and Holman applied the rhetoric of naval supremacy to advance
their own interests in educating the public about the realities of naval
life and in lobbying the Admiralty for better pay and work reforms.
After all, Holman reminded his readers, 'ships would be useless without

men', and 'the *material* worthless without the *personnel*'.[24] In *Our Fighting Seamen*, Yexley argued that the men's contribution was 'largely forgotten in the mad rush to build ships'.[25] By educating the British public about the naval man's service to, and sacrifice for, the nation, lower-deck reformers like Yexley intended to create public support to pressure Parliament for naval personnel reforms that would improve lower-deck conditions. He contended that 'The nation itself – if it is determined to do justice by its fighting sea men – must take the task in hand before it is too late'.[26] Otherwise, 'we're living in a fool's paradise – if everything depends on human element, can we meet crisis which must come – if it fails us in the crisis then the British Empire passes away to the region of have-beens'.[27] In his writings, Holman encouraged recruiting and sought to convince the public that the navy was a worthy profession for their sons to join. According to Holman, the technological restructuring of the navy meant that 'the men are being altered as rapidly as the material, and are in every way fit to take such huge and delicate boxes of machinery into action against an enemy'. Yet, stronger recruits were necessary to man the latest technology, 'the public cannot too soon demand that its fleet shall be re-manned by the picked youth of the nation, who can be trained in the use of our new armament in the Navy, and in whose hands both it and the country will be safe'.[28] The 'altered conditions of naval warfare' necessitated that 'the coming fleet shall be manned with the best of the coming men'.[29]

According to naval writers, the effect of education had changed the whole character of the lower deck. The advances in the education of naval personnel had resulted in part from the development of national education in the 1870s and the provision of naval instruction on ships.[30] A chief gunner of the Gunnery School at Sheerness at the turn of the century, Henry Capper, noticed the changed quality of naval men,

> With respect to the character and status of the men with whom I was much in touch . . . it was clear that the Education Act of 1870 – passed after my own entry into the Service – had had a considerable influence, illiterates being entirely unknown, while the habits, associations, and general character of the great body of the men demonstrated how great was their social advance.[31]

Thomas J. Spence Lyne, who entered the navy in 1885 and became the first naval rating to be promoted to an admiral's rank since 1818, also agreed that the introduction of compulsory education after 1876 had benefited the entire service,

> With new times came new men and new methods which brought about the disintegration of the abuses of the past and proved that the customs

of the nineteenth and twentieth centuries could not run side by side. There was no question which should give way to the other. The presence of compulsory education, the potency of whose power could not be gauged, though it was destined to create industrial and political changes all over the world and possibly reconstruct the map. So far as the education of the lower deck of the Navy was concerned, the country was beginning to get value for its money.[32]

For Lyne, educational changes produced better skilled naval men, lessened the need for harsh discipline, and contributed to the maintenance of Britain's naval supremacy.

According to lower-deck advocates, naval men wanted to be valued for their brains, rather than be judged solely for their physical stamina or their worth as 'deckhands'. In a letter to the *Fleet*, a naval correspondent asserted that, 'The age of spit and polish has gone, brains are as necessary as bravery'.[33] The *Bluejacket* claimed that 'education had changed the naval man who had become a thinking and intelligent man, who despised all mistaken coddling, and was determined to assert his manhood ashore as well as afloat, and look for and expect the same rewards and honours as all other good citizens were given for good service to their country'.[34] The intelligence, professionalism and independence of naval men served as the crucial foundation for claiming a masculine social status concomitant with citizenship.

The emphasis on education underscored the argument of these lower-deck advocates that the development of a professionalised labour force had enabled the technological transformation of the navy. By the last third of the nineteenth century, steam power had replaced sail, armour plating had superseded wooden-hulled ships, and breech-loading guns had outperformed muzzle-loaders. The introduction of new ship designs, from the mastless *Devastation* in 1871 to the first modern battleship *Dreadnought* in 1906, and new weaponry, from torpedoes, mines to submarines, demanded technically competent men to man the fleet. For these naval writers of the lower deck, these changes ushered in a new type of seaman. The combination of new technologies, which demanded new skills and an educated labour force, and educational developments, which supplied a literate population, contributed to better qualified naval recruits. According to the *Bluejacket*, this new navy required and received a new breed of seamen to 'man the New Fleet – who adjust the gun sights, manipulate the torpedos, and tend the boilers and machinery'.[35]

'Sailors' in the traditional sense of the word were no longer needed for hulks of steel reliant on steam from coal-fed boilers. Yexley contended that,

The present century ushered in an entirely new era. The sea man was no longer a mere hewer of wood and drawer of water. Mechanical science was rapidly changing a ship-of-war into a huge box of complicated machinery which required ever and ever more skill and intelligence for its successful manipulation. Submarines, wireless telegraphy, turbines, modern guns of precision, torpedoes, dirigibles, all demanded and had attention bestowed on them, till the sea man was turned into a student: brawn had to give way to brain, and our sea men had to be more carefully selected to enable them to meet the strain of the new conditions.[36]

Education and applied mechanical knowledge had replaced the hands-on experience gained by seamen of sailing fleets. Sail training for naval ratings finally ended in 1903 when it was replaced by further mechanical instruction.[37] Yet, boarding pikes were still carried on board ships and cutlass drills continued to be taught, despite the fact that the navy had not engaged in ship-to-ship combat since Navarino in 1827.[38]

Navalism and naval scares

The interests of lower-deck advocates intersected with the concerns of navalists who were active in extra-parliamentary organisations like the British Navy League and the Imperial Maritime League. During the Navy League's campaigns to increase naval expenditures, it argued that the future health of Britain and its empire rested on the strength and fitness of the navy, the merchant marine, and its men. The Navy League brought maritime and naval concerns, and specifically the life of the modern naval man, to the public through a media campaign of lectures, writings and celebrations. The health and physical strength of the naval man personified a powerful navy ever ready to protect Britain and Empire. The writings of Rudyard Kipling, Frank Bullen, Archibald Hurd and Fred Jane not only refashioned naval masculinity, emphasising the physical prowess and straightforward integrity of British naval men, but they also cast naval manhood as a model for imperial manhood.

By the turn of the century, navalism was like a religion, practised by its proponents with varying degrees of fervour and orthodoxy. Its small band of devout followers firmly believed that British naval supremacy was vital to British security at home and abroad. The establishment of the Navy League, spearheaded by the *Pall Mall Gazette*'s editor Henry Cust, reflected the increased effectiveness of navalist journalism to stir up public opinion since W. T. Stead's first writings had compelled the government to spend an extra £5 million on warships and ordnance in 1884.[39] The immediate origins of the League's formation lay in the public agitation caused by the naval scare of 1893, which had pressured the Liberal government under Gladstone to, once again, increase the naval estimates. Although the new extra-parliamentary organisation claimed by its constitution to be 'absolutely distinct from all party politics', with its main purpose 'to secure as the primary object of the National Policy, "The Command of the Sea"', most of its leadership, membership, and outlook were decidedly Conservative and Unionist.[40] Yet, Liberal politicians like Charles Dilke, and Liberal ship owners like Thomas Brassey, supported the Navy League because they agreed that the navy was vital to securing British trade routes and protecting their own commercial interests within the Empire.

With its main support coming from the middle and upper classes, the League successfully courted membership and patronage of men and women of social rank and standing from the monarchy and aristocracy, admirals, generals, politicians, imperialists, prominent writers, to headmasters and leading churchmen.[41] In 1911, King George V congratulated the League for 'arousing patriotic feeling throughout the country'.[42] Other notable members included Admiral Lord Charles Beresford, Rudyard Kipling, the Harmsworth brothers, Sir Charles Dilke, Leo Maxse, Alfred Milner, Thomas Brassey, Arnold White, Fred Jane, Arthur Conan Doyle, the Duke of Devonshire, the Duke of Hamilton, the Earl of Minto, the Duke of Westminster and Field-Marshal Lord Roberts.[43] By1908, Navy League could boast the membership of 112 MPs.

By the turn of the century, navalism had become a popular political platform. One Liberal paper commented in 1896 that 'all classes of the nation appear to be bitten by the craze'.[44] The few protests by Radicals like Sir Wilfred Lawson and Henry Labouchere about the exorbitant Naval Estimates of 1896 conceded the popularity of navalism with voters. To the derision of Parliament, Labouchere admitted that peace, retrenchment and reform had become a joke and that 'working men were as keen on spending this money as the House of Commons'.[45] H. W. Wilson, the editor of the *Navy League Journal*, as well as a naval correspondent for the *Daily Mail*, did not miss the opportunity to claim a victory for the Navy League when Parliament passed an expansive naval budget in 1896, 'It is significant that the only protest against the increase of Navy Expenditure in the House of Commons so far was accompanied by an admission that the masses were in favour of a strengthened Navy. This is no doubt in a great measure due to the wholesome literature that has been disseminated by our League'.[46] It was doubtful that the Navy League, only a year since its formation, was responsible for converting the British public to a navalist agenda.

Pro-naval sentiment was probably as easily roused in 1896 as it had been in previous scares.

As navalist campaigns mounted, it was clear that the Navy League was not the society for all navalists, many of whom believed that the invasion scares nurtured by League publications were detrimental to internal domestic stability and that the League went too far in its interference in Admiralty affairs. At its formation, the Navy League did not consider the current navy adequate to protect either Britain or the Empire whether in peace or war. As a consequence, the Admiralty saw the League as an adversary rather than as an ally because it believed that the League only undermined its authority. Similarly, the Navy Records Society, itself only established in 1893 as a scholarly organisation of naval affairs, initially viewed the Navy League as a non-representative rancorous interloper in national affairs.[47] Philip and John Colomb, brothers and naval strategists, and others like John Knox Laughton, a founder of the Navy Records Society, dropped out of the League because they condemned the League's scare-mongering tactics.[48] Yet, there were certain diehard navalist members like Admiral Lord Charles Beresford, Fred T. Jane, L. G. Horton-Smith, Rudyard Kipling, Arthur Conan Doyle and Harold Frazer Wyatt who believed that the Navy League was not critical enough of the government and no longer acted as a watchdog of Admiralty policies.[49] Internal dissension over Fisher's policies as First Sea Lord led to the splintering of the League and the formation of the 'navier' Imperial Maritime League in 1908, an even more rabidly navalist organisation than the Navy League.[50]

Despite the splintering of the navalist camp, the Navy League grew with the intensification of Britain's naval race with Germany and the engorgement of British naval estimates. In 1907, the League was convinced that 'there can be no doubt that popular interest in the navy, and knowledge of naval affairs, has grown visibly throughout the Empire during the past ten years, and the League claims that this result is one of the most valuable fruits of its efforts'.[51] The League's campaign brought new strands of navalism to the public and did influence British opinion but the degree of that influence is debatable. With around 1000 members in 1896, the Navy League grew dramatically between 1901 and 1914 – from 14,000 to 100,000 members.[52] By 1912, the Navy League claimed to have over 120 branches and, by the war, had formed over 150 branches, with strongholds in Hertfordshire and Oxfordshire, marked growth in urban working-class districts like Manchester, Liverpool, Birmingham and Glasgow and a presence in imperial outposts like Cape Town, Hong Kong, Durban and Toronto.[53] While the overall growth of the Navy League during the

Edwardian period is impressive, it pales when compared to the 600,000 members of the German Navy League, the *Flottenvereins*.[54]

In many ways, the British Navy League faced a tougher task than the German Navy League, whose organisation was founded in April 1898, alongside the German navy. Within Britain, navalism was an ideology of consensus; while the British public may have needed 'reminding', they did not require 'conversion'.[55] Thus, many individuals who agreed with the Navy League's agenda of greater naval estimates most likely never felt the compulsion to join its membership.

To the Navy League, manning the navy was crucial to its success and strength. Initially, the Navy League was less concerned with the maintenance of active naval personnel, whose organisation appeared sound, than with the administration and manning of the naval reserve. The League feared that without a strong, plentiful, skilled British-born merchant marine for the reserve, the navy's success in wartime was untenable. However, augmenting the reserves with British-born merchant seamen was a difficult task because of the rising number of foreign seamen on board British merchant vessels by the late-nineteenth century.[56] Such trends, according to the League, spelled disaster for Britain's command of the seas. As a result, it proposed a variety of schemes to reform the merchant service in order to boost the employment of British-born seamen and thus to add to the ranks of the reserve. Apart from lobbying Parliament, shipping firms, and the Admiralty, the League appealed to the public not only to join the reserves but also to pressure the government to find domestic solutions to the manning problem. In its appeal, the Navy League manipulated xenophobic sentiments in order to create public rancour against the presence of foreign seamen on British ships. At the turn of the century, the outcry of 'British men for British ships' made the naval reserve issue not simply an issue of British sea power, but transformed naval reform into the popular issue of the day – jobs and Empire.[57]

Navy Leaguers saw the Royal Navy as a model from which the British merchant service could fashion itself. Early navalist rhetoric blamed the poor quality of British merchant seamen rather than profit-seeking shipowners for the rising numbers of foreign seamen in the merchant service. Captain S. M. Eardley-Wilmot, a prolific Navy League writer, asked in an article in the *Navy League Journal*,

Why have we so many foreigners in our merchant ships? And why do owners prefer such crews? It is because English merchant seamen as a rule are less reliable and less sober. Bring them under the influence of discipline and the excellent system of the navy, and they would become a different class, eagerly sought after by the owners of merchant ships.

Nor would the navy suffer, because we should still rely on long-service men for a great portion of the force when war broke out, but we should have seamen to augment it who had served in warships and been trained in the only recognised method of forming an efficient reserve.[58]

This assessment of merchant men stood in sharp contrast to the debates over naval reserves and naval manning that had taken place in the early 1870s when merchant seamen were considered superior in certain aspects to naval men.[59] But according to many navalists, all that had changed by the turn of the century as British merchant seamen were considered poor rivals to naval men in terms of skill, discipline and respectability. Frank Bullen, maritime novelist and navalist, commented that merchant men looked towards naval men as 'the poor and badly used usually regard the comfortable and well-to-do'.[60]

The debates about the state of merchant seamen highlighted the progress of naval men. At a 1901 Navy League meeting on manning, Admiral T. S. Brand had noted how education, discipline and naval training had transformed both the character and ability of naval men serving in the new navy. Brand argued 'that if the result which has been obtained in the Navy could be obtained in the mercantile marine, we should all of us be most anxious to advocate any change in that direction'.[61] John Knox Laughton, a naval historian and founder of the Navy Records Society, attested that naval men differed 'from their countrymen mainly in being finer specimens of the race'.[62] The ascendant reputation of naval men as dutiful, disciplined and skilled eclipsed the perceived character of merchant men who, as Eardley-Wilmot asserted, now were considered less disciplined, reliable and sober.

By reforming the character of the merchant marine, the Navy League intended to attract a better quality of British recruits into the merchant service. The lack of stable employment in the merchant marine distinguished it from the Royal Navy, which compelled men to sign on for long periods of service and offered career sailors an opportunity to earn pensions. As a shipowner, politician, former Secretary to the Admiralty and navalist, Thomas Brassey was a leading authority on both the state of the merchant marine and the naval reserve. He had previously recommended financial inducements for shipowners who hired British-born seamen and advertised the opportunities of the Royal Naval Reserve in their firms.[63] Brassey argued that many families did not consider sending their sons to merchant service because continuous and steady employment appeared unlikely. At an 1899 Navy League meeting on the topic of manning a naval reserve, Brassey as the chair suggested that the mercantile marine could offer new labour opportunities, 'We want to improve the mercantile marine as an opening for the British working classes by securing continuity of employment'.[64]

For Colonel Mc L. McHardy, a Navy League member, the problem of manning British ships with British men did not lie with the inadequacy of British seamen or the hesitancy of families to submit their sons to service. The onus lay with shipowners who turned qualified British applicants away in order to hire cheaper foreign adult labour. McHardy believed,

> there are thousands of respectable lads who would be glad to take to a seafaring life for a livelihood, but who cannot get into the mercantile marine. I could give you instances that have come under my own direct observation, where men have taken their boys to the docks; have gone from ship to ship only to find that the owners do not want apprentices, preferring to ship full-grown men; as the lads could not get into the Navy they have been obliged to take to some other occupation.[65]

The Navy League's solution to entice more British boys into merchant service was to turn the apprenticeship system into a competitive and viable programme that shipowners would rely on to fill their manning needs.

To boost the numbers of British merchant seamen, the Navy League funded training ships that prepared boys for careers in the merchant marine and the navy and encouraged city councils to establish their own training ships.[66] As early as 1897, the Navy League considered a plan to sponsor the costs for boys interested in the merchant marine to be sent to a training ship for twelve months, followed by three years at sea, and then entry into the Royal Naval Reserve. The Navy League justified its plans: 'The reason we want apprentices entered is to increase the number of British seamen; and the reason we want the number of British seamen to be increased is to make our food supply in war-time safer, and to have a reserve of men that the Royal Navy can fall back upon in time of war'.[67] The Navy League's focus on apprentices also partly explains its particular interest in youth education. In this light, their naval brigades for boys were really opportunities to entice them to join the merchant marine, the navy and the reserves.

In the wake of turn-of-the century invasion scares and the Boer War, the Navy League redoubled its efforts to pressure the Admiralty to increase both active and reserve personnel in order to protect both island and empire. In particular, both the vulnerability of the Empire exposed by the difficulty of winning the Boer War, and the success of naval brigades fighting in South Africa, emboldened navalists to demand the strengthening of the navy, Britain's first line of defence.[68] The popularity of the coronation naval review of 1902 at Spithead provided the Navy League with an opportunity to convince a wider public of the need to expand the naval reserves. Navalists like Charles Dilke had argued for a large trained reserve since 'all authorities agree that it is useless to pretend to fill the gap by mere figures of wholly untrained men, lacking in discipline and *esprit de corps*'.[69] In an article entitled 'The Passing of our Mercantile Marine Supremacy', Frank Bullen argued that the Admiralty delayed what was necessary, 'A very slight exercise of statesmanship would have built up a splendid reserve of British seamen capable of reinforcing the *personnel* of the Fleet in time of war, or what is just as important, manning the swift food-bearing ships without which we die'.[70] Responding partly to the League's demands to expand the naval reserve, First Lord of the Admiralty, Lord Selborne, formed the Royal Naval Volunteer Reserve (RNVR) in 1903. However, the RNVR disappointed Navy Leaguers since it recruited civilians, rather than skilled seamen, for naval positions.[71] As a result, the League continued to press for a greater commitment by both the Admiralty and shipping firms to boost the employment of British merchant seamen.

The League's campaign to secure British seamen for British ships not only pressured the Admiralty, but was also intent on securing popular support for its campaign and, for that reason, must also be seen as a strategy that linked social reform to the Empire. As imperialists like Joseph Chamberlain depicted the Empire as an outlet for British employment, navalists portrayed the maintenance of naval supremacy as vital to safeguarding jobs in Britain.[72] Through its xenophobic rhetoric and its celebrations of naval strength, the Navy League appealed to the patriotism and to the self-interest of British working families as it lobbied for reform of the merchant marine. By advocating that only British men serve in British ships, the Navy League held out the promise of jobs to working-class men and drew upon virulent anti-immigration and anti-Jewish sentiment within Edwardian Britain. Navalist xenophobia was similar to that used by other anti-alien political groups that aimed to safeguard 'English' employment like the anti-Semitic British Brothers' League, established in 1901 to push for anti-alien legislation that targeted the entry of Eastern European Jews, and the Tariff Reform League, founded in 1903 to restrict both the immigration of foreign workers and trade of foreign goods into Britain.[73]

With a mission to convert the public to navalism, the Navy League targeted the fears of newly enfranchised working men from working-class families. One essential aim of the Navy League was 'to spread information, showing the vital importance to the British Empire of the Naval supremacy upon which depend its trade, empire, and national existence' to both 'public men' and politicians.[74] To Navy Leaguers, working men's support of navalism was crucial to winning parliamentary seats for navalists and to maintaining naval supremacy. To secure their support, the Navy League urged that working-class voters 'sink your party feelings for a day; be neither Conservatives, nor Liberals, but something greater and better, be ENGLISHMEN'.[75] Navalism required patriotic fealty because naval supremacy protected Britain's commerce and its food supply. H. W. Wilson argued that the England's future rested in the hands of the working classes. In an alarmist pamphlet entitled 'The Meaning of Defeat', Wilson warned that the decision rested on the 'working-man (who) has to choose whether he will have lighter taxation for the moment, starvation and irretrievable ruin for the future'.[76] To help him choose his fate, navalists saw it as their responsibility to steer the misguided working man to patriotism and to convert him to their agenda.

> His clubs echo with socialistic denunciations and detractions of the value of our Empire, and but a lukewarm supporter of large Naval Budgets. We must be at him and teach him. It is the duty of the better educated amongst us to go down into the market place and refute the sophistries of the blind leaders of the blind. The lower classes can be led, but they want leaders, men with the courage of their opinions, men with devotion to the great ideals at which this nation should aim. For our end is to strengthen that England which has made us what we are: to retain the inheritance of greatness which our fathers bequeathed to us: to confirm that proud national position without which many of us feel that life in this smoky island would be intolerable; and to do this by making the Navy strong. For by the Navy we stand or fall.[77]

To win the support of working men, the Navy League began a campaign in 1897 to target and recruit workers through lectures, leaflets and pamphlets, and less expensive membership fees.[78]

Recruitment into the Navy League was one step towards convincing men of the Navy's importance, 'If the work of the Navy League can be so pushed that we can form strong branches in towns throughout the Kingdom, this "Little Navy" spirit should be killed', since working men and their leaders would 'have the sense to see that their welfare and prosperity depend upon the upkeep of an efficient Navy'.[79] But Navy League intentions were difficult to realise. In 1909, the League admitted that it had 'failed so far to establish a firm hold upon the interests of those in whose hands lies in the last resort the responsibility for the maintenance of our supremacy of the sea – the lower middle and wage-earning classes'.[80] Following the introduction of a number of measures to increase working-class membership, such as reducing subscription fees and erasing distinctions between 'members' and 'associates', working-class membership increased as branch membership rose throughout the country before the outbreak of war.[81] Despite inroads in urban districts like Manchester and Liverpool, working-class membership in the Navy League remained marginal until the First World War; which questions the extent to which the Edwardian working classes were actively jingoistic.[82]

In particular, the Navy League felt that its advocacy of many naval personnel reforms would help in its efforts to win over working-class support. By lobbying for better service conditions for naval men, the League hoped to quell any discontent – often labelled socialist within navalist circles – that would detract from naval efficiency and imperial strength. Admiral Lord Charles Beresford argued that:

> the more the public knows about the navy the more certain it is that comfort and efficiency will be increased. The fleet would never have arrived at its present strength if the question had been left to authority. It was public opinion that compelled authority to awake, and find out if the Empire had a fleet sufficient for its needs.[83]

The state of the personnel was an important component to maintaining naval supremacy and war readiness, and while 'the "lower deck" is good enough, no fleet will be able to fight successfully, no matter how good its personnel, unless all the details inseparable from proper organisation for war in these modern days are perfect and complete'.[84]

A key detail upon which navalists focused was feeding the fleet. Arnold White, the staunch navalist correspondent for the *Daily Express* and the *Referee*, was an unfailing advocate of lower-deck reforms.[85] Arnold White and Robert Yerbugh, the League president, took a brief tour in 1901 with the Mediterranean Fleet where they learned about life on board a man-of-war. White and Yerbugh ate alongside the men and were shocked to discover that the quality and quantity of naval food was so poor. In the 1902 *Navy League Guide to the Coronation Review*, White lobbied the Admiralty for better victualling conditions for fleetmen.[86] White explained that feeding men properly was as important to naval strength as arming ships or increasing fleet size. Invoking navalist rhetoric, White argued that,

> We owe too much to the men of the Fleet to delay justice. In this Coronation year it is not too much to ask that the food of the bluejackets should be improved and brought up to the standard of living that is

common among all classes on shore. If British sea-power is to be assured British bluejackets must be better fed, and that without delay.[87]

Lobbying by White and others had helped pressure the Admiralty to organise a committee under Commodore Spencer Login to reform victualling. The recommendations of the Login Committee eventually resulted in significant victualling reform introduced in 1907 under Fisher's administration.[88]

White was able to explain the importance of British maritime supremacy and therefore the urgency of greater naval expenditure by personifying the navy through the life of the seaman. Even technological improvements could be advanced by considering the well-being of naval personnel. For example, the League emphasised issues of men's safety when it advocated retro-fitting ships with breech-loading guns rather than keeping the older, less accurate, and more dangerous muzzle-loaders. To garner public attention and to shame politicians into action, the League employed sandwich-board men to parade outside Whitehall in April 1900 carrying signs that declared the dangers of muzzle-loaders.[89] By implying that the Admiralty endangered both the safety of naval men and the Empire because it failed to invest in newer safer technologies, the League proved itself to be a skilful propagandist.

Charting naval manhood afloat

Although navalists kept up unofficial correspondence with officers and sailors, the Navy League's official access to the navy really depended on Admiralty predilection. During the 1890s, hoping to secure favourable publicity, the Admiralty invited navalist journalists and writers like Rudyard Kipling, Frank Bullen and Archibald Hurd to visit naval ships during manoeuvres or on foreign stations.[90] Although the writers received no official direction about what to write, they each focused on the lives of lower-deck men.[91] Best known for his imperial and army fiction, Kipling was also an ardent navalist who made two trips with cruisers in the Channel Squadron in 1897 and 1898, which were later described in *A Fleet in Being*. Frank Bullen, who wrote both journalism and popular maritime fiction, had once been a merchant seaman. Assigned to the HMS *Mars* to report on the naval manoeuvres of 1899, Bullen wrote *The Way They Have in the Navy* with the goal of imparting 'an ordinary man's understanding, a man who, like myself, would be glad to know how our huge Naval Machine works'.[92] A Navy League member and a naval correspondent for the *Daily Telegraph*, Hurd wrote *How Our Navy is Run* in 1902.

Through their tracts, Kipling, Bullen and Hurd wanted to share a world little known to the British public. Hurd's stated purpose was to reveal the lives of naval men 'who guard our shores, protect our very daily bread as it is borne over the ocean from far distant lands, and safeguard the oversea empire'.[93] Through his account, Kipling intended to bring 'the daily life of our naval defenders more in touch with those, who, under God, are indebted to them for all the peace and security they enjoy'.[94] Like the lower-deck advocates who had served in the navy, these writers agreed that the public did not know enough of the duties and responsibilities of the men upon whom the safety of Britain rested. For Hurd, the public misunderstood the sailor as a class apart and did not appreciate 'the highly technical character of their training and duties'.[95] According to Bullen, what was 'hardly realised by the great majority of people was that in the personnel of the Navy we have a force of warriors that on land as well as at sea have not their equals in the world'.[96] He admitted that part of the problem lay in the nature and location of naval men's work: 'Like the deeds of all true heroes, the work of our sailors is done out of sight; there are no applauding crowds to witness the incessant striving after perfection that goes on in our ships of war. We rarely see a company of bluejackets ashore unless we have the good fortune to live at some of the ports favoured by men-o'-war'.[97]

While their writings intended to uncover a world hidden from public view with the hopes of winning general readers to the navalist cause, Kipling, Bullen and Hurd also portrayed naval masculinity as a model for imperial manhood. Their reverence for naval men celebrated their physical strength, discipline, hard work, adaptability and communal spirit. In their descriptions of naval routines and rituals, Kipling, Bullen and Hurd extolled naval men's bodies for their fine physique and strength. As British ambassadors, naval men conveyed the strength and health of the nation and empire. Long gone were the days of scurvy-ridden, malnourished sailors. On the contrary, according to Bullen, these men were 'all models of health and strength' so much so that 'the first thing that strikes a casual observer is their superb health'.[98] The modern bluejacket's strong physique was proof that discipline and order had permeated the service. On the ship, masculinity was tamed by the ritualised imposition of discipline. Through the eyes of the navalist observers, daily gymnastic exercises accentuated the controlled harmonisation of men's bodies, imparted the order of the ship, and conveyed the strength of the fleet (figure 4.4).[99]

In the absence of sail, gymnastics had become part of naval routine as a way to keep men fit aboard highly mechanised battleships. In an

GYMNASTICS ON BOARD THE BATTLESHIP "HOWE."

4.4 'Gymnastics on board the Battleship *"Howe"*', *Navy & Army Illustrated*, 15 May 1896.

article from the *Spectator*, Bullen described the ritual of naval men performing gymnastics,

> they put down their dumb-bells and went through the exercise bare-handed in a rhythmical swing to the music and with an energy that I thought wonderful . . . to those who enjoy the spectacle of a body of men at the highest pitch of physical development, clothed in garments that permit the utmost freedom of limb, and actuated . . . by an intelligent desire after perfection, the sight is worth any trouble to obtain. Really, it is 'hardy' as strong wine. To the dash and enthusiasm of public-school boys the men unite an intense pride in their profession and an intellectual obedience that is amazing to the beholder.[100]

To Bullen, the rhythmic synchronised movement of bodies displayed the intoxicating individual physical strength of the men, their professional status and the reassuring discipline of this homosocial attachment, all of which conveyed the strength of the fleet in its service defending nation and empire. The exercises at once both exhibited and tempered the power of the men in a display that, for Bullen, rivalled the public school ethos. Rather than being a cause for concern, these

[143]

homosocial displays could be celebrated for distinguishing the respectability of naval manhood, in its approximation to the idealised middle-class masculine camaraderie of the public school.[101]

Hurd encouraged men to volunteer for service because 'those who wish to live long cannot do better than serve under the white ensign and join in the healthy sports that develop and strengthen the body, while the mind is expanded by visits to all parts of the world, not as ordinary tourists, but as bearers of the red, white, and blue'.[102] Writings like Hurd's had a potential threefold effect given that they were written during the Boer War – a war that exposed Britain's weakness and isolation in the series of defeats that British troops suffered at the hands of outnumbered Boers. They encouraged men to volunteer for naval service, they highlighted the strength and value of the navy at a time when the army's performance was tarnished, and they extolled naval manhood as strong and healthy enough to defend Britain and its Empire.

In the wake of the war, the Report of the 1904 Interdepartmental Committee on Physical Deterioration had exposed the physical deficiencies of the British army and the general unfitness of the British population. Such studies seemed to confirm eugenicist fears that racial decline would undermine the vitality of empire.[103] Unlike the army, the navy escaped such derision and was lauded for its contribution during the Boer War, like the naval brigade from HMS *Powerful* which attacked Boer positions to relieve the Boer siege of General White's troops at Ladysmith in late October 1899. The end of the siege in late February had brought accolades from press and public for the navy's crucial contribution to the war effort, and the 7 May 1900 parade in London drew thousands who lined the streets to catch a glimpse of the sailors and marines from the *Powerful* brigade.[104] In the *Bluejacket*'s coverage of the parade, Lionel Yexley contended that there was hardly a parallel for the crowds gathered (the parade occurred less than two weeks before Mafeking night) and admitted that 'Londoners rarely have an opportunity of showing how "they all love Jack", but they made up for lost time with a vengeance'.[105]

At the ceremony at the Horse Guards Parade, Captain Hedworth Lambton of the brigade praised his men, 'you have done your duty as became the representatives of the Royal Navy, called on to fight on shore. You have not only had your baptism of fire; you have, most of you, been under fire for months by night and by day . . . by the defence and the relief of Ladysmith, you have saved the country from such a disaster as has never befallen British arms.'[106] Other speakers made similar assertions that the relief of Ladysmith had saved Natal, South Africa and the Empire.

Given the adulation of naval efforts in the war, it is not surprising to find that naval manhood was also extolled. By 1902, *The Times* argued that the navy was an 'almost incomparable school' in character building.[107] In a 1907 book on the Navy League's progress in schools, E. L. Churchill, the Assistant Master at Eton and Navy League member, believed that the navy offered important lessons in manhood:

> surely nowhere can more types be found of what a boy should aim at being and a man should be than in the British Navy. The two leading characteristics of that service are modesty and devotion to duty. The adventurous nature of the life, the patient endurance of discomfort and hardship, the readiness to meet all emergencies – to go anywhere and do anything – and the self-abnegation which disclaims merit, together produce a type of man that must command the admiration of all boys; (while beyond all this lies the knowledge that this quiet performance of duty may lead to a degree of fame hardly to be attained in any other sphere of life). . . .[108]

For Churchill, the epitome of manhood was embodied in the naval man.

In addition to a healthy physique, the naval man had the reputation for cleanliness and sharp attire – all of which contributed to his images as respectable, domesticated and dutiful. After a conversation with a naval man about shipboard life, the female columnist of the *Navy League Journal* commented that 'he admitted a great dislike to the penetrating grime – a glance at his extreme trimness suggested a fondness for soap and water'.[109] The sailor's reputation for cleanliness was well-known because of accounts which described sailors holystoning shipdecks, polishing brasswork, or washing their own clothes. In an age when cleanliness was revered, this image of the clean, well-groomed sailor presented the naval man as respectable and virtuous defender of empire. Advertisements for cleaning products often featured the sailor's image. A Colman's Starch advertisement from the early 1900s, featured a naval man, shown in his crisp white uniform, carrying his son, also donning a sailor's costume, aloft on his shoulders (see figure 4.5). The advertisement suggests that an application of Colman's starch not only cleans the clothes but also helps to make the man. Such advertisements contributed to what Anne McClintock has referred to as a larger 'consumer spectacle' in which imperial and domestic duties intersected to assert the benefits of empire and civilisation.[110]

The crispness of the naval uniform particularly conveyed the image of imperial strength. Hurd commented that 'there are few pleasanter and more refreshing sights than a smartly dressed seaman of his

4.5 Colman's Starch advertisement.

Majesty's navy; nor is he unconscious, as a rule, of the admiring eyes that are fixed on him as with an easy roll he passes along. There is a saying that fine clothes do not make a man, but sailors of the King's fleet have reason to know how important a matter their uniform is'.[111] Hurd agreed that the 'the men of the navy well know that the smart appearance of the force depends on all the men being dressed alike'.[112]

Equally impressive to Hurd was the adaptability and domesticity of naval men. Hurd was amazed at the prospect that naval men were still responsible for making and maintaining their own uniform: 'who that has seen Jack, the manly boy in blue, dragging his guns along on parade, or knows anything of the stiff training in seamanship, guns, and torpedoes . . . would suppose that he is often also a skilled tailor, almost as adept with the needle as with the rifle'.[113] According to Hurd, all would agree that the naval man was a handyman, a jack of all trades; 'there are few things he cannot do, from defending the Empire to making his clothes, and preparing a savoury stew. Of course he does his own washing, and is a capital "housemaid", if the term may be used of a *man* who lives in a *ship*'.[114] The domestic virtues of the naval man further reinforced the dexterity of his manhood.

For writers like Bullen, Kipling and Hurd, the sailor was a national asset where living on ship provided the medium to cultivate his manhood. According to Hurd, the secret to the naval man's impressive character was that he was 'caught young, younger than in any other navy in the world', and while 'still undeveloped', he was like 'clay in the potter's hands'. After being 'moulded and polished while still a lad, both physically and mentally', the sailor boy grew into the modern naval man who was the 'splendid product of a splendid system'.[115] For Kipling, work on board ship was like a democratised hive in its closeness and sense of purpose where men's speech was 'soft', 'their gestures' few, and their steps 'noiseless'.[116] The men's quarters reflected a 'general democracy' where 'the men smoke at the permitted times, and in clubs and coteries and say what they please of each other and their superiors'.[117]

To capture the ship's energy, Kipling animated all that he observed. For Kipling, the relationship between the ship and its men was gendered – the ship was a feminine vehicle that both nurtured and submitted to naval manhood. Everything about the ship awakened to the 'life hot in her' with the sailor's touch.[118] While life in the modern navy may have appeared distant and impenetrable to the public, Kipling roused the ship and its men to life through lush sexualised imagery. For Kipling, the ship that engaged in the 'Big Sea Dance' was a woman who coyly revealed herself to the men of the fleet: 'As the ship rolls in her descent you can watch curve after new curve revealed, humouring and coaxing the water. When she recovers her step, the long sucking hollow of her own wave discloses just enough of her shape to make you wish to see more'.[119]

For Kipling, naval men possessed the skills to subdue the ships and control the ship's movements. During gunnery practice, Maxim guns 'waked to life' after the skilful working of gunners caused the 'lips' of the guns to cry 'a shrillish gasping wail – exactly like the preliminary whoop of an hysterical woman – as the little shell hurried to target'.[120] Even torpedoes were transformed by men – Kipling related, 'when you have been shown lovingly over a torpedo by an artificer skilled in the working of its tricky bowels, torpedoes have a meaning and a reality for you to the end of your days'.[121] Such passages did not merely romanticise life in the modern navy, they transformed the ship into a site of arousal in need of manly control.

Bullen also commented on the high level of discipline maintained aboard ship, 'where 800 men are living in so small a space as even this huge ship affords, it is easy to see that discipline must be adamantine if things are to go as they should'.[122] With rigid discipline in place and a better class of men, the navy had improved, according to Bullen. The commander of the *Mars* attested that the 'decrease in punishable cases since he has been in the service has been enormous'.[123] Bullen attributed declining punishments to 'the spread of temperance, the advance of education, the vastly improved treatment, and doubtless many other causes have contributed to this happy result, which ought to be a source of the most complete gratification to every lover of our country'.[124] Hurd also admitted that the 'bad old times' of flogging and rough treatment were gone from the navy. The naval man's character changed with 'the abolition of the press-gang, the closing of the navy to the criminal classes, and the institution of the long-service system'. As a result, naval discipline was easily maintained because the lower deck was comprised only of 'men of good character' who were 'among the best behaved and most sober of the classes ashore'.[125] Kipling defended the skills of warrant and petty officers who, he argued, would successfully lead the navy to victory 'if any accident removed every single Commissioned Officer'.[126]

Naval manhood was distinguished by hard work; there was no room for romanticising the life on the ocean wave. Dashing away any false illusions of the sailor's breezy life at sea, Hurd asserted that,

> bluejacket, stoker, engine room artificer, or marine, they all love the sea and its life, though it is far from realising many landsmen's dreams of lazy days on the ocean, while the ship glides over gently rippling waters, and past strange romantic coasts . . . Bluejackets work as hard as horses,

and they seldom know what it is to sleep more than four hours at a stretch afloat.[127]

Describing the extra preparations required for the war manoeuvres, Kipling commented that the crew 'worked like sailors – there is no stronger term'.[128] Such descriptions helped to redefine naval manhood in terms of hard work rather than playful excess. In an article written for the 1902 coronation review of the fleet at Spithead, a female Navy League member shared the humble words of a naval man who admitted that dying for his country was part of a day's work: ' "But you see the work is very interesting, it's got to be done by some of us, and" – this with an apologetic laugh – "it's for the good of the country" '.[129] According to the correspondent, the patriotism of naval men lay not in their word but in their deeds. The hard work and humility of these men 'hidden amongst these warships' was 'the secret of our existence as an empire'.[130]

The naval man repeatedly proved himself as a capable soldier of empire. He enjoyed the reputation, according to Admiral Lord Beresford, of 'splendid courage in critical moments, readiness of resource, individuality, a loyal sense of duty, combined with a chivalrous idea of honour and a cheery demeanour under all circumstances'.[131] The modern naval man distinguished himself as both sailor and soldier, as proved by the performance of the naval brigade at Ladysmith during the Boer War. Writing in the wake of the war, Hurd commented that the naval man was indeed a handyman with his capabilities of fighting afloat as well as ashore. Although his training was unproved in a naval war, the naval man proved himself as an imperial soldier,

> It is satisfactory however, to know that as a fighter Jack upheld his character so splendidly during the siege of Ladysmith, and through the earlier part of the South African campaign; as in China, Egypt, Ashanti and elsewhere. His nickname of 'the handy man' is only too well-merited, and, as has been told over and over again, the beleagured Natal town owed its salvation to the naval brigade and naval guns which had proceeded across country from Durban. Although none of our bluejackets have had an opportunity of engaging in a sea battle, naval detachments have many times, during the past ten years or so, distinguished themselves in land fighting. . . . He seems to have the happy knack of adapting himself to varied circumstances in perhaps a greater degree than his comrade in the Army and it is for this reason that he is so often selected for the work of chastising a coast tribe or a chief of the interior of the Dark Continent.[132]

His adaptability for fighting afloat or ashore had not only made the modern sailor a 'handyman' but also made him a more valuable defender of empire than an army soldier. In an article in the *Spectator*, Bullen also commented upon the dexterity of the naval man as both sailor and soldier,

> It would be well for landsmen reading of the doings of a Naval Brigade ashore to remember this, – to bear in mind that if Jack excels as a soldier, preparation for which duty is made in the merest fag-ends and scraps of his time, he is super excellent in the performance of his main business which he does in the privacy of the sea, with only the approval of his superior officers – and his pride in the British Navy – to encourage him.[133]

Kipling extolled these men as defenders of nation and empire because they possessed 'such strength and such power as we and the World dare hardly guess at'.[134] Their strength defended Britain and protected the sea, Britain's most significant, yet neglected, possession. There was little question that the sea belonged to Britain, defining its culture and its people. For Kipling, an appreciation of Britain's naval heritage was a bond that all 'white' Britons shared – the realisation of a shared past erased class divisions and united Britons in common purpose. 'The speech on the deck below was mine, for the men were free white men, same as me, only considerably better . . . we had a common tradition, one thousand years old'.[135] Kipling's words aimed at reminding his readers to value those 'things one takes for granted'. His words helped define naval manhood as a democratised and desirable manly ideal for Britain and its empire. The model of naval manhood then served to inculcate British patriotism by constructing a shared British heritage based on freedom, whiteness and admiralty of the seas.

The writings of Kipling and Bullen informed a public who rarely came into contact with the navy or its men apart from song or fiction. In their accounts, which were well-spun yarns about their time on board a man-of-war, Kipling and Bullen hoped to demystify the lives and customs of seamen as if they composed an exotic tribe. Kipling counselled his readers that the

> next time you see the 'blue' ashore you do not stare unintelligently. You have watched him on his native heath. You know what he eats, and what he says, and where he sleeps, and how. He is no longer a unit; but altogether such as one as yourself – only, as I have said, better.[136]

After reading about the exploits of such men, readers, according to Kipling, would come to realise that the 'majesty' of the Fleet was not its ships or its armament but that 'Men live there'.[137] Writers such as Kipling, Bullen and Hurd had animated a navy by personifying it as a naval man, and in so doing, they popularised and refined the image of the sailor as the stalwart defender of nation and empire. By idealising the manhood of common seamen, they had also furthered the project of democratising British manliness; while British manliness had been typified by an elite manly ideal, it now could be conceived within the reach of all.

Naval manhood as 'real manhood'

The democratisation of the manly ideal took place within fiction as well as journalistic accounts. Popular literature depicted naval manhood as a model for all Britons, even monarchs, to emulate. In these representations, the navy possessed the power to turn any man into a 'real man' through rigorous military training and strong discipline. In 1908, Fred T. Jane, an outspoken navalist and journalist, published *A Royal Bluejacket*, a novel about a contemporary naval romance.[138] Jane, who had already written several novels with maritime themes, had recently left the Navy League for the Imperial Maritime League and was a critic of Tories and Liberals alike as well as the British monarchy. In *A Royal Bluejacket*, Prince Arthur, an honorary naval officer, forsakes his birth and privilege to enter the navy as a common seaman in order to win over the love of Princess Margaret, who has questioned his virility.

The novel begins as Prince Arthur and Princess Margaret are having lunch aboard the royal yacht and are looking out upon the naval dockyard and moorings. Stirred by the sight of naval men rowing past their yacht, Margaret exclaims, 'What splendid men they are!' as the sailors pulled against the tide.[139] When Arthur, uninterested, mutters that they are only common seamen, Margaret retorts: 'They are men . . . Real men, who *do* things'. In contrast, she asks Arthur, 'What do *we* do?'[140] Arthur cannot offer an answer and can only accuse Margaret of socialist sympathies for defending common sailors. Margaret admits that her attraction to common naval men rests in their simplicity and naturalness, 'I do sometimes envy ordinary people. To – to be able to love a man because he was a *man*–'[141] Arthur explains that there is nothing particularly heroic or manly about naval men because they are little more than mercenaries, hired by the state to perform a task, 'They get an ample reward over and above their pay by being called the "Handy Man" and cheered by the crowd, and so forth'. At the end of the argument, Margaret challenges Arthur to become a real man by joining the navy as a common sailor: 'You are a royal sailor', she cried. 'Be a *real* sailor, instead of a sham one . . . Go unknown and be a real sailor, win distinction as a *man*. And then, – when you have done that, – tell me again that you love me! . . . Till then *au revoir*'.[142] The implication was that royal sailors and officers were not real men. Real manhood was attained on the lower deck rather than the quarter deck. Most likely this was Jane's indictment of King Edward VII, who had earned the reputation for enjoying 'fleshly pleasures' and revelling in material extravagance.[143]

In *A Royal Bluejacket*, Jane argues that action and daring were better proof of manhood than birth, ritual and pomp. Jane's critique of elite British manhood as effeminate and his emphasis on instilling 'real manhood' through naval training were part of a larger Edwardian movement that sought to prevent national decay and degeneration by reinvigorating British manhood through martial training. Robert Baden-Powell's Boy Scouts movement was an emblematic attempt to regenerate the nation by nurturing a martial manliness. Whereas Kipling in his 1902 poem 'The Islanders' denounced the British at the close of the Boer War for becoming too 'soft', distracted in the selfish pleasures of idle leisure rather than motivated by duty to defend the nation, Jane indicted the monarchy for becoming too soft and offering no proper model for the British public to emulate.[144]

Arthur's quest for manhood is the main theme of the book. Although Arthur was a naval officer, it is soon apparent that Arthur knows little of shipboard life and less of the manly virtues encouraged in the navy. In fact, after Arthur joins the navy, he earns the nickname of 'Puffy' from one of his messmates, 'Nosey' Trott who is repulsed by Arthur's physical weakness and his bloated arrogance. It is Nosey's mission to turn Arthur into a real man, 'I hopes to make a man of 'im yet. It's the object of 29 Mess'.[145] To attain manhood, Arthur is forced to do the work of common sailors – scrubbing decks, polishing brasswork, and coaling ship – and is also subject to the ship's discipline just as the others. Although Arthur is tempted to complain and whine about the conditions, he learns that grumbling is a dishonourable trait among seamen.

Nearing the end of the ship's commission, Arthur works hard, without complaint, and enjoys the simple life of his mess. By the end of the tour, Nosey congratulates Arthur on his transformation by exclaiming 'Puffy, You're a Man!'[146] For Arthur, Nosey's compliment is the best tribute that he could receive, 'Nosey had called him a *man;* he had fought and suffered enough now to value that appreciation'. By serving in the navy as an ordinary seaman, Arthur was stripped of his pretensions and had earned his manhood, 'the selfish Princeling, with his petty little hates, his belief that the world was made for him, his selfish creed that he was a little centre of the Universe, was gone for ever . . . Meagre his pay and hard his lot, at least he earned his right to live'.[147] Although Arthur had entered the navy to win the love of a woman, by the end it was his manhood which was his most important victory.

Jane's tale of 'Puffy' clearly posits that masculinity is intimately linked with action, rather than appearance or words. Arthur realised that action and modesty were the essential components of naval manhood. By working alongside real naval men, Arthur also realised that only 'poets made them (naval men) talk in high-faluting terms of duty and of country. Duty, Country, Empire, those were the things they sang of in music-halls and spouted about to catch votes with on political platforms. The men who *did* things needed something less fanciful than that'.[148] Arthur understood that such jingoist prattle was worthless to naval men whose sense of duty meant that they unfailingly performed their jobs as a matter of course without boasting.

A Royal Bluejacket warned its audience that empty patriotism and effete manhood would weaken the nation. For Jane, Britain's salvation rested upon real manhood where men were trained to act. As a result of foreign challenges to Britain's naval supremacy and its empire, the manly and brave British bluejacket represented Britain's best defence. Jane's rhetoric was hardly different from the contemporary demands of Lord Roberts, Lord Meath, or Baden-Powell who all emphasised that a new disciplined manhood was necessary to ensure the security of Britain and its empire. But for Jane, the navy offered the best protection for Britain's future.

Over the course of the nineteenth century, the reputation of the British naval man was transformed. Older popular images of the sailor as a 'Jolly Jack Tar' whose character was defined by an insatiable thirst for grog and women were reduced to parody and were overshadowed by patriotic representations of the sailor as a British bluejacket whose duty, discipline and hard work came to the defence of nation and empire.

The glorification of the navy and its men at the turn of the century responded to the naval scares and imperial challenges that fuelled concerns that Britain's naval supremacy like its empire was illusory. By the Edwardian period, the idealisation of the sailor's rugged manhood marked a process that democratised the manly ideal from elite manliness to a manliness that was attainable by all male Britons. Given the new demands of empire, such models of naval manhood were needed if nation and empire were to be secured from challenges within and without.

Notes

1 Jan Rüger, 'Nation, Empire and Navy: Identity Politics in the United Kingdom, 1887–1914', *Past and Present* 185 (Nov. 2004), 160.

2 Herbert Hayens, *Ye Mariners of England: A Boy's Book of the Navy* (London: Thomas Nelson and Sons, 1901), 10; James Anthony Froude, *Oceana: Or, England and Her Colonies* (New York: Scribner, 1888), 14. Quoted in Cynthia Behrman, *Victorian Myths of the Sea* (Athers, Ohio: Ohio University Press, 1977), 28.
3 Spenser Wilkinson, *The Secret of the Sea* (London: Swan, 1895), 2.
4 Alfred Lord Tennyson, 'The Fleet: Or its Reported Insufficiency', *The Times*, 23 April 1885.
5 Alfred Lord Tennyson, 'Opening of the Indian and Colonial Exhibition by the Queen', in *Poems of Alfred Lord Tennyson*, ed. Christopher Ricks, vol. 3 (Berkeley: University of California Press, 1987), 147–8.
6 Alfred T. Mahan, *The Influence of Sea Power on History, 1660–1783* ([1889] New York: Sagamore Press, 1957).
7 *Navy League Journal*, July 1895, 1.
8 Cynthia Behrman elaborates on the mythic importance of the Royal Navy to British identities of the late nineteenth century. See Cynthia Behrman, *Victorian Myths of the Sea* (Athens, Ohio: Ohio University Press, 1977).
9 'Some Naval Memories' by an Englishwoman in *Navy League Guide to the Coronation Review*, ed. H. W. Wilson (London: A. Constable and Co., 1902), 15.
10 Bovril advertisement, registered by Albert Hildesheimer, 13 August 1902, Public Record Office.
11 Archibald Hurd, *How our Navy is Run: A Description of Life in the King's Fleet* (London: C. Arthur Pearson, Ltd, 1902), 91.
12 *Bluejacket*, June 1901, 137.
13 *Bluejacket*, June 1901, 122.
14 *Bluejacket*, January 1906, 14.
15 *Bluejacket*, March 1906, 70.
16 *Bluejacket*, March 1906, 70.
17 *Bluejacket*, June 1901, 137.
18 Tosh, *Manliness and Masculinities in Nineteenth-Century Britain* (Harlow, England: Pearson Longman, 2005), 36–7.
19 Lieutenant-Commander Henry D. Capper, *Aft-from the Hawsehole: Sixty-two Years of Sailors' Evolution* (London: Faber & Gwyer, 1927), 253.
20 Stephen Reynolds, *The Lower Deck: The Navy and the Nation* (London: J. M. Dent and Sons, 1912), 13.
21 *Bluejacket*, June 1901, 137. Lionel Yexley was a pseudonym; his real name was James Woods.
22 *Bluejacket*, June 1901, 122.
23 Tosh, *Manliness and Masculinities*, 71; John Tosh, *A Man's Place: Masculinity and the Middle Class Home in Victorian England* (New Haven: Yale University Press, 1999), 27–50, 123–42; Leonore Davidoff and Catherine Hall, *Family Fortunes: Men and Women of the English Middle Class, 1780–1850* (Chicago: University of Chicago Press, 1987).
24 Thomas Holman [A Ranker, pseud.], *Life in the Royal Navy* (Portsmouth: G. Chamberlain, 1891), viii.
25 Lionel Yexley, *Our Fighting Seamen* (London: Stanley Paul, 1911), 15.
26 Yexley, *Our Fighting Seamen*, 14.
27 Yexley, *Our Fighting Seamen*, 16.
28 Holman, *Life in the Royal Navy*, ix.
29 Holman, *Life in the Royal Navy*, ix.
30 Capper, *Aft-from the Hawsehole*, 168. The navy also demanded and promoted a higher standard of education for all its ranks. The navy provided education for boy ratings and, once in the service, it offered further instruction afloat and ashore for naval men pursuing a specialised branch like gunnery.
31 Capper, *Aft-from the Hawsehole*, 166.
32 Rear-Admiral Sir Thomas J. Spence Lyne (1870–1955), *Something about a Sailor: From Sailor Boy to Admiral* (London: Jarrolds, 1940), 106.

33 *Fleet*, May 1905, 16.
34 *Bluejacket*, July 1901, 147.
35 *Bluejacket*, August 1905, 224.
36 Lionel Yexley, *Our Fighting Seamen*, 49.
37 The passing of sail instruction and the increased amount of port-based training of naval men had provoked a wave of criticism from navalists like J. R. Thursfield, who later founded the Imperial Maritime League. See J. R. Thursfield, 'The Training of Seamen', *The Journal of the Royal United Service Institution* 44, no. 271 (September 1900), 969–1025.
38 Anthony Carew, *The Lower Deck of the Royal Navy, 1900–1939* (Manchester: Manchester University Press, 1981), xvi.
39 Andrew Thompson, *Imperial Britain: The Empire in British Politics, c.1880–1932* (Harlow, England: Longman Pearson, 2000), 45; Raymond L. Schults, *Crusader in Babylon: W. T. Stead and the Pall Mall Gazette* (Lincoln: University of Nebraska Press, 1972).
40 *The Navy League* (August 1896), Navy League Pamphlets, British Library; Marder, *The Anatomy of British Sea Power*, 49; Frans Coetzee, *For Party or Country* (Oxford: Oxford University Press, 1990), 32–7, 163. Founder Henry Cust was a Conservative backbencher and Robert Yerburgh, the League's first president was the Unionist MP for Chester.
41 *The Navy League* (August 1896), Navy League Pamphlets, British Library; Marder, *The Anatomy of British Sea Power*, 54; Anne Summers, 'The Character of Edwardian Nationalism: Three Popular Leagues', in *Nationalist and Racialist Movements in Britain and Germany Before 1914*, ed. Paul Kennedy and Anthony Nicholls (London: Macmillan Press Ltd, 1981), 69.
42 Hamilton, *The Nation and the Navy*, 145.
43 Arnold White, *The Navy League and the Public* (London: Navylague, c. 1914); W. Mark Hamilton, 'The "New Navalism" and the British Navy League, 1895–1914', *Mariner's Mirror* 64 (February 1978), 38; A. J. A. Morris, *The Scaremongers* (London: Routledge & Kegan Paul, 1984), 409.
44 Marder, *The Anatomy of British Sea Power*, 57.
45 *Hansard's Parliamentary Debates*, 4th ser., vol. 38 (6 March 1896), col. 402.
46 *Navy League Journal*, March 1896, 2.
47 Once the League could claim popular support, it continued to be a thorn in the administration of Admiralty affairs. See *Admiralty and Horse Guard Gazette*, 27 December 1894, 2 March 1895; *National Review*, December 1895; Marder, *The Anatomy of British Sea Power*, 50.
48 Marder, *The Anatomy of British Sea Power*, 55.
49 L. G. H. Horton-Smith Papers, National Maritime Museum (hereafter NMM), HSM/1. Lionel Graham Horton-Smith (1871–1953) and Harold Frazer Wyatt (1858–1925) led the exodus to the Imperial Maritime League. Together they produced alarmist pamphlets like *The Passing of the Great Fleet* (London, 1909) and *Britain's Imminent Danger* (London, 1912) to alert the public about Britain's naval vulnerability.
50 Coetzee, *For Party or Country*, 83–4; Hamilton, *The Nation and the Navy*, 154, 159. In 1911, the IML sponsored navalist plays held in London's Royal Court Theatre entitled 'Secrets of State' and 'Admiral Peters' and used those opportunities to include the League's objectives in play programmes.
51 *The Navy League Report for the Year 1906*, NMM, HSM MSS/1.
52 Coetzee, *For Party or Country*, 138. By 1910, the Navy League's journal, *The Navy*, had reached circulation of 21,000.
53 Coetzee, *For Party or Country*, 138; Hamilton, *Nation and the Navy*, 126–7.
54 See Geoff Eley, *Reshaping the German Right: Radical Nationalism and Political Change after Bismarck* (New Haven: Yale University Press, 1980), and Geoff Eley, 'Reshaping the Right: Radical Nationalism and the German Navy League, 1898–1908', *Historical Journal* 21 (1978), 327–54.
55 Marder, *The Anatomy of British Sea Power*, 55.

56 See Laura Tabili, *'We ask for British Justice': Workers and Racial Difference in Late Imperial Britain* (Ithaca: Cornell University Press, 1994).

57 *British Seamen for British Ships: Report of Conference of Representatives of Public Bodies and of Others Interested in the Training of British Seamen* (8 May 1901), L. G. H. Horton-Smith Papers, NMM, HSM/1; Coetzee, *For Party or Country*, 26; Bernard Semmel, *Imperialism and Social Reform: English Social-Imperial Thought, 1895–1914* (Cambridge: Harvard University Press, 1960), 223.

58 S. M. Eardley-Wilmot, 'Our Naval Supremacy – is it assured?' *Navy League Journal*, September 1895, 2–3.

59 Public Record Office, Kew (hereafter PRO), ADM 1/6216, 'Men from the Merchant Service having ceased to enter the Royal Navy for some time past', November 1871.

60 Frank T. Bullen, *The Way They Have in the Navy* (London: Smith, Elder, and Co., 1899), vii.

61 *British Seamen for British Ships* (8 May 1901), NMM, HSM MSS/1.

62 John Knox Laughton, *The Study of Naval History* (London: Royal United Service Institute, 1896), 5.

63 Lord Thomas Brassey, *Papers and Addresses: Mercantile Marine and Navigation: From 1871 to 1894* (London: Longman's Green and Co., 1894).

64 *Navy League Journal*, April 1899, 67.

65 C. McL. McHardy, *British Seamen, Boy Seamen, and Light Dues* (London: Navy League, 1899); *Navy League Journal*, April 1899, 68.

66 Summers, 'The Character of Edwardian Nationalism', 69.

67 *Navy League Journal*, April 1899, 68.

68 Similarly the National Service League lobbied for conscription in order to ensure the necessary numbers of trained men for wartime.

69 H. W. Wilson, ed., *Navy League Guide to the Coronation Review*, 28 June 1902, 28 June 1902 (London: A. Constable and Co., 1902).

70 Frank T. Bullen, 'The Passing of our Mercantile Marine Supremacy', in *Navy League Guide to the Coronation Review, June 28, 1902*, ed. H. W. Wilson (London: A. Constable and Co., for the Navy League, 1902), 29–30.

71 Frank C. Bowen, *History of the Royal Naval Reserve* (London: Lloyd's, 1926).

72 Wilfried Fest, 'Jingoism and Xenophobia in the Electioneering Strategies of British Ruling Elites before 1914', in *Nationalist and Racialist Movements in Britain and Germany Before 1914*, ed. Paul Kennedy and Anthony Nicholls (London: Macmillan Press, Ltd, 1981), 175; E. H. H. Green, *The Crisis of Conservatism* (London: Routledge, 1995), 317–19.

73 Coetzee, *For Party or Country*, 96; Andrew S. Thompson, *Imperial Britain: the Empire in British Politics, c.1880–1932* (Harlow: Longman, 2000), 41–4, 53–5; Anne J. Kershen, *Strangers, Aliens and Asians: Huguenots, Jews and Bangladeshis in Spitalfields, 1660–2000* (London: Routledge, 2005), 221.

74 *The Navy League* (August 1896), Navy League Pamphlets, British Library.

75 Navy League Pamphlet, C1, 1895, quoted in Summers, 'The Character of Edwardian Nationalism', 77.

76 H. W. Wilson, 'Meaning of Defeat', NMM, WHI MSS/75. Along similar lines, see Arnold White's 'England Expects', NMM, WHI MSS/75; Hamilton, *The Nation and the Navy*, 133. In 'The Meaning of Defeat', the consequences of England's loss of maritime supremacy is war, defeat, loss of empire, and the ruin of British civilisation, marked by 'grass-grown streets, ruined mills, bankrupt cities, social revolution'.

77 *Navy League Journal*, July 1895, 1.

78 Leaflets like 'England Expects' and 'Our Next War' were targeted to working men and 'for all those who care for their country'. Admiral Lord Charles Beresford, a frequent lecturer for the Navy League, spoke at Canning Town in the spring of 1897 on the subject, 'The Navy and the Working Man'. See *Navy League Journal*, June 1897, 4–5. Navy League Lecturers like Lt Henry T. C. Knox spoke in Workmen's Clubs in London. See Hamilton, *The Nation and the Navy*, 148.

79 *Navy League Annual Report*, 1908, quoted in Hamilton, *The Nation and the Navy*, 132.
80 *Navy*, August 1909, 229, quoted in Coetzee, *For Party or Country*, 111.
81 Thompson, *Imperial Britain*, 55.
82 Fest, 'Jingoism and Xenophobia', 174; Richard Price, *An Imperial War and The British Working Class: Working-Class Attitudes and Reactions to the Boer War* (London: Routledge, 1972).
83 Charles Beresford, preface to *How our Navy is Run*, by Archibald Hurd, xv.
84 Beresford, preface to *How our Navy is Run*, xvi.
85 Arnold White had proclaimed that the *Daily Express* was 'the only Tory paper that is read by working men'. See Morris, *Scaremongers*, 367.
86 Arnold White, 'The Feeding of the Fleet', in *Navy League Guide to the Coronation Review, June 28, 1902*, ed. H. W. Wilson (London: A. Constable and Co., for the Navy League, 1902), 10–12.
87 White, 'The Feeding of the Fleet', 12.
88 *Fleet*, April 1907, 116; Wells, *The Royal Navy*, 65. Among the reforms were a greater and healthier variety of rations like fresh bread, more meal times allotted, more time given during meals, and the free provision of mess utensils.
89 Hamilton, *The Nation and the Navy*, 141; Coetzee, *For Party or Country*, 21, 111.
90 Rudyard Kipling, *A Fleet in Being* (London: Macmillan, 1898); Frank T. Bullen, *The Way They Have in the Navy* (London: Smith, Elder & Co, 1899); Hurd, *How our Navy is Run*.
91 Hurd, *How our Navy is Run*, ix.
92 Bullen, *The Way They Have in the Navy*, viii.
93 Hurd, *How our Navy is Run*, ix.
94 Bullen, *The Way They Have in the Navy*, viii.
95 Hurd, *How our Navy is Run*, xii.
96 Frank T. Bullen, 'Our Amphibious Army', *Spectator*, 6 January 1900, 10.
97 Bullen, 'Our Amphibious Army', 10.
98 Bullen, 'Our Amphibious Army', 10.
99 Contemporary newspapers and periodicals featured stories and photos of men at drill. See the *Navy and Army Illustrated*, 15 May 1896, and the *Navy League Journal*, September 1899.
100 Bullen, 'Our Amphibious Army', 10.
101 Tosh, *Manliness and Masculinities*, 37–8; Paul Deslandes, *Oxbridge Men* (Bloomington: Indiana University Press, 2005); Michael Hatt, 'Uranian Imperialism: Boys and Empire in Edwardian England', in *Art and the British Empire*, ed. Tim Barringer, Geoff Quilley and Douglas Fordham (Manchester: Manchester University Press, 2007). In describing the ordered physical displays of naval manhood, writers like Bullen could celebrate male camaraderie without arousing connotations of proscribed male desire.
102 Hurd, *How our Navy is Run*, 253. While the Army's death rate was 12 per thousand, the civilian death rate was as high as 17.6 per thousand, and the Navy was only 4.9 per thousand. Hurd seemed to discount the fact that the navy was a youthful service with most of its members under the age of forty.
103 G. R. Searle, *Eugenics and Politics in Britain, 1900–1914* (Leyden: Noordhoff International Publishing, 1976); Greta Jones, *Social Darwinism and English Thought* (Brighton, Sussex: Harvester Press, 1980).
104 Jacqueline Beaumont, 'The British Press During the South African War: The Sieges of Mafeking, Kimberley and Ladysmith', in *War and the Media: Reportage and Propaganda, 1900–2003*, ed. Mark Connelly and David Welch (London: I. B. Tauris and Co., 2005), 1–18. See also Donal Lowry, ed., *The South African War Reappraised* (Manchester: Manchester University Press, 2000); Paula M. Krebs, *Gender, Race and the Writing of Empire: Public Discourse and the Boer War* (Cambridge: Cambridge University Press, 1999).
105 *Bluejacket*, June 1900, 485.

106 *The Times*, 8 May 1900, 10.
107 *The Times*, 19 July 1902.
108 E. L. Churchill, BA, Assistant Master at Eton College, 'Public Schools and the Navy League', in *The Work of the Navy League in Schools* (London: Navy League, 1907), NMM, HSM MSS/1.
109 'Some Naval Memories by an Englishwoman', in *Navy League Guide to the Coronation Review*, 15.
110 Anne McClintock, *Imperial Leather: Race, Gender and Sexuality in the Colonial Contest* (New York: Routledge, 1995), 33.
111 Hurd, *How our Navy is Run*, 187–8.
112 Hurd, *How our Navy is Run*, 194.
113 Hurd, *How our Navy is Run*, 187. Ready-made uniforms were not introduced until the early 1900s and then were criticised by many men for shoddy tailoring and styling. Hurd included a photo of two naval men in their uniform for the tropics, referred to in the caption as their 'cool-looking costume'. Another photo featured sailors making and mending clothes with a sewing machine and needle.
114 Hurd, *How our Navy is Run*, 187.
115 Hurd, *How our Navy is Run*, 155–6.
116 Rudyard Kipling, *A Fleet in Being* published in *The Bombay Edition of the Works of Rudyard Kipling*, vol. 5 (London: Macmillan, 1913), 205–6.
117 Kipling, *A Fleet in Being*, 205–6.
118 Kipling, *A Fleet in Being*, 268.
119 Kipling, *A Fleet in Being*, 268
120 Kipling, *A Fleet in Being*, 218, 219.
121 Kipling, *A Fleet in Being*, 233.
122 Bullen, *The Way They Have in the Navy*, 85.
123 Bullen, *The Way They Have in the Navy*, 87.
124 Bullen, *The Way They Have in the Navy*, 87.
125 Hurd, *How our Navy is Run*, 212.
126 Kipling, *A Fleet in Being*, 248. Kipling argued that naval men did not receive enough attention from the public: 'The public is apt to lump everything that does not carry the executive curl on its coat-sleeve as some sort of common sailor.'
127 Hurd, *How our Navy is Run*, 92.
128 Kipling, *A Fleet in Being*, 209.
129 'Some Naval Memories' by an Englishwoman, in *Navy League Guide to the Coronation Review*, 15.
130 'Some Naval Memories', 15–16.
131 Beresford, preface to *How our Navy is Run*, xiii.
132 Hurd, *How our Navy is Run*, 62.
133 Bullen, 'Our Amphibious Army', *Spectator*, 6 January 1900, 11. Other contemporary books about the Navy's performance in the Boer War included Surgeon T. T. Jeans, RN, ed., *Naval Brigades in the South African War* (London: Sampson, Low, Marston, 1899–1900).
134 Kipling, *A Fleet in Being*, 228.
135 Kipling, *A Fleet in Being*, 228.
136 Kipling, *A Fleet in Being*, 233.
137 Kipling, *A Fleet in Being*, 233.
138 Fred T. Jane, *A Royal Bluejacket* (London: Sampson and Low, 1908); Morris, *The Scaremongers*,156; *The Fleet*, June 1909, 20. Lionel Yexley reviewed Jane's book in the *Fleet* and belittled it as mere fantasy. F. T. Jane was the founder of *The Naval Annual* as well as *All the World's Ships*, first published in 1910. An ardent Germanophobe, he had a penchant for being on the lookout for German 'spies' in England and claimed to have captured one in his car in Portsmouth.
139 Jane, *A Royal Bluejacket*, 12.
140 Jane, *A Royal Bluejacket*, 13.
141 Jane, *A Royal Bluejacket*, 14.
142 Jane, *A Royal Bluejacket*, 16.

143 Samuel Hynes, *The Edwardian Turn of Mind* (Princeton: Princeton University Press, 1968), 7.

144 Rudyard Kipling, 'The Islanders', in *The Complete Verse*, with a foreword by M. M. Kaye (London: Kyle Cathie, 1990), 244–6.

145 Jane, *A Royal Bluejacket*, 174.

146 Jane, *A Royal Bluejacket*, 345.

147 Jane, *A Royal Bluejacket*, 377

148 Jane, *A Royal Bluejacket*, 382.

CHAPTER FIVE

Lessons in manhood: boyhood, duty and war

On 29 July 1916, thousands of mourners travelled to East Ham in east London to attend the funeral of Jack Cornwell, the boy sailor who had died in early June from wounds sustained during the Battle of Jutland. A 16-year-old sight-setter in a gunnery crew aboard the HMS *Chester*, John Travers Cornwell had been hit by shrapnel during the first hour of the battle but, nevertheless, stood beside his gun during his ship's engagement with the German High Seas Fleet. The delayed July publication of the official battle dispatch by Vice-Admiral Sir David Beatty brought Cornwell's actions and death to the attention of both media and public, who quickly clamoured to memorialise his sacrifice. The revelation in early July that Cornwell had been buried in an 'unmarked' grave at Manor Park Cemetery, near his family's East Ham home, sent the media into a frenzy of demand for a more fitting tribute to his sacrifice. After mounting public pressure, the Admiralty exhumed Cornwell's body from the grave, and arranged for a public funeral with naval honours to be held at the same cemetery. Despite the frequency of funerals and the continuous state of mourn- ing in wartime Britain, Cornwell's naval funeral garnered national attention and marked a distinctive collective moment in public mourning.

The press had publicised the coming funeral and provided wide coverage of the event. On the day of the funeral, stores in East Ham closed and thousands lined the neighbourhood streets as the funeral procession left from Jack's house, progressed past his school and through the town centre before reaching its destination at the ceme- tery. To help keep order among the throngs of mourners, 300 Boy Scouts, several hundred constables, and a detachment from Jack's father Eli Cornwell's 10th Essex Volunteer Regiment lined the course.[1] As the naval gunners drew the carriage carrying the flag-draped casket along procession route, Girl Scouts sold song sheets of 'Brave Jack

Cornwell', from which proceeds were donated to the newly formed Cornwell Memorial Fund begun by the Navy League.[2]

The sombre spectacle included detachments of soldiers and sailors, groups of children, among them eighty of Cornwell's schoolmates from the Walton Road School, a local group of Naval Cadets, and Cornwell's old Boy Scout troop as well as its Scoutmaster. The boy's school headmaster, his former employer from Brooke Bond Teas, and his Plymouth naval instructor also marched in the lengthy procession. Following the marchers in open carriages were Cornwell's family, along with T. J. Macnamara (the Parliamentary Secretary to the Admiralty), the Lord Mayor of London, and other dignitaries from London, East Ham, Parliament, the Navy League, the church, and the newly formed memorial committee. Six boys from the *Chester* carrying wreaths from the ship accompanied the family's carriage as an honour guard.

The funeral service itself intended to serve as testament to Cornwell's heroic act and celebrated duty, obedience and sacrifice. In the course of it, Cornwell would be presented as a fusion of the patriotic and religious virtues represented respectively by Admiral Horatio Nelson and Jesus Christ. The Bishop of Barking conducted the re-committal service and noted that Cornwell had distinguished himself by his signal devotion to duty in taking to heart Nelson's words: 'England expects that every man will this day do his duty'.[3] Duty was not simply a patriotic devotion; rather the bishop argued that Cornwell was true till death so that he might receive the 'crown of everlasting life'.[4] The bishop encouraged mourners to consider how they could be dutiful in life by learning from Cornwell's service, 'Might they all in their different spheres try to do their duty, to do their bit for the glory of God, as he did his, even to the laying down of his life as a good soldier of Jesus Christ'.

After the Bishop conducted the graveside religious service, T. J. Macnamara eulogised Cornwell for laying 'the hopes and aspirations of early youth, the expectations of vigorous manhood, the dreams of life – its affections, its adventures and its opportunities', upon 'the altar of duty'.[5] Macnamara proclaimed that Cornwell's 'grave shall be the birthplace of heroes. From it shall spring inspiration that shall make heart more strong, spirit more dauntless and purpose more noble for generations of British subjects yet unborn, all the wide world over'.[6] Cornwell's death, Macnamara contended, sanctified the British cause.

Think of him. Seek to emulate him, for by his sacrifice and those of the good company of heroes to whom he belongs, heroes of land and sea and air, heroes who sleep beneath the waves, on the plains of Flanders, amid the rugged slopes of Gallipoli, on the banks of the Tigris, away on the far off African veldt, and in the valley of the Somme – by their sacrifices our British ideals of freedom will be maintained and flourished and not perish in our midst. For freedom they went forth to fight and to die; by freedom shall their sacrifice be justified.[7]

Macnamara's words evoked a pantheon of nameless war heroes whose deaths had become sacramental acts of sacrifice for nation and empire.

Although funerals and memorial services were all too frequent during the war, this one served both state interests and individual desires to mourn collectively. In reviews of the funeral, the press remarked that 'there could be no finer epitaph or a more striking testimony to the sterling qualities of the rising generation', and that this was 'the most impressive funeral which has yet taken place in connection with the Great War'.[8] In the days following the funeral, hundreds of visitors from London and Essex came to pay further respects to Cornwell's grave. There was perhaps no boy more famous, nor more extensively commemorated, during the First World War than John Travers Cornwell, but by the war's end he was largely a forgotten figure.

Commemorative efforts did not end with the staging of the funeral. From the moment that the press ran Cornwell's story, individuals, organisations and authorities began to consider appropriate memorials to Cornwell. Once the public learned of Jack Cornwell's service at Jutland from the widely published Admiralty dispatches, there ensued a commemorative frenzy to memorialise the boy that heralded his devotion to duty and propelled the 16-year-old to heroic stature. His life was commemorated intensely by state authorities, private organisations and individuals – in eulogies, awards, newspaper accounts, speeches, monuments, poems and paintings. Notably, Cornwell had received a posthumous Victoria Cross in September 1916. Additional tributes included the Boy Scouts' creation of the Cornwell Badge; a poem that summer by the popular formalist poet John Oxenham; the Navy League's celebration of 'Jack Cornwell Day' in British schools in September 1916; the installation of his wax figure in Madame Tussaud's museum that autumn; the declaration in October by the *National Review* that the 'imperishable boy Cornwell' was 'already a national hero'; the distribution of Frank O. Salisbury's portrait of him to schools in the spring of 1917; and even, in 1918 the dedication of Mount Cornwell in Canada's British Columbia.[9]

In his treatment of Lawrence of Arabia, Graham Dawson notes that 'heroes are made not by their deeds but by the stories that are told about them'.[10] Such was clearly the case with Jack Cornwell; the proliferating stories about his service aboard the *Chester* helped to cast his heroic legend. The aim of this chapter is not to recount Cornwell's service at Jutland but to contextualize the significance of his mythic heroism. The First World War was not the war that Edwardian naval-ists had predicted, but the death of a naval boy had animated the nation in the summer and fall of 1916. Rather than charting portrayals of naval manhood during the course of the war, this chapter offers a case study that delves into the life and death of one boy sailor in order to illuminate how a new egalitarian vision of manhood was best expressed through a naval example and how this emerging form was not cast anew but aligned with Victorian models of heroism defined by duty, honour and sacrifice.

Sacrifice and the manly ideal

Some historians have argued that as a result of the experience of con-scription, mass mobilisation, and the Somme, 1916 sounded the death knell to romantic views of wartime sacrifice.[11] Yet the commemora-tion of Cornwell in 1916 and 1917 demonstrates that the opposite was true; state and society were still seeking out heroes and defining them – telling their stories, in Dawson's phrase – in terms of the familiar pre-war manly ideals. The intensity of the commemorations arose in an atmosphere of war crisis at home and abroad, social and psychologi-cal: the demands of mass mobilisation, the realities of a failed Somme offensive, wartime challenges to masculinity, and the perception that the war was interminable. In a total war where stalemate and attrition increasingly threatened to erode British resolve, celebrations of Corn-well's obedience heralded him as a beacon to inspire the nation.

The romantic visions of adventure and glory, best captured in Rupert Brooke's poetry, led to an enthusiastic outpouring of support for the war, prompting thousands of men to volunteer for service in 1914. But, by 1916, as the war increasingly became a battle of endurance, the state found itself mobilising public opinion in ways it had not yet consciously done, in order to strengthen British resolve and combat war-weariness.[12] Brock Millman has noted that even politicians were increasingly pessimistic about the state of the war.[13] As the indecisive Jutland victory undermined the mythic reputation of British naval mastery, the circumstances that led to Jack Cornwell's death offered a strategic opportunity for state and society to romanticise and cele-brate traditional manly sacrifice in chivalrous and religious language. Jack Cornwell's age and the circumstances that led to his death offered a strategic opportunity for both state and society, and his youth became a focal point for the idea that the next generation of men ready to defend the nation and its empire could be animated by the 'Cornwell spirit'. Memorials continued the process, of democratising the heroic manly ideal by celebrating Cornwell's humble origins. Thus, as the war dragged on, the propagation of the language of heroic sacrifice became more, rather than less, intense.

The commemoration of Jack Cornwell offered state authorities, private organisations, and bereaved individuals the opportunity to resurrect, reinvigorate and celebrate older gendered ideals of duty, obedience and sacrifice that were being brought into question by the new realities of total war. Although trench warfare had challenged romanticised visions of soldiering, the obscure nature of modern naval warfare enabled the authorities to continue to extol Victorian values of patriotism, courage and duty as masculine ideals in a manner that paradoxically still proved useful even in a modern industrialised war of attrition. Interestingly, the commemoration of Cornwell highlights how state interests, private concerns and public pressure worked simultaneously, whether intentionally or not, towards similar patriotic ends. Despite the different motivations of the Admiralty, Parliament, the Boy Scouts, the Navy League, and the popular press, their memorials to Cornwell highlighted the virtues of his noble sacrifice to the nation. In time, these tributes demanded that Britons, in order to demonstrate their own citizenship, should not only admire Cornwell's deed but also offer similar sacrifice. The commemoration of Jack Cornwell served many different ends, but one common goal was to elevate the sailor boy as a model to inspire the youth of the Empire for generations to come.

Democratising the manly ideal for total war

From a contemporary vantage point, the Cornwell story also serves to shed light on one particular aspect of the First World War that has generated differing interpretations. Historians have argued about the extent to which the war stimulated a modernist turn or confirmed traditional sensibilities.[14] In particular, historiography of the First World War has questioned the degree to which the war, and specifically trench warfare, redefined Edwardian manliness.[15] Although the battle of Jutland was a terribly modern battle with disastrous losses, naval warfare retained a mystique and adventure that was denied to the land campaigns by the experience of trench warfare. The First World War may not have been a naval war but the experience did not end the romanticisation of naval heroism. A close reading of the Cornwell commemorations reveals that is memorials were steeped not only in the rituals of mourning but also in the language of chivalry and the imagery of Christian sacrifice, beginning with the funeral orations.[16]

In the face of a total war defined by mass attrition and mass conscription, Cornwell's humble origins served to democratise that, hitherto, elite manly ideal but retained Victorian conceptions of martial manliness that stressed duty, sacrifice and martyrdom.

The eulogies, newspaper accounts and poems about Cornwell's death were saturated with a hyperbolic patriotism that Ted Bogacz has termed the 'language of high diction'. Celebrations of Cornwell's heroism bolster Bogacz's claims that the war offered the opportunity to resurrect 'hallowed traditional values' and to promote neglected manly chivalric virtues.[17] Accounts of his sacrifice often compared him to historic heroes, evoking the language of manly sacrifice that combined religious and patriotic imagery. In writings, speeches and paintings Cornwell was described as the modern reincarnation of the young Musgrave from the sinking *Aboukir*, Nelson at Trafalgar, Casabianca at the Nile, Havelock at Lucknow, Gordon at Khartoum, and even the legend of the faithful Roman sentry at Vesuvius. Stories of Cornwell's heroism, building on the model first provided by Bishop Barking and T. J. Macnamara, made it possible to cast the celebration of his suffering, salvation and sacrifice as both patriotic and Christian virtues.

The irony was that these traditional tropes were made to serve modern ends. The demands of total war meant that the British state required the loyalty, hard work and obedience of the entire population. In comparing Cornwell to past heroes, memorials elevated the boy sailor as a model of manhood for Britons young and old to emulate. Cornwell's youth and innocence were central to his widespread commemoration; however, he was just one of eight boy seamen to die serving on the *Chester* during the battle. Although all the tributes used Cornwell's example as proof that Victorian manly ideals of duty, hard work and courage were still alive in the next generation of Britons, such commemorations, amid heavy wartime losses, were also attempts to confront anxieties about the vitality of the nation, the state of British boyhood, and the questionable fate of the British empire. Memorials sought to portray Cornwell's sacrifice as proof that a boy could take a man's role and as assurance of the inevitable victory and the future stability of the Empire.

Although one might expect to see the death of chivalry in the face of industrialised warfare, Jay Winter, Joanna Bourke and Allen J. Frantzen, placing themselves firmly in the camp of those who believe that tradition remained strong in the face of the modern, have contended that the older hallowed rhetoric of chivalry and Christian sacrifice was well suited to the demands of fighting a modern total war.[18] In this war of attrition, celebrations of Jack Cornwell's innocence and chivalric sacrifice similarly rescued British manhood from the experiences of unimaginable brutality in the trenches of France. Cornwell's com-memoration was not merely the resurrection of an older manly ideal but the reinvigoration and adaptation of older romanticised forms to correspond with the new requirements of mass mobilisation. Given the realities of mass conscription, the commemoration of Cornwell democratised the idea of chivalrous manhood, implicitly rejecting the idea of the hero as elite, simply by enlarging the ranks of those who could possess these virtues and achieve heroic stature. In contrast to figures like Gordon and Nelson, whose stories displayed a mythic heroism, memorials to Cornwell celebrated his modest background and the attainable character of his deeds. Here was the boy who had learned how to be a man, and in the process became a humble hero. Thus, rather than inculcating a new heroic ideal, tributes to Cornwell, organised by both state and private interests, democratised an older rhetoric of patriotic duty, imperial fealty and Christian sacrifice, which helped redefine manliness for total war and encourage further wartime sacrifice by the wider British public.

The fervour of the commemorative discourse, which celebrated the tragic heroism of Cornwell, might appear incongruous when set in the context of 1916, with the controversial introduction of conscription, devastating casualties in France and Britain's mounting difficulties in Ireland, where Britain faced interminable challenges precipitated by the Easter Rising and worsened by the imposition of martial law, the executions of the Rising's fifteen leaders, and Unionist intransigence over home rule. The initial enthusiasm for the war, born from faith in a short contest and certain victory, faded with continued fighting, mounting casualties, and no end in sight two years after it had begun. The introduction of conscription in spring 1916 indicated the state's recognition of the grim realities of total war and its determination to win at all costs. Its monumental passage also signalled that greater sacrifice was required of Britons if the war was to be won. And while the passage of the May Military Service Act acknowledged the war's seemingly unquenchable thirst for soldiers, conscription was unable to provide the military with the number of soldiers needed to replace the men lost in the fighting.[19]

The Battle of the Somme was undertaken in order to relieve the French fighting at Verdun and to offer the allies the 'breakthrough' necessary for victory, but the experience of the Somme, which began one month after Jutland, came at a devastating cost that military con-scription alone could not hope to redress. On the first day, the British lost over 60,000 casualties with nearly 20,000 dead. By the end of the campaign in November, they had suffered 420,000 casualties.[20] Coming on the heels of the implementation of military conscription, the

Somme confirmed the inadequacies of the Military Service Act. As a consequence, national service remained the main topic of a debate that would divide Parliament for the better part of the year. The question of amending and extending conscription to civilian war work contributed to the fall of Asquith and the rise of David Lloyd George as Prime Minister.

The summer of 1916 also witnessed the shocking death of Earl Horatio Herbert Kitchener, the popular war minister, whose death came only three days after Cornwell's, Lord Kitchener had drowned on a mission to Russia, when HMS *Hampshire* struck a mine off the Orkney islands on 5 June 1916.[21] While memorials to Kitchener abounded because of his legendary reputation, tribute to Cornwell resulted from the confluence of his humble origins, his youth and the sacrificial nature of his death. As John Bethell, MP from Romford had noted, Britons 'were proud of their Jellicoe, their Beatty, their Kitchener and their Haig; but they could accomplish very little if it were not that throughout the length and breadth of the land in every city and in every hamlet were to be found youths and young men inspired with what he [Bethell] would call the Jack Cornwell spirit'.[22] Cornwell's headmaster reminded his pupils that Cornwell was a 'poor boy, a boy of the masses, who rose to the heights of bravery and self-sacrifice'.[23]

Thus, the commemorations of Cornwell and Kitchener served different ends. Commemorations of Kitchener lauded the legacy of his character, leadership and heroism, but the nature of his death and the inability to recover his body led newspapers to see the event as a tragic ending to a heroic life.[24] In the case of Cornwell, it was his death itself, resulting from the dutiful act of standing by his post that, for contemporaries, made him a hero, and his sacrifice – seemingly voluntary – deserving of esteem. Despite these differences, the impulse to commemorate them both would lead St Botolph's Church in Bishopsgate to erect a monument to both Kitchener and Cornwell in August 1916 – the first war memorial in the City.[25]

In need of a hero

Biographical sketches of Cornwell's life were retold countless times in newspaper stories, memorial campaigns and books, during and shortly after the war. Nevertheless, a detailed narrative of Jack Cornwell's life remains lacking.[26] Born on 8 January 1900 in Leyton, Jack, the second of four children, moved to Manor Park with his family in 1910. His father, Eli Cornwell, who had thirteen years' military service with engagements in the Sudan and South Africa, drove a tram for a living until the outbreak of war when he joined the army as a reservist in the 10th Essex Regiment. Jack Cornwell, a boy scout, attended the local council school, leaving at the age of 14 to work as a delivery boy.[27] According to Chief Petty Officer Daniels, Cornwell's recruiting officer, Cornwell was keen on joining the navy from the outbreak of the war but had been rebuffed in these earlier attempts because of his age.[28] Cornwell finally entered the navy in July 1915 when he reached 15½, giving up his job for an opportunity to fight in the war.

Once Cornwell had volunteered as a boy seaman, he trained at the Keyham Naval Barracks at Plymouth where he earned a 'very good character' and received high marks in seamanship and gunnery. Later accounts noted that he attended church service, sang in the choir, signed the temperance pledge, and received his confirmation.[29] After passing his seamanship exam in February 1916, Cornwell completed the rest of his training by late April and on 1 May boarded the train for Rosyth, Scotland to join the HMS *Chester*, a newly commissioned light cruiser under the command of Captain Robert Lawson.[30] In the last week of May, gunnery crews were assigned. On 23 May 1916, Cornwell confided in his last letter to his father that 'they have just put me as sight-setter at a gun'.[31] A week later, he would put those recently acquired skills to test in the waters off Jutland.

While we can view the powerful impulse to commemorate Cornwell's sacrifice through a prism of stalemate, attrition and domestic instability, the battle of Jutland provides a crucial vantage point to understanding the elevation of Cornwell as a heroic figure. In the days and weeks that followed the battle of Jutland, the press was divided about its outcome. Many papers claimed that the battle dealt a decisive blow to German forces; others saw it as 'a defeat' and criticised naval leadership after news emerged about the heavy loss of British ships. Increased mistrust of the press led the Admiralty to discuss the possibility of newspaper censorship and to delay publication of John Jellicoe's official dispatch of the battle in order to produce a report that would dispel criticism.[32] As a result, the public did not receive official details until the publication of Jellicoe's official dispatch in the *London Gazette* on 6 July 1916, more than a month after the battle's end. Although there is no conclusive evidence, the Admiralty may have deliberately fastened on to the story of Cornwell in order counter potential bad publicity surrounding the battle.[33]

The publication of Jellicoe's report was accompanied by a special dispatch by Vice-Admiral David Beatty, who commanded the battlecruiser squadron. As well as recounting the performance of his squadron, part of Beatty's account recognised the actions of particular officers and men, like Cornwell, whose service had been distinguished in captains' reports. In their lists of recommendations, most commanding officers distinguished their sailors for some kind of active participation in the battle, while the *Chester*'s Captain Robert Lawson gave special recognition to 'Boy Cornwell's' more passive dutiful service. As part of his list of recommendations, longer than that of any other captain, Lawson had requested on 9 June 1916 that Cornwell receive 'special honours' for 'steadily standing alone at a most exposed post', despite mortal injury.[34]

To ensure honours for Cornwell, Lawson's superior officer Rear-Admiral Trevelyan Napier of HMS *Falmouth* sent a second letter to Beatty on 18 June 1916, which reiterated 'that the services of Boy Cornwell (since dead), are specially deserving of recognition, both in justice to his memory and as a high example to his shipmates'.[35] In recommending honours for his men, <u>Beatty</u> singled out Cornwell's character during the battle, restating Lawson's commendation:

> A report from the Commanding Officer of *Chester* gives a splendid instance of devotion to duty. Boy First Class John Travers Cornwell of *Chester* was mortally wounded early in the action. He nevertheless remained standing at a most exposed post, quietly awaiting orders till the end of the action, with the gun's crew dead and wounded all round him. His age was under 16 1/2 years. I regret that he has since died, but I recommend his case for special recognition in justice to his memory, and as an acknowledgement of the high example set by him.[36]

Beatty's remarks, which had highlighted Cornwell's youth and passive sacrifice, would serve as the founding text for commemorations of Cornwell. Although details about the British navy's performance during the battle of Jutland filled newspaper columns for the next week, Beatty's brief but special mention of Cornwell in his supplementary report immediately captured the headlines in most newspapers. Numerous illustrated papers like the *Daily Mirror*, *Daily Sketch* and *Daily Express* also featured photos of Cornwell in their initial reporting of the dispatches.[37] Newspaper coverage of the dispatches not only sparked a reassessment of the battle of Jutland, but also stirred public interest in the life and death of young Jack Cornwell.[38]

With the information from Beatty's dispatch, scant as it was, newspapers began to endorse Cornwell's bravery and appeal for proper commemoration of his heroism. In describing Cornwell's service, newspaper accounts relied on comparisons with historical examples of manly heroism familiar to Britons from literary works and history books. Newspapers like the *Daily Mirror*, *Daily Sketch* and the weekly *Spectator* particularly stressed how Cornwell's bravery recalled the 'Epic of the Modern Casabianca'.[39] The English poet Dorothea Hemans had made the true story of young Casabianca famous in an 1826 poem called simply 'Casabianca', but better known as the 'Boy Stood on the Burning Deck'.[40] The poem celebrated the death of Giocante Casabianca, the 12-year-old son of the commander of *L'Orient*, the flagship of the French Admiral de Brueys. Casabianca died when his father's ship went up in flames during the battle of the Nile in 1798. In comparing Cornwell to Casabianca, the *Spectator* acknowledged 'that British boys and girls who have forgotten almost every other line of poetry they ever learnt remember verses of "Casabianca"'.[41]

Although Casabianca was a Spaniard, papers like the *Spectator* recognised that his appeal was universal, and they sought the same for Cornwell. Familiar with Hemans's tale, the British public were told how Cornwell, like Casabianca, was also 'a creature of heroic blood/ A proud, though child-like form'. As Casabianca refused to leave his post and save himself as flames engulfed his ship 'without his Father's word', the press described Cornwell heroically standing by his gun as he awaited orders.[42] The allusions to Casabianca's faithful devotion helped to cast Cornwell's death as a similar testament to duty and sacrifice. To the British public familiar with traditional heroic tropes of martyrdom, duty and sacrifice, the portrayal of Cornwell's last hours by his post were perhaps more recognisable than the contemporary accounts that depicted death in the trenches as the 'Great Sacrifice'.[43]

A widely republished letter sent from Captain Robert Lawson to Cornwell's mother in early June recalled her son's sacrifice. His description of Cornwell's service during the battle elaborated on his official commendation to Beatty. Lawson wrote to Mrs Cornwell,

> I know you would wish to hear of the splendid fortitude and courage shown by your boy. His devotion to duty was an example for all of us. The wounds which resulted in his death within a short time were received in the first few minutes of the action. He remained steady at his most exposed post at the gun, waiting for orders. His gun would not bear on the enemy; all but two of the crew were killed or wounded, and he was the only one who was in such an exposed position . . .[44]

For Lawson, Cornwell's devotion to duty had withstood the test of battle. In noting that 'his gun would not bear', Lawson's depiction of Cornwell's service evoked selfless sacrifice and purity, characteristic of Christian manliness. Cornwell's young age also enhanced the image of innocence. And yet, as a boy, he proved himself worthy of emulation by the ship's crew. Although Captain Lawson had not witnessed Cornwell standing by his gun during the battle, he explained to Jack's mother that the reason her son remained at his post was because 'he felt he might be needed . . . so he stayed there, standing and waiting, under heavy fire, with just his own brave heart and God's help to support him'. This testament to Cornwell's faith served to portray the boy's action as obedience to both nation and God. In closing, Lawson added that he hoped 'to place in the boy's mess a plaque with his name on it, and the date, and the words, 'Faithful unto death'.[45] By invoking this phrase from Revelations 2:8, Lawson was further reinforcing the view of Cornwell as a martyr for God, for king and for country.

In echoing the sacrificial trope, commemorations of Cornwell compared his death to the martyrdom of Victorian military heroes such as General Henry Havelock from the Indian Mutiny and General Charles Gordon at Khartoum.[46] Although Havelock died of dysentery in November 1858 two weeks after the press reported the relief of Lucknow, initial press accounts imagined him 'falling at his post' during the siege.[47] With this mythic hero in mind, Robert Baden-Powell saw his former scout, Cornwell, as a modern Havelock whose sacrifice would inspire other scouts. In August 1916, the Boy Scouts' *Headquarters Gazette* even altered Tennyson's lines from his Havelock poem to envision how, 'Bold Cornwell died/ Plucky, and straight, and good,/ And every Scout in Britain says/ I am of Cornwell's blood.'[48] For Baden-Powell, Cornwell's blood sacrifice had served to unite and reinvigorate the brotherhood of scouts.

From the start, the press served as the catalyst for commemorating Cornwell's life. While the passage of the Defence of the Realm Act in 1914 prevented the press from publishing anything that could benefit the enemy, it would be difficult to claim that 'government coercion' rather than 'willing acquiescence' best explained why the press so often served as a mouthpiece of official wartime propaganda.[49] Early suggestions by correspondents to newspapers were focused either on erecting a monument, supplying portraits to schools, or hanging plaques in schools.[50] *Teachers' World* enclosed in its July issue an engraved portrait of Cornwell for teachers to hang in their classrooms accompanied by the poem 'Promoted', a Christian elegy dedicated to Cornwell's duty and written by John Oxenham, the immensely popular war poet whose poem 'Hymn: For the Men at the Front' had sold over seven million copies during the course of the war.[51] In its July issue, the *Spectator* considered how a Cornwell sculpture could be used to 'inspire' and 'teach' children. For the *Spectator*, the Cornwell sculpture would be similar to Gordon's statue in Trafalgar Square where 'children stood enchanted and compelled to ask questions' about whether in reality Gordon had stood before his death as patiently and calmly as did his statue.[52]

The *Spectator* writer imagined that a sculpture of Cornwell would capture him enduring 'the bout of "passive strife"' as he waited dutifully by his damaged gun and 'would turn all youths into pilgrims'. Although such a sculpture was never cast, the intention behind most commemorative efforts was to reaffirm Britons' sense of duty and obligation to the nation by evoking a reverence to Cornwell. By heralding the values of obedience and holding up Cornwell as a model, commemorative tributes like the *Spectator*'s served the demands of a total war that required unremitting adherence to duty from the entire population.

The intense campaign to memorialise Cornwell, illustrated by these hagiographic accounts and commemorative suggestions, was generated with remarkable speed. It was initially fuelled by a sensational newspaper article that was published only two days after the Jellicoe dispatch appeared in the *Gazette*. This was a story that would spark public outrage and provide momentum. On 8 July 1916, the *Daily Sketch* sensationally revealed on its cover page that Cornwell's body lay in an unmarked grave in Manor Park Cemetery close to his parents' home in north-east London.[53] With a histrionic headline exclaiming, '323: ALL THAT MARKS THE COMMON GRAVE OF THE BOY HERO OF JUTLAND BATTLE', the *Daily Sketch* began its campaign to secure a more fitting tribute to the boy than the numbered little wooden peg affixed to his grave. A couple of days later, the *Daily Sketch* reported that Cornwell's grave was still nameless but no longer unknown since it had become a place of pilgrimage for the people who 'paid their tribute to the hero whom the Navy honoured and the authorities forgot'.[54]

In the wake of the discovery, editorials and correspondents in a variety of papers suggested that Cornwell's body be exhumed and prepared for a proper funeral with full naval honours. Some suggested that Cornwell be buried in Westminster Abbey. According to Reverend G. H. East of Bradford, the war had shown that it was time to break 'away from the convention that reserves Westminster for kings'. In a war of mass mobilisation and conscription, he acknowledged, 'this is the day of the people. England is being delivered, in this her hour of need, by the splendid devotion of humble men and women.'[55] Ralph Whitfield, the manager of Cornwell's old school who served as the Cornwell family's public representative, suggested that Cornwell be buried in Westminster because the national burial place 'would help to keep his memory and the bravery and noble discipline of his life before the thousands of our boys who will visit the Abbey'.[56] Mrs Cornwell later that month rejected suggestions to bury her son in a naval port cemetery, 'I could not have that. I felt that I must have my boy lying near me, somewhere where I know I can go to at any time.'[57] By mid-July, the Admiralty had bowed to public demands and Mrs Cornwell consented to the Admiralty's offer to re-inter her son in a private grave at Manor Park with naval honours and at the Admiralty's expense.[58] Although this state funeral now came at Admiralty expense, it was a welcome disruption for the navy to eulogise its service to the nation. In addition, Cornwell's funeral offered the nation a hero to mourn and a model to champion in the months ahead.

Duty and endurance in total war

The campaign to honour Cornwell with a state funeral was concurrent with efforts in military, political and civic circles to reward Cornwell's sacrifice with even greater honours. Lord Charles Beresford was instrumental in pressuring the government to award Cornwell a posthumous Victoria Cross and in organising a national memorial fund in Cornwell's honour. Beresford, former Commander-in-Chief of the Mediterranean Fleet, had retired from the Admiralty but was active both in the House of Lords and in the Navy League. A popular but unconventional figure, Beresford remarked during a parliamentary debate that the military rarely gave medals posthumously, or awarded them to naval men whose actions were distinguished at sea rather than ashore.[59] Thus, in spite of the special mention of Cornwell in Beatty's dispatch, Beresford questioned whether the government would do what he believed should be done. Beresford advised the government that a Victoria Cross for Cornwell would pay practical dividends across the Empire. 'An honour paid to Cornwell's memory would be an example to the boys of the Empire at their most susceptible age. It would encourage that splendid specimen of humanity, the British boy.'[60]

In his remarks, Beresford cited the historical (though unusual) precedent of awarding the Cross posthumously. The passively obedient nature of Cornwell's service, however, was particularly uncharacteristic of posthumous wartime Victoria Cross holders, who typically distinguished themselves by sacrificing their own lives to save others, or by actively fighting on despite mortal injury.[61] British soldiers fighting in Europe had tragically proved themselves worthy of Cornwell's sacrifice, but only rarely received the honour of the Cross. Although the numbers of Victoria Crosses awarded had increased dramatically since the start of the war, such honours were still rare. In the battle of Jutland, where 6000 men died, only four sailors received the Victoria Cross; and on the first day of the battle of the Somme, where 20,000 died, only ten soldiers received such honour. Why was Cornwell's death – perhaps equally tragic but surely no more so than these – to

[173]

be distinguished by medals and memorials? With little surviving documentation, it is not clear what finally influenced the War Office to nominate Cornwell for a posthumous Victoria Cross; but the award became certain once King George endorsed the boy's candidacy later that summer. The official announcement, along with other Cross winners, was made in the *London Gazette* on 15 September 1916 and quickly became front-page news.[62]

The publicity attending the Victoria Cross awards also provided a much-needed opportunity for government and a sympathetic press to drum up patriotic support for the war. A day later, the *Daily Mirror* assured its readership that *Gazette*'s list of naval honours would 'serve to quicken British pride in the deeds of Britain's Navy and to remind us of that unconquerable British heroism which has walked the deep since the outbreak of war'.[63] On the same day, the paper reported on the 'Great Somme Advance', boasting of the capture of 2300 German prisoners and the seizure of 'nearly all important high ground'.[64] Yet, despite euphoric claims made about such progress, the outcome of Britain's great Somme offensive remained inconclusive, and by the autumn of 1916 the end of the war was still not in sight. The announcement of military honours like Jack Cornwell's Victoria Cross presented an occasion to celebrate examples of British heroism, kindle patriotism, and reassure the public of future victory. In metaphorical language neatly calculated to present the navy's role (and, by extension, that of boy hero Cornwell) as equal to the army's in pursuing the war, the *Daily Mirror*, 'All of us who sleep comfortably in our beds at home, serene and secure behind those great sea trenches which are held by our battalions of seamen, realise that while the Navy remains unchallenged and unbroken our ultimate victory is secure'.[65] Clearly, the citation of Cornwell's proven mettle and that of his military comrades, as well as the celebration of his heroism and his Victoria Cross award, all aimed to strengthen public confidence and resolve. Concomitantly, this coverage provided good press for the navy.

Although the earliest and most notable honours were organised by military and state authorities, the wartime commemoration of Cornwell was not simply a reflection or a product of political interests. In their analysis of wartime commemoration, T. G. Ashplant, Graham Dawson, and Michael Roper maintain that the study of war remembrance has suffered from the historian's desire to overemphasise either the significance of state control or the experiences of civil society.[66] The wartime memorials to Cornwell support this argument: this was surely a case where commemoration was negotiated among the myriad interests of the bereaved, the state and private extra-parliamentary organisations.[67] True, acts of commemoration often expressed themselves in state-sponsored forms – a state funeral, the award of a Victoria Cross, the establishment of a school holiday – and the state mobilised the public to participate in them. But such acts also reflected public initiative. After all, the Admiralty's undertaking of the state funeral – though the event certainly came to serve government purposes – was itself belated and reluctant, resulting solely from the mounting pressure applied by both press and public. The intense mid-July coverage of the Cornwell story was a product not simply of the desire of to sell papers, but also of the public's fascination with the story. The subsequent overwhelming turnout for the funeral demonstrated that collective mourning could represent both genuine public feeling and state interests, while even more people were able to participate vicariously through press coverage of the event. Furthermore, the Cornwell commemorations clearly demonstrate that, by intent or by coincidence, state interests and public concerns worked simultaneously towards similar ends.

Among the most prominent extra-parliamentary and civic efforts to commemorate Cornwell's life were those of the Navy League and the Boy Scouts. Although the impulse behind their memorial efforts may have sprung from different motives from those of the Admiralty, their activities often involved the participation of state authorities, and promulgated a similar message of noble sacrifice. And these civic memorial efforts augmented the military honours that Cornwell had received. The Navy League quickly organised a Jack Cornwell Memorial Fund with the aim of using schoolchildren's donations to build a wing in his name at the Star and Garter Home in Richmond.[68] By mid-September, authorities in central London and East Ham were also spearheading the National Memorial Fund, which raised funds to build semi-detached cottages in Hornchurch for infirm or disabled sailors and their families, to provide naval scholarships to train deserving boys for service, and to commission a portrait of Cornwell for the Admiralty by Royal Academy painter Frank Salisbury, copies of which would then be distributed to schools across the empire.

The National Memorial Fund formally commenced its activities with a meeting at Mansion House on 14 September, thus offering another opportunity to memorialise Cornwell through speeches and letters, including one by Lady Beatty, wife of the Vice-Admiral. Published widely in the press, her letter characterised Cornwell as a 'real hero' because he had 'exhibited the qualities of a hero: hardiness, endurance, reliance, obedience. We can all do well to copy the qualities of Jack Cornwell'.[69] For John Bethell, MP, the fate of the empire rested on common 'humble' soldiers and sailors like Cornwell. 'For nine hundred years no conqueror had set his foot on these shores. While they had heroes such as John Cornwell, England would never be at the proud foot of a conqueror'.[70]

The Navy League's Jack Cornwell Memorial Fund also launched its formal campaign in September. One of the League's major goals was to educate British youth about the navy's role in securing the health and stability of the Empire.[71] Historically, one of the Navy League's aims had been to highlight the significance of naval power to the Empire; among other activities, the League pressured educational authorities to include more naval history in school curricula. The Cornwell Memorial Fund thus offered a further opportunity to spark children's interest not only in the heroic Jack Cornwell but also in patriotism and the strategic importance of the British Navy.[72]

Just as the Jack Cornwell Memorial Fund served to increase the public profile of the Navy League, the Boy Scouts' celebration of Cornwell's heroism helped to distinguish the character of the scouting movement and call attention to the thousands of Scouts in wartime service.[73] By early August 1916, Robert Baden-Powell and the Boy Scouts had also started their own memorial fund to endow a Cornwell Badge to be granted annually to the extraordinary scout who displayed special sacrifice and heroism.[74] For Baden-Powell, Cornwell embodied the scouting ethos. The bronze badge in the shape of a 'C' would then be synonymous for both 'Cornwell and Courage'. At a September Scout rally in Nottingham, Baden-Powell announced that the Cornwell Scout would be one who had 'saved life under exceptional circumstances' or who had 'undergone great suffering in a heroic manner'.[75] Jack Cornwell's story stood at a crucial intersection, where it served to underscore changes in the society while upholding traditional values: in the face of a total war defined by mass attrition and mass conscription, Cornwell's humble origins served to help democratise an elite manly ideal, while retaining Victorian conceptions of martial manliness of duty, sacrifice and martyrdom.

The impulse to memorialise Cornwell was intense and the tributes abundant. Predictably, the many depictions of the boy hero were almost interchangeable: The image of Cornwell remaining at his post was central to all the commemorative efforts – not only the formal activities organised by the National Memorial Fund, the Navy League, and the Boy Scouts, but also the tributes both commercial and informal that abounded in the late summer and autumn of 1916. He became the subject of paintings, illustrations, sculpture, poems, songs, stories, postcards, boys' stories, pottery and cigarette cards. This iconography of duty and sacrifice was best captured in the myriad portraits, both formally commissioned and commercially produced, that began appearing soon after the funeral. In addition to the Salisbury portrait, the

[176]

town of Grimsby, home to the hospital where Cornwell had died, and periodicals like the *War Illustrated*, *Answers* and *Sphere* all commissioned commercial portraits, and war artists like Frederick Elwell and Fortunio Matania to produce portraits of the boy hero at his post on the *Chester*.[76]

Like other tributes, the commemorative portraits promoted the twin virtues of duty and sacrifice. After correspondence with Captain Lawson of the *Chester* about the ship's design, Baden-Powell, who illustrated both scouting literature and British war posters, produced a watercolour portrait in September (figure 5.1).[77] His picture sought to portray the boy's steadfast determination, standing by his gun as shells burst in the water just beyond the deck, and two of his mates lie nearby, either wounded or dead. Cigarette companies like Gallaher and Copes Brothers featured Cornwell in their card series of wartime heroes and Victoria Cross winners.[78] His iconic status was further secured that fall when Madame Tussaud's opened a Cornwell exhibit. Short moralistic biographies, written by popular and prolific authors like John Ernest Hodder-Williams, were being published both during and shortly after the war.[79] Even souvenir accounts of Jutland, recounting tactical battle details, found space to include Cornwell's photograph, accompanied by Beatty's famous dispatch describing his deed.[80]

The most notable and famous of all Cornwell portraits was the Salisbury painting (figure 5.2), because it was so widely viewed, and on display for a time at the Royal Academy. After it was returned to the Admiralty, which had commissioned it, the National Memorial Fund Committee continued to provide reproductions for schools, and also made sure that they would also be on sale to the public, with proceeds forwarded to the Navy League's Cornwell Memorial Fund.[81] Inscribed at the top of the reproductions were verses from John Oxenham's poem, 'Promoted', a very early tribute that was written in the same month as the funeral. A generation of school children would have been familiar with the lessons of Cornwell's sacrifice whether by seeing his portrait or by reading the last lines of the poem that 'There was his duty to be done/ And he did it.'[82]

A youth for all youths

One common goal served by the Cornwell commemorations was the inspiration of young people. In voicing their support for the National Memorial Fund, both T. J. Macnamara and John Jellicoe had asserted that Cornwell's heroism would serve as an example to inspire the 'youth of the Empire' – 'for all time', not because it was unusual but rather because it was characteristic (or perhaps expected), embodying

5.1 Reproductions of Robert Baden-Powell's water-colour portrait of Jack Cornwell featured in a 1916 Scouts Christmas card distributed as a reward to scouts who raised funds for the scouts' memorial to Cornwell.

5.2 Reproduced poster of Frank Salisbury's portait of Cornwell, Spring 1917. Copies of the portrait were distributed to schools across Britain and the empire in spring 1917.

a 'lofty and self-forgetting ideal of duty' and a 'spirit of true and serious patriotism'.[83] The example of Cornwell would then ensure that 'the youth of the Empire . . . are filled with the deepest sense of responsibility for the safeguarding of the heritage into which they have entered'.[84] In short, Jack Cornwell's life would serve as a didactic testament to the vitality of the nation and its empire.

The inculcation of this sense of national purpose and 'responsibility' in British youth was particularly critical during the war, as the state of male adolescence came under increasing scrutiny. Adolescence as a developmental stage and its accompanying disorder of juvenile delinquency had become areas of scientific enquiry only in the late-nineteenth century. Justified by science and Social Darwinian racial ideas, Edwardian social reformers endowed adolescence with the responsibility of saving both nation and empire. Charles Russell, a social reformer who helped pioneer the boys' club movement in Britain, noted that, 'with its adolescents from age to age rests the destiny of the nation, the race'.[85] When reports of juvenile crime began rising during the First World War, that destiny appeared in jeopardy.

Before the war, an average of 37,500 British youths under the age of 16 appeared annually in juvenile courts; by 1917, that number had climbed to 51,000.[86] Authorities and reformers from governmental offices and voluntary organisations dedicated to juvenile welfare attributed the rise in delinquency to the decline in active boys' clubs and the deterioration of parental control during the war. By December 1916, the Home Office had formed the Juvenile Organisation Committee to encourage and coordinate activities by local juvenile organisations, seeking to reverse the trend.

In the midst of wartime uncertainties, the worries about delinquency led to general concerns about the state of British youth and British boyhood. In addition to delinquency and juvenile crime, authorities worried about post-war social reconstruction and whether young men and working-class youth, in particular, would be ready and able to carry out the duties of post-war citizenship and revitalise the nation in the wake of the war.[87] Educational authorities were principally apprehensive and met in conferences in the summer of 1916 to discuss whether the schools were sufficiently nurturing the character and developing the skills that boys and young men needed in wartime and those they would require at war's end.

The story of boy hero Cornwell clearly resonated with those who saw a crisis of youth. The popular press was certainly of the opinion that his example could prove valuable. Already in mid-July, a *Daily Mirror* editorial about an educational conference at Oxford entitled the 'Study of the Boy', observed how 'the example of the brave boy John

Cornwell . . . is being proposed for admiration now to countless little boys in Britain'.[88] The *Daily Mirror* argued,

> those whose mission it now is to give the small boy good advice will certainly find it harder to make dullness seem as heroic as death amongst the shells. Yet they may succeed if they point out the true moral of young Cornwell's happy end – if they show that he could die so, because to be gallant and modest and faithful was to him a habit: that he lived from a formed character which was continual inspiration to his bravery, not on sudden impulses.[89]

The story of Cornwell's heroism may not have been endowed with an exhilarating tale of combat that would excite a boy reader, but his 'happy end' was within the reach of any British boy whose character was good and steady. The *Daily Mirror* went on to say that Cornwell's humble roots and previous obscurity would help 'to form that brave character in little people who, humble today, have the future of our country within them'. In celebrating his ordinariness, memorials to Cornwell's heroism served to mark how the war contributed to the democratisation of popular portrayals of heroism. One letter in the *The Times* suggested that schoolchildren should learn the story of Cornwell's life so that 'all children – not of this generation only – may read, mark and learn from this simple story of one of the bravest acts of devotion to duty which the whole record of this war has given to us'.[90]

Cornwell's death presented educational authorities with the opportunity to extol the heroic conduct of Cornwell as a model of boyhood. At an August conference on New Ideals in Education', held at Oxford, Baden-Powell noted that Cornwell's heroism and the service of thousands of other Boy Scouts during the war demonstrated the success of scouting in developing a boy's character and provided a model for how the state could educate boys in character building.[91] A few weeks prior, Baden-Powell had emphasised the need for character building in boys because 'the boy of today is the father of the Empire. He has to fill blank spaces left by those, the flower of our manhood, who have fallen'. Otherwise, he warned that the British empire would go the way of the Roman Empire in its 'want of men – men in character and in numbers'.[92]

For the Navy League, seemingly less concerned about delinquency than about the future health of the nation, Cornwell's act of heroism was not only a singular act by an exemplary boy; but also a reassurance that such character ran deep through the ranks of British boyhood. A September article published in the league's monthly periodical cited Cornwell as the embodiment of the 'coolness, calm courage, and heroism' that most British boys possessed.[93] The league celebrated Cornwell's character, marked by courage and discipline because, it argued, he exemplified the true character of the British boy. Cornwell was

> but the impersonation of the spirit which animates hundreds of British boys, and it is the pride and glory of British hearts that this spirit, so long as England endures, shall remain untainted and inviolate. To those who prate of the decadence of England, of her lost traditions and dead ideals, examples of heroism but recently displayed by British boys give the direct lie.[94]

With the hope that Cornwell's 'heroism' would be an 'inspiration to the youth of our race', the League's Jack Cornwell Memorial Fund committee encouraged schools in Great Britain and across the empire to honour the boy by participating in a celebration of his life. On Cornwell Day, 21 September 1916, schools held recitals about his life and death and collected donations for his memorial fund.[95] To raise money for the memorial, the committee provided school authorities with a booklet about Cornwell's life, which was intended 'as a useful "reader" before the collection', and stamps, which bore Jack's likeness, for students to sell and purchase at a penny each. Noting the campaign's early success, the Navy League claimed that schoolchildren had raised over two million pennies just during the week following the celebration.[96]

The portrait of Jack Cornwell, sketched in July by one of his *Chester* mates, had initially appeared in an August issue of the *Scout* magazine and then was reproduced in Navy League publications including its memorial fund booklet. The booklet, 'Faithful unto Death', was probably penned by Lord Beresford. It offered a moralistic tale of Cornwell's life and, in a section called 'How you can copy him', directly encouraged students to emulate the boy hero.[97] While few schoolchildren would have found themselves in similar straits as Cornwell, the booklet argued that Cornwell's bravery offered lessons that all could follow in their daily lives,

> It may not fall to the lot of every boy or girl to prove so devotedly the obedience, discipline, and self-sacrifice of Jack Cornwell. Yet the lesson remains. Every boy and girl can endeavour to live up to his example by practising discipline and being obedient in small things. In this way character is formed and we are enabled, when the crisis of our fate arises, and there are big things to be done – to do them. This is the British way – and the best way.[98]

As the booklet instructed, celebrating Cornwell's heroism would serve little purpose if young Britons did not take his example to heart and try to emulate his character.[99] By October, the Navy League claimed that several hundred thousand copies of the booklet, at a penny each, had already been sold and purchased by schoolchildren.[100]

The Boy Scout Association offers perhaps the best example of a youth organisation that realised how Cornwell's death offered opportunity to inculcate moral lessons to their young members.[101] The newly created Cornwell Badge was intended both to remind Scouts to keep Cornwell as their moral guide and to reward similar acts of heroism displayed by other Boy Scouts. Just as other memorials had done, the Boy Scouts distributed publications about Cornwell, suggested activities to honour him, and awarded successful fundraising scouts and troops with his portrait.[102] Informed by an ideology of Social Darwinism, eugenics and national efficiency, the Boy Scouts saw the heroism of Cornwell as hopeful proof that 'we are not a decadent race. Every day brings the most wonderful stories of courage and cheerfulness in men of all ranks'.[103] According to Geoffrey Elwes, a leading member of the Scouting Council and editor of the *Headquarters Gazette*, the success of British scouting and the experience of the war had put to rest any fears that 'our race was getting "soppy"'.[104] Scouting memorials to Cornwell were at the same moment tributes to scouting's efforts at sustaining the 'health of the race' and future of the Empire.

Although scouting literature recounted the already well-rehearsed life of Cornwell, it also underscored the importance of scouting to Cornwell's character formation. For Baden-Powell, Cornwell's death afforded young scouts valuable lessons about character, obedience and leadership. Like Beresford's remarks to schoolboys, an August *Scout* article advised scouts, 'Don't think of him as someone different from yourselves. He was a boy like you – with your hopes and plans, and love of jokes, and your temptations. What his example should help you to do is to keep his ideals before you, so that, when your hour of trial comes, you may be proved of the same stout stuff as Jack Cornwell'.[105] If only they remained disciplined, dutiful and obedient, other boys could distinguish themselves as Cornwell had done. Cornwell's 'ideals' would serve as an attainable model for all boys.

A youth for the nation

By 1916, the call to duty was not merely a lesson for children. The implementation of military conscription and the discussion about extending conscription to war work on the home front demonstrated that 'greater sacrifices would be required from the civilian population'.[106] Although the commemorations primarily cast Cornwell as a model for children to emulate, they also noted how his death could inspire every Briton to do his part. At the September inaugural meeting of the National Memorial Fund, T. J. Macnamara noted that even a boy could lead men in realising their patriotic duty:

> And we children of larger growth, let a child lead us too. Let us each, whoever we may be and whatever our function in life, catch the spirit of this great act of renunciation and submission to duty. Let us each resolve anew that until this struggle is brought to final and conclusive victory for the sacred cause of the Allies, we will know no thought, speak no word, do no deed in which duty to our country does not come first.[107]

The commemoration of Cornwell had provided Macnamara with the opportunity to rally Britons to follow this youthful model of sacrifice and to remind Britons that their 'renunciation' to the nation would lead to certain victory. For Macnamara, it was only by obeying Cornwell's model of willing sacrifice, whether on the home or war front that, 'the supreme sacrifice of our heroes of land and sea and air shall not have been made in vain'.[108] The message of Macnamara's speech was clear: in order to win the war and ensure Britain's imperial future, everyone, no matter their age, needed to emulate Cornwell's model of heroic sacrifice to the nation.

And greater sacrifice was needed by spring 1917. Even with military conscription, the manpower shortage remained acute through 1917 and spurred the coalition government, now led by David Lloyd George, to review the framework of the Military Service Act. By the spring, the government had debated introducing a new Military Service Bill that would limit the work exemptions men could claim to avoid enlistment and would tighten medical exemptions and enable the re-examination of medically rejected men.[109] After Labour leaders had cast the bill to workers as an attempt to introduce general national service upon the civilian population, the final act that was passed in late March focused upon re-examination of medically rejected men.

In the midst of these debates, the story of Cornwell's heroism was offered to soothe labour unrest by inculcating a model of sacrifice that would resonate with working men. In a speech at the public unveiling of Salisbury's portrait in March 1917, Edward Carson, the Unionist leader and, by 1917, the First Lord of the Admiralty, sought to use Cornwell's story to silence shipyard workers' discontent. His words were intended for all but especially the ship workers across Britain whose agitation over conditions and wages had increased by 1917 to such an extent that a major government inquiry was established to investigate the situation.[110] On 7 March 1917, Lynden Macassey, director of shipyard labour for the Admiralty, had requested in a letter to the First Lord that either Carson or Jellicoe send a message to inspire men to work without rancour.[111] To the crowd gathered at Mansion House for the unveiling, Carson admitted that he was

> from time to time disappointed with some men in our shipyards. I am not talking of the whole body of them, but of some of the men who from time to time delay the repairing of our ships by strikes and other matters of that kind. I ask them to think of John Travers Cornwell. It is not a question between capital and labour . . . – think of the men who are dying while you will not send them the necessary relief: think of the men who are perishing on the seas from the cold and the elements while you are in comfort and in warmth.[112]

Carson believed that Salisbury's painting would help to re-energise those who had not 'put every inch of their muscle' into working to victory. Carson then told the crowd that Cornwell's message to the 'people of the Empire' would be to; 'Obey your orders, cling to your post, don't grumble, "stick it out"'. In the face of total war, total victory would require obedience and sacrifice. Carson advised his audience against 'grumbling' for better conditions: 'The high example of this boy standing by the gun might well be taken to heart by every man in the U. K. and throughout the Empire at the present time . . . The man who is not prepared to do all that is necessary in the way of sacrifices to bring about the results that this boy was aiming at is not worthy to be counted as a British citizen'.[113] In the midst of total war, citizenship would not merely inspire sacrifice; it would now demand it.

Although many of the memorials to Cornwell would not be completed until the 1920s, the unveiling and circulation of the commemorative Salisbury portrait would be the high-water mark for tributes and fundraising efforts to Cornwell. In the post-war years, despite the Navy League's hopes that 'Jack Cornwell's exploit' would go down to history and 'his noble deed' would inspire 'British boys and girls for generations to come', Cornwell's heroic legacy faded.[114] War memorials, like the Cenotaph and the tomb of 'An Unknown Warrior', now commemorated the universality of wartime sacrifice rather than the individual heroism of someone like Cornwell.[115] The contrast in intensity between wartime and post-war commemoration of Cornwell reveals the changing needs of British state and society in the aftermath of the war. By its end, the democratisation of heroism was made redundant by the democratisation of suffering. The cult of individual heroism, as shown in Cornwell's case, was cast aside as the public sought new outlets to express their collective grief.

Since the totality of this war blurred the traditional lines between war front and home front, tributes to Cornwell served the useful state ends of celebrating patriotic and obedient sacrifice whether on the battlefield, in the workplace, or in the classroom. In the context of attrition and conscription, the rhetoric of Cornwell's memorials helped to redefine citizenship as sacrifice and demanded the loyalty and obedience of both public and soldiers if victory was to be secured.[116] Thus, though commemoration enabled the public to mourn his loss and the deaths of thousands like him, Cornwell's memorials, whether organised by state authorities or private groups, best reflected the interests of a modern state fighting a total war. While various groups like the Navy League and the Boy Scouts seized on and memorialised Cornwell to suit their own purposes, the consequence of their memorials resulted in the proliferation of stories and images about how a boy instinctively served and died for his country without complaint.

Tributes to Cornwell held up his sacrifice as an example to be followed by all Britons interested in a British victory. While it was hoped that memorials to Cornwell would help in recruiting soldiers for battle, the tributes were intended also to bolster morale and reassure the British public that Cornwell's character was emblematic of the fighting spirit of Britain's military forces. Ironically, such acts of submission and duty were rehearsed daily in the trenches; however, these Somme 'heroics' did not capture the British imagination in the summer and autumn of 1916. Instead, the navy resurfaced as a site to inspire the nation. Unlike Trafalgar, Jutland produced the model of the dutiful common sailor boy (rather than of the dutiful admiral) who would animate the public to defend nation and empire. Cornwell's very youth and innocence underscored the weight of his sacrifice and endowed him with universal appeal. In order to ensure that British youth would be ready to defend these interests, classrooms recounted tales of his heroism and promulgated the 'Cornwellian' virtues of duty, obedience and sacrifice. The commemoration of Cornwell even provided the Government with the occasion to exhort shipyard labour to help secure the economic front in the spring of 1917. The myth of Cornwell's unflinching obedience and tragic innocence was intended to inspire and strengthen British resolve to continue fighting and working without complaint until victory. And during the autumn of 1916, with no end to the war in sight, such renewed blind devotion was needed.

Notes

1 *Echo and Mail*, 4 Aug. 1916, 5. The account of the funeral reported mourners in the 'hundreds of thousands'.
2 *Echo and Mail*, 4 Aug. 1916, 5.

3 *Daily Express*, 2 Aug. 1916.
4 *Daily Express*, 31 July 1916, 5.
5 *Daily Express*, 31 July 1916, 5; *Echo and Mail*, 4 Aug. 1916, 5.
6 *Daily Express*, 31 July 1916, 5; *Echo and Mail*, 4 Aug. 1916, 5.
7 *Echo and Mail*, 4 Aug. 1916, 5.
8 *The Times*, 31 July 1916, 3; *Daily Express*, 2 Aug. 1916.
9 *National Review*, Oct. 1916, 193. Madame Tussaud's display of Cornwell ran from the autumn of 1916 until the 1960s. See Madame Tussaud's Archives, London. Mount Cornwell is 2972 metres (9750 feet) and is located along the Alberta and British Columbia border at the continental divide at the headwaters of the Henretta Creek.
10 Graham Dawson, 'The Blond Bedouin: Lawrence of Arabia, Imperial Adventure and the Imagining of English-British Masculinity', in Michael Roper and John Tosh, eds, *Manful Assertions: Masculinities in Britain since 1800* (London: Routledge, 1991), 138.
11 Andrew Gordon, *The Rules of the Game: Jutland and British Naval Command* (Annapolis: Naval Institute Press, 1996), 513; Mark Girouard, *The Return to Camelot: Chivalry and the English Gentleman* (New Haven: Yale University Press, 1981), 290. Girouard claims that though the First World War initially revived chivalric rhetoric, the war experience dealt a 'death-wound' to chivalry. He suggests that 1916 offered disillusionment to elites like Lt Raymond Asquith, the Prime Minister's son, who noted in a letter to his wife in July 1916, 'the suggestion that it (the war) elevates character is hideous'. Asquith was killed during the battle of the Somme on 15 September 1916, the day that the *London Gazette* announced Cornwell's VC.
12 M. L. Sanders and Philip Taylor, *British Propaganda during the First World War, 1914–1918* (Houndmills, Basingstoke: Palgrave Macmillan 1982), 11.
13 Brock Millman, *Pessimism and British War Policy, 1916–1918* (London: Frank Cass, 2001); Brock Millman, *Managing Domestic Dissent in First World War Britain* (London: Routledge, 2000).
14 Paul Fussell, *The Great War and Modern Memory* (Oxford: Oxford University Press, 1975); Girouard, *The Return to Camelot*; Ted Bogacz, '"A Tyranny of Words": Language, Poetry and Antimodernism in England in the First World War', *Journal of Modern History* 58 (1986), 643–68; Modris Eksteins, *Rites of Spring: The Great War and the Birth of the Modern Age* (Boston: Houghton Mifflin, 1989); Samuel Hynes, *A War Imagined: The First World War and English Culture* (New York: Atheneum, 1991); Adrian Gregory, *The Silence of Memory: Armistice Day, 1919–1946* (Oxford: Berg, 1994); Jay Winter, *Sites of Memory, Sites of Mourning: The Great War in European Cultural History* (Cambridge: Cambridge University Press, 1995); Alex King, *Memorials of the Great War in Britain: The Symbolism and Politics of Remembrance* (Oxford: Berg, 1998); T. G. Ashplant, Graham Dawson and Michael Roper, eds, *The Politics of War, Memory, and Commemoration* (London: Routledge, 2000).
15 For a review of recent historiography, see Michael Roper, 'Between Manliness and Masculinity: The "War Generation" and the Psychology of Fear in Britain, 1914–1950', *Journal of British Studies* 44, no. 2 (April 2005), 343–62. Eric Leed, *No Man's Land: Combat and Identity in World War I* (Cambridge: Cambridge University Press, 1979); Elaine Showalter, *The Female Malady: Women, Madness and English Culture, 1830–1980* (London: Virago Press, 1987); Joanna Bourke, *Dismembering the Male: Men's Bodies, Britain, and the Great War* (Chicago: University of Chicago, 1996).
16 Richard Schweitzer, *The Cross and the Trenches: Religious Faith and Doubt among British and American Great War Soldiers* (Praeger: Westport, Conn., 2003); Daniel Todman, '"Sans Peur et sans Reproche": The Retirement, Death and Mourning of Sir Douglas Haig, 1918–1928', *Journal of Military History* 67 (2003), 1083–1106; Allen J. Frantzen, *Bloody Good: Chivalry, Sacrifice, and the Great War* (Chicago: University of Chicago, 2004); Max Jones, *The Last Great Quest:*

Captain Scott's Antarctic Sacrifice (New York: Oxford University Press, 2003); Stephanie Barczewski, *Antarctic Destinies: Scott, Shackleton, and the Changing Face of Heroism* (London: Hambledon Continuum, 2008). Barczewski's study was not released in time to consider it more fully for this book.

17 Bogacz, '"A Tyranny of Words"', 659. See also Girouard, *Return to Camelot*, 275–93.

18 See Winter, *Sites of Memory*; Bourke, *Dismembering the Male*; and Frantzen, *Bloody Good*.

19 R. J. Q. Adams and Philip P. Poirier, *The Conscription Controversy in Great Britain, 1900–18* (Athens, OH: Ohio State University Press, 1987), 175.

20 Adams, *The Conscription Controversy*, 174.

21 Bourke, *Dismembering the Male*, 237; *The Times*, 31 July 1916, 3; *The Times*, 13 Sept. 1916, 11; *Navy League Letter*, 15 Dec. 1916, and Charles Beresford's Letter to School Boys, Imperial War Museum (hereafter IWM) C94, VC Box 18. Bourke notes that 1.5 million people bought copies of the *Daily Mirror* to read of the announcement of his death. Kitchener's death led to an immediate outpouring of grief and donations for his memorial. By the end of July 1916, relief efforts in Kitchener's name exceeded £164,000. By mid-September, donations totalled more than £281,000. Donations to Cornwell's memorial fund, which began in late July, were paltry in comparison, only totalling around £29,000 by December.

22 *Echo and Mail*, 15 Sept. 1916, 5.

23 Quoted in Mark Connelly, *The Great War, Memory and Ritual: Commemoration in the City and East London, 1916–1939* (Rochester, NY: Boydell and Brewer, 2002), 92.

24 Bourke, *Dismembering the Male*, 237–42. The failure to recover his body from the North Sea waters fostered conspiracy theories in the 1920s and served as the basis for Frank Power's Kitchener hoax of 1926.

25 King, *Memorials of the Great War*, 46; Connelly, *Great War, Memory and Ritual*, 30.

26 Stuart Sillars, *Art and Survival in First World War Britain* (Houndmills, Basingstoke: Macmillan, 1987), Connelly, *The Great War, Memory and Ritual*, 91–7.

27 Alastair Maclean, 'John Travers Cornwell', in *Fifty World Famous Heroic Deeds* (London: Odhams Press, 1938), 351.

28 *Echo and Mail*, Friday 14 July 1916, 5.

29 Maclean, 'John Travers Cornwell', 352–3.

30 With an armament of ten 5.5-inch guns, the newly built light cruiser was attached to the Third Battlecruiser Squadron under the command of Admiral Horace Hood within Admiral David Beatty's battlecruiser squadron.

31 John Cornwell to Eli Cornwell, 23 May 1916, IWM, Cornwell Papers, C94, VC Box 18. Based on gunnery practice schedules from the *Chester* log, it is probable that this appointment took place on 17 May 1916. See Public Record Office, Kew (hereafter PRO), ADM 53/37664.

32 Letter from Jellicoe to Admiralty, 6 June 1916, National Maritime Museum (hereafter NMM), Jellicoe Papers, ADD MS 49008; *Spectator*, 15 July 1916, 55.

33 NMM, Jellicoe Papers, ADD MS 49008.

34 HMS *Chester* Reports, 9 June 1916, NMM, Jellicoe Papers, ADD MS 49008. Lieutenant H. E. Morse had reported Cornwell's service to Lawson. See IWM, Cornwell Papers, C94, VC Box 18.

35 Letters of Robert Lawson, 10 June 1916 and 18 June 1916, NMM, Jellicoe Papers, ADD MS 49008; Letters of Rear Admiral Trevelyan Napier to Beatty, 18 June 1916, NMM, Jellicoe Papers, ADD MS 49008.

36 *London Gazette*, 6 July 1916, 6726.

37 *Daily Mirror*, 7 July 1916, 1.

38 *Great European War Week by Week*, 15 July 1916, 49.

39 *Daily Mirror*, 7 July 1916, 3; *Daily Sketch*, 14 July 1916, 2; *Spectator*, 15 July 1916, 68.

40 Felicia [Dorothea] Hemans, *Poetical Works of Mrs Felicia Hemans* (New York, 1902), 324–5. The popular poem first appeared in 1826 in *Monthly Magazine*.
41 *Spectator*, 15 July 1916, 68.
42 *Daily Mirror*, 7 July 1916, 3; *Daily Sketch*, 8 July 1916; *Spectator*, 15 July 1916, 68.
43 Bourke, *Dismembering the Male*, 213.
44 Robert Lawson to Mrs Cornwell, June 1916, IWM, Cornwell Papers, C94, VC Box 18; *The Times*, 7 July 1916, 5.
45 *The Times*, 7 July 1916, 5; *Echo and Mail*, 14 July 1916, 5.
46 In addition, the Navy League compared Cornwell to John Moyse, the legendary soldier who refused to prostrate himself before a Chinese mandarin when taken prisoner during the China war of 1860. Adapting the lines from Sir Francis Hastings Doyle's popular poem 'The Private of the Buffs' about Moyse, the Navy League edited the lines so that England's greatness rested upon 'the strong heart of her sons', the rising generation of boys like Cornwell. The League proclaimed the nobility of Cornwell's humble birth, 'So let his name through England ring/ A boy of mean estate/ Who died as great as England's King/ Because his soul was great.' See *Navy*, Sept. 1916, 242.
47 Graham Dawson, *Soldier Heroes: British Adventure, Empire, and the Imagining of Masculinities* (London: Routledge, 1994), 103. Dawson notes that part of the problem of reporting Havelock's death was the delay of communications.
48 *Headquarters' Gazette*, August 1916, 212.
49 Sanders and Taylor, *British Propaganda*, 31.
50 *The Times*, 8 July 1916, 11; *The Times*, 11 July 1916, 9; *Spectator*, 15 July 1916, 68.
51 *Teachers' World*, 15 July 1916. John Oxenham was the pseudonym for William Arthur Dunkerley, who was inspired by the character of the same name in Charles Kingsley's novel *Westward Ho!* Mabel C. Edwards and Mary Booth, eds, *The Fiery Cross: An Anthology of War Poems* (London: Grant Richards, 1915). The edition, reprinted in 1917, originally sold for the benefit of the Red Cross.
52 *Spectator*, 15 July 1916, 68.
53 *Daily Sketch*, 8 July 1916, 1.
54 *Daily Sketch*, 10 July 1916, 1.
55 *Echo and Mail*, 14 July 1916, 5.
56 *Echo and Mail*, 14 July 1916, 5.
57 *Echo and Mail*, 14 July 1916, 5; Letter from Captain Lawson to his mother, IWM, Cornwell Papers, C94, VC Box 18; Stephen Snelling, *Naval VCs* (Phoenix Mill: Alan Sutton, 2002), 117. The East Ham *Echo and Mail* revealed that Cornwell's mother had declined help by the Admiralty to cover expenses for a naval funeral in order to bury her son in a cemetery quickly and close to her home. Without money to cover burial costs, Jack's grave was only distinguishable by a numbered marker. In the wake of the scandal, Captain Lawson in a private letter to his own mother noted, 'If Mrs Cornwell had not elected to have his body moved from the hospital to her own house, there would have been a funeral with full naval honours'.
58 *Daily Sketch*, 14 July 1916, 2; *Echo and Mail*, 14 July 1916, 5; *Daily Express*, 26 July 1916, 5.
59 M. J. Crook, *The Evolution of the Victoria Cross: A Study in Administrative History* (Tunbridge Wells, Kent: Midas Books, 1975), chapters five and eight.
60 *Hansard's Parliamentary Debates* (Lords), 5th series, 26 July 1916, cols 920–1.
61 Crook, *Evolution of the Victoria Cross*, 170; John Smyth, *The Story of the Victoria Cross* (London: Frederick Muller, 1963), 206; Rupert Stewart, *The Victoria Cross: The Empire's Roll of Valour* (London: Hutchinson, 1928), 30. Although Britain's military and its lines of engagement had grown dramatically by 1916, 33 fewer Crosses were issued in 1916 than in 1915. Of the 84 Victoria Crosses issued in 1916, only 6 were won by the Royal Navy and Cornwell was the lone non-commissioned rating.

62 *Daily Mirror*, 16 Sept. 1916, 1.
63 *Daily Mirror*, 16 Sept. 1916, 5.
64 *Daily Mirror*, 16 Sept. 1916, 3. The *Daily Mirror* termed the front a 'success' at least half a dozen times in the one-page summary.
65 *Daily Mirror*, 16 Sept. 1916, 5.
66 Ashplant et al., *Politics of War, Memory, and Commemoration*, 9.
67 Bourke, *Dismembering the Male*, 210–52.
68 The Jack Cornwell Memorial Fund was set up on 20 July 1916 and registered as Charity Trust in 1921. It also enabled East Ham schoolchildren in East Ham to raise funds to erect a permanent monument for Cornwell's grave.
69 *Echo and Mail*, 15 Sept. 1916, 5; *The Times*, 14 Sept. 1916, 9.
70 *Echo and Mail*, 15 Sept. 1916, 5; *The Times*, 14 Sept. 1916, 9.
71 Stephen Heathorn, *For Home, Country, and Race: Constructing Gender, Class, and Englishness in the Elementary School, 1880–1914* (Toronto: University of Toronto Press, 1999), 180; W. Mark Hamilton, *The Nation and the Navy: Methods and Organization of British Navalist Propaganda, 1889–1914* (New York: Garland Publishing, 1986).
72 *Navy*, Aug. 1917, 112.
73 *The Times*, 19 September 1916; F. Haydn Dimmock, *Scouts Book of Heroes* (London: C. Arthur Pearson, 1919), 128–46; *Boy Scouts and the Great War* (London: Aldine Pub. Co., 1915). A laudatory article in *The Times* estimated that 35,000 Scouts served in the Army and Navy during the war. In addition, thousands of Scouts, too young for enlistment, offered wartime services to families, local authorities, and Coast Guard stations.
74 Proceedings of a Meeting of the Committee of the Council held on 3 Aug. 1916, Scout Association Archives (hereafter SAA), Minute Book, vol. 5.
75 SAA, POR 1917 edition, paragraph 54. In addition to such demonstrations of bravery or suffering, the Cornwell Scout had to be a first-class scout who had obtained numerous badges and received a reference of effusive praise. Baden-Powell awarded the first Cornwell badge in December 1916 to scout Arthur Shepherd who had saved a man from drowning. See Proceedings of a Meeting of the Committee of the Council Held on 2 Nov. 1916, SAA, Minute Book, vol. 6.
76 Within a year of his death, at least three portraits of Cornwell were commissioned and a full-page illustration of Cornwell alone or by his gun was featured in at least seven periodicals. See *War Illustrated*, 22 July 1916; *Teacher's World*, July 1916; *Fleet: The Journal of the British Navy*, Aug. 1916; *Scout*, 19 Aug. 1916; *Answers*, 28 Oct. 1916; *Sphere*, 18 Nov. 1916; and *Boy's Own Paper*, Jan. 1917.
77 CSBI/12/3/71, SAA. The original watercolour is located at Scout Association Headquarters, Gilwell Park, Chingford.
78 Cornwell cigarette cards, SAA. Cornwell was featured in at least three series of cigarette cards during the war. In addition to Copes and Gallaher, a photograph of 'Boy Cornwell' appeared in the Weekly Welcome's 'Lest We Forget' series 1916. For the perceived connection between cigarettes, cards and the 'boy labour problem' see Matthew Hilton, *Smoking in British Popular Culture 1800–2000: Perfect Pleasures* (Manchester: Manchester University Press, 2000).
79 John Ernest Hodder-Williams, *Jack Cornwell: The Story of John Travers Cornwell, VC* (London: Hodder & Stoughton, 1917); Harry Golding, *The Wonder Book of the Navy for Boys and Girls* (London: Ward, Lock & Co., 1917); Dimmock, *Scouts Book of Heroes*; Alastair Maclean, 'John Travers Cornwell'; Hodder-Williams's biography was reprinted in Canada the following year and Dimmock's work was updated and reissued in 1924.
80 John Leyland, 'Souvenir of the Great Naval Battle and Roll of Honour' (London, 1916); John Buchan, *The Battle of Jutland* (London: T. Nelson and Sons, 1916); W. H. D. Boyle, ed., *Gallant Deeds* (Portsmouth: Gieves, 1919).
81 Frank O. Salisbury, *Sarum Chase: New and Enlarged Edition of Portrait and Pageant*, revd edn (London: John Murray, 1953), 222. The National Memorial Committee had announced on 14 September 1916 that Frank O. Salisbury, the

Royal Academy portrait painter, would paint Cornwell's portrait for the National Memorial Fund. Both Lord Balfour, as First Lord of the Admiralty, and Sir John Bethell, as Member of Parliament for Romford, had persuaded Salisbury to paint Cornwell's portrait. Salisbury had previously received a parliamentary commission to produce a series of paintings to grace the halls of Westminster. Among Salisbury's best-known works are his paintings of the burial of the Unknown Warrior.

82   John Oxenham, *Selected Poems of John Oxenham* (London: T. F. Unwin, 1924), 242.
83   *Echo and Mail*, 15 Sept. 1916, 5.
84   *Echo and Mail*, 15 Sept. 1916, 5.
85   Quoted in John Gillis, *Youth and History* (New York: Academic Press, 1974), 143. Charles Russell, 'Adolescence', in *Converging Views of Social Reform: no. 2. Being a series of lectures on the industrial unrest and the living wage given at the Interdenominational Summer School, held at Swanwick, Derbyshire, June 28th–July 5th, 1913* (London: Collegium, 1913), 55.
86   Victor Bailey, *Delinquency and Citizenship: Reclaiming the Young Offender, 1914–1948* (Oxford: Clarendon Press, 1987), 17.
87   Harry Hendrick, *Images of Youth: Age, Class, and the Male Youth Problem, 1880–1920* (Oxford: Clarendon Press, 1990), 219–20.
88   *Daily Mirror*, 10 July 1916, 5.
89   *Daily Mirror*, 10 July 1916, 5.
90   *The Times*, 11 July 1916, 9.
91   Robert Baden-Powell, 'Boy Scout Movement in Education', New Ideals in Education Conference, Oxford, 1 Aug. 1916, SAA, TC/28, Founders Files; *Manchester Guardian*, 2 Aug. 1916.
92   Robert Baden-Powell, 'The Boy Scout Movement and the Future', 1916, Gilwell, SAA, TC/28, Founders Files.
93   *Navy*, Sept. 1916, 242.
94   *Navy*, Sept. 1916, 242.
95   *The Times*, 21 Sept. 1916, 11; *Navy*, Sept. 1916, 242. A later date was announced for a variety of schools unable to organise the memorial day (e.g., Irish and Welsh schools, and certain English schools that were not in full session because of hop picking). Both John Winton and Dictionary of National Biography mistakenly attribute 30 Sept. 1916 as Cornwell Day. See John Winton, *Victoria Cross at Sea* (London, 1978), 128; Richard Davenport-Hines, 'John Travers Cornwell', in H. C. G. Matthew and Brian Harrison, eds, *Oxford Dictionary of National Biography* (Oxford, 2004), 13, 493–4.
96   Beresford Letter to Secondary Schools, 11 Oct. 1916, Navy League Publication, IWM, Cornwell Papers, C94, VC Box 18.
97   Given the similarity of this booklet to his other writings about Cornwell and his personal investment in Cornwell's memorial, it is probable that Beresford, as President of the Jack Cornwell Memorial Fund, had penned this pamphlet. See letter by Beresford in *Boy's Own Paper*, January 1917, 138.
98   'Faithful unto Death' booklet, IWM, Cornwell Papers, C94, VC Box 18.
99   Beresford's Broadsheet Letter to School Boys, 'Will You Honour a Boy Hero?' 15 December 1916, IWM, Cornwell Papers, C94, VC Box 18. In its conclusion, the booklet encouraged its readers to: 'Let us all try to follow the noble example of the hero of this story, and thus will Britain – the land we love – always remain great, in the only one real way – the greatness of her sons and daughters'.
100   *Navy*, Oct. 1916, 255.
101   *Headquarters Gazette*, Sept. 1916, 252.
102   'Cornwell Memorial' pamphlet, 4 Aug. 1916, SAA, Cornwell Papers. In the first week of August Robert Baden-Powell had already issued a three-page pamphlet entitled 'Cornwell Memorial'. The *Scout* had issued a special 'Jack Cornwell Number' on 19 Aug. 1916.

103 *Headquarters Gazette*, Sept. 1916, 236; Michael Rosenthal, *The Character Factory: Baden-Powell and the Origins of the Boy Scout Movement* (New York: Pantheon books 1986), 253–5; Robert H. MacDonald, *Sons of the Empire: The Frontier and the Boy Scout Movement, 1890–1918* (Toronto: University of Toronto, 1993), 176–202.

104 *Headquarters Gazette*, Sept. 1916, 236.

105 *Scout*, 19 Aug. 1916, 995; Press Release, Autumn 1916, SAA, Cornwell Papers.

106 Sanders and Taylor, *British Propaganda during the First World War*, 65–6.

107 *Echo and Mail*, 15 Sept. 1916, 5.

108 *Echo and Mail*, 15 Sept. 1916, 5.

109 Adams and Poirier, *The Conscription Controversy*, 202.

110 Noel Whiteside, 'Population at War', in John Turner, ed., *Britain and the First World War* (London: Routledge, 1988), 94.

111 Lynden Macassey to Edward Carson, 7 March 1917, Belfast, Carson Papers, Public Record Office, Northern Ireland, D/1507/B/22/25.

112 *The Times*, 24 March 1917. The transcription from the newspaper noted that this brought cheers from the crowd.

113 *The Times*, 24 March 1917.

114 In fact, in the wake of the war more attention was paid to the Navy League's neglect of the Cornwell family's impoverishment despite the League having raised over £20,000 for the Cornwell Memorial Fund. The death of Mrs Cornwell on 31 October 1919 led the surviving members to emigrate to Canada. Efforts to raise money to alleviate travelling costs led to renewed outrage in the press over the League's abandonment of the Cornwell family. See Connelly, *Great War, Memory, and Ritual*, 94–6.

115 Gregory, *Silence of Memory*, 8–50; George Mosse, *Fallen Soldiers: Reshaping the Memory of the World Wars* (New York, 1990), 94–106.

116 Nicoletta Gullace, *'The Blood of Our Sons': Men, Women, and the Renegotiation of British Citizenship during the Great War* (Houndmills, Basingstoke: Palgrave Macmillan, 2002), 145–66.

Conclusion

As this book has tried to show, the new depictions of naval manhood that emerged in the late nineteenth century were not a matter of the triumphant supplanting of the libertine Jack Tar for the figure of the respectable dauntless British bluejacket defending home and empire. However, what was remarkable in the late-Victorian and Edwardian period was the proliferation of positive depictions of naval men and how these newly fashioned representations aligned themselves around the ideals of naval and imperial manhood. Older stereotypes of the rollicking sailor still existed and, in fact, have endured; but newer images emerged that valorised the modern bluejacket, who was cast as a manly ideal, virtuous both afloat and ashore. The rhetoric of naval manhood was reconstructed in part because older images of it were irreconcilable with the demands of empire.

The emergence of the naval man as an appropriate symbol of empire became a possibility only after a series of naval reforms, beginning with the introduction of continuous service, produced the conditions to imagine a new type of sailor. By the late-Victorian period, naval reforms, in conjunction with the revolutionary changes in naval technology, professionalised the lower deck and created a modern industrialised fleet that was celebrated in popular culture for its defence of Britain and its empire. Within this context, the British bluejacket served as part of an imperial panoply of icons from Tommy Atkins, Britannia, to John Bull, that projected an image of confidence, of a united strong empire sharing a common past and motivated by a national purpose. The advent of mass culture combined with the various displays of imperial pageantry facilitated the appearance of representations that depicted the 'manly' and patriotic bluejacket.

In fact, as charted in these chapters, constructions of sailors' masculine social status or celebrations of imperial manliness were not static, but responded to new conditions and contexts that emerged during the fifty years of this study. Characterisations of Victorian naval manhood imparted the virtues of the imperial manly ideal, valorising discipline, duty and a moral Christian ethos. However, notions of manliness were recast by the turn of the century in the wake of intense imperial competition, the experience of war and the advent of mass politics. While manliness now celebrated the body, action and feeling, naval manhood as envisaged by writers like Rudyard Kipling or Fred Jane heralded a rugged masculinity that embraced physical strength and imparted a straightforward integrity. These popular portrayals of the British bluejacket valorised naval manhood for defending home and empire and provided an egalitarian model of the manly ideal.

Although the First World War was not a naval war, representations of naval manhood responded to and served the war effort, even if in contradictory ways. Celebrations of Jack Cornwell's heroism, forged in the naval battle of Jutland, helped to revive an older vision of manliness defined by duty, discipline and sacrifice in the face of the war's challenge to masculinity. Despite its nostalgic embrace of traditional forms, the idealisation of Cornwell's sacrifice reshaped the elite character of manliness, democratising it as an attainable model for all Britons who served the war effort whether on the seas, in the trenches, or in the factories.

This study has noted a particular interest in the changing rhetoric depicting naval men in late-Victorian and Edwardian Britain, but to contextualise this discourse, it has attempted to illuminate what men's lives were like when serving in the navy during this period. In his fascinating social study of the lower deck, Christopher McKee makes a playful argument where he conjectures that, apart from the technological gap that separated them, a mid-nineteenth-century sailor held much in common with a sailor from 1939.[1] While there is some truth in this statement, the British navy had not only made marked changes since the introduction of continuous service in 1853 but, more importantly, career naval men by the early twentieth century saw themselves differently from their predecessors in the early Victorian or Georgian fleets. Increasingly, naval men saw themselves as professionals. The establishment of long-term service and its concomitant reforms paved the way for the career naval rating whose masculine social standing was defined by his independence and his ability to maintain a home and family.

By the turn of the century, naval men frequently heralded the qualitative improvements of the lower deck, particularly as they petitioned for personnel reforms. The monthly service paper, the *Bluejacket*, whose publication was itself proof of the growing professional consciousness of naval ratings, proclaimed that the British seaman of 1900 had the same 'courage' as their 'pig-tailed sires' but, at the same time 'in all these respects there is yet a difference . . . it is an asset that makes him [the British bluejacket] a thinking as well as a fighting man. The asset of primary, and in many cases secondary, education. In the old days, a sailor did his duty without any idea of the value of the service he was performing for the country. Today the sailor is as conscious of his worth to the state, as the soldier or civil servant'.[2] While popular discourse championed sailors' bodies, naval men's writings repeatedly emphasised their intellectual acumen. Countless claims to the educational improvement of the naval ratings served as the basis from which the emergent lower-deck reform movement appealed to the Admiralty to improve personnel conditions in the early twentieth century.

As we have seen, in their writings, naval men justified their claims to professional standing and attendant improved benefits in the name of home and family. Although stereotypes of Jack Tar evoked the sailor as a libertine, naval men rejected such aspersions and attested their domestic devotion to wives and children. Their masculine social standing was determined by their ability to establish and maintain a household. The ship may have been a world away from a sailor's home back in Britain, but there's every indication that the idea of 'home' was central to men's minds. Given the key position of the home to sailors' masculine identities, it is little wonder that naval ratings were so critical of the Weston's charitable remonstrations about the threats posed by men drinking. While sailors' contact with home society had increased during the late-Victorian period, sailors' distance and time away from family most likely intensified their need to assert their control over the home.[3] In part, this explains their vociferous defence of their abilities to maintain domestic responsibilities as husbands and fathers in their response to Weston's ministrations.[4]

As the lower-deck reform movement developed in the first decade of the twentieth century, it sought to persuade both Admiralty and Parliament to redress long-standing grievances over pay and allowances as well as to provide the lower deck with parliamentary representation.[5] Using the familiar language of a bread-winning wage, naval men petitioned for formal recognition for their wives through the addition of marriage allowances and provision of widow's pensions. While the first round of reforms had begun in earnest in 1912, the upheaval of the First World War brought long-awaited changes to sailors with improvements in pay and pensions and the provision of a marriage allotment. In addition, the passage of the Representation of the People Act in 1918 had meant that sailors and soldiers now had the vote.[6] With the vote, naval men now could finally claim the full rights of their citizenship. Rather than serving as a summative moment that brought the close to the reform movement, the war's end marked a new beginning of struggle for naval men to claim their just rewards for their service and sacrifice to the nation.

Notes

1 Christopher McKee, *Sober Men and True: Sailor Lives in the Royal Navy, 1900–1945* (Cambridge: Harvard University Press, 2002), 5.
2 *Bluejacket*, April 1900, 439.
3 John Tosh, *Manliness and Masculinities*, 17.
4 Anna Clark, 'The Rhetoric of Chartist domesticity: Gender, Language and Class in the 1830s and 1840s', *Journal of British Studies* 31 (1992), 70–1.
5 Anthony Carew, *The Lower Deck of the Royal Navy, 1900–1939* (Manchester: Manchester University Press, 1981), 1–99. Residency restrictions before 1918 disqualified most sailors from voting.
6 Nicoletta Gullace, *'The Blood of Our Sons'*, 169–94.

Select bibliography

Manuscript collections

Bodleian Library, University of Oxford
British Library, London
Imperial War Museum, London
National Maritime Museum, Greenwich
Portsmouth City Records Office, Portsmouth
Public Record Office, Kew (now The National Archives)
Public Record Office, Northern Ireland, Belfast
Royal Naval Museum, Portsmouth
Royal Sailors Rest, Portsmouth
Scout Association Archives, Gilwell

Contemporary newspapers and periodicals

Bluejacket
Boys of the British Empire
Boys of Our Empire
Boy's Own Annual
Boy's Own Magazine
Boy's Own Paper
Brassey's Naval Annual
Comrades
Cornhill Magazine
Daily Mirror
Daily Sketch
Daily Telegraph
English Review
Fleet
Headquarters Gazette
Miss Weston's Ashore and Afloat
National Review
Naval and Military Record
Navy & Army Illustrated
Navy League Journal
Scout
Spectator
Teachers' World
The Times

Printed primary sources

Adams, W. H. Davenport. *England on the Sea: Or the Story of the British Navy, Its Decisive Battles and Great Commanders*, 2 vols. London: F. V. White, 1885.

Ashton, John, ed. *Real Sailor-Songs*. London: Leadenhall Press, 1891.

Bechervaise, John. *Thirty-Six Years of a Seafaring Life by an Old Quarter Master*. Portsea: W. Woodward, 1839.

Beresford, Admiral Lord Charles. *The Memoirs of Admiral Lord Charles Beresford*, 2 vols. London: Methuen and Co., 1914.

Brassey, Thomas A. *Papers and Addresses: Mercantile Marine and Navigation: From 1871 to 1894*. London: Longman's Green and Co., 1894.

——'The Manning of the Navy in Time of War'. *The Naval Annual* (1898), 102–17.

Bullen, Frank T. *The Way They Have in the Navy*. London: Smith, Elder, and Co., 1899.

——'The Passing of our Mercantile Marine Supremacy'. In *Navy League Guide to the Coronation Review, June 28, 1902*, edited by H. W. Wilson. London: A. Constable and Co., for the Navy League, 1902.

Capper, Lieutenant-Commander Henry D. *Aft–from the Hawsehole: Sixty-two Years of Sailors' Evolution*. London: Faber & Gwyer, 1927.

Clowes, William Laird, ed. *The Royal Navy, A History: From the Earliest Times to the Present*, 7 vols. London: Sampson, Low, Marston and Co, 1897–1903.

Couch, Arthur Quiller ['Q.', pseud.], ed. *Story of the Sea*, volume 1. London: Cassell, 1895.

Crowe, George. *The Commission of the H.M.S. 'Terrible' 1898–1902*. London: George Newnes, 1903.

Dimmock, F. Haydn. *Scouts Book of Heroes*. London: C. Arthur Pearson, 1919.

Eardley-Wilmot, Stanley Morrow. *The British Navy, Past and Present*. London: E. Stanford, 1897.

Firth, C. H. *Naval Songs and Ballads*. London: Navy Records Society, 1908.

Froude, James Anthony. *Oceana: Or, England and Her Colonies*. New York: Scribner, 1888.

Gilbert, W. S. *The Bab Ballads*, edited by James Ellis. Cambridge: Belknap Press of Harvard University Press, 1980.

——and Arthur Sullivan. *H.M.S. Pinafore*. In *The Compete Annotated Gilbert and Sullivan*, introduced and edited by Ian Bradley, 113–85. Oxford: Oxford University Press, 1996.

Gildea, Colonel Sir James. *Historical Record of the Work of The Soldiers' and Sailors' Families Association from 1885 to 1916*. London: Eyre and Spottiswoode, 1916.

Giraldus [Gerald O'Driscoll]. *Awful Disclosures of a Bluejacket: A Book of Naval Humour*. Devonport: Marlboro' Publishing Co., 1929.

Goodenough, Rev. G., RN. *The Handy Man Afloat and Ashore*. London: T. Fisher Unwin, 1901.

Hayens, Herbert. *Ye Mariners of England: A Boy's Book of the Navy*. London: Thomas Nelson and Sons, 1901.

Henty, G. A. *Do Your Duty*. London: Blackie and Son, 1900.

——*Sturdy and Strong or How George Andrews Made His Way*. London: Blackie and Son, 1900.

Hodder-Williams, John Ernest. *Jack Cornwell: The Story of John Travers Cornwell, VC*. London: Hodder & Stoughton, 1917.

Holman, Thomas [A Ranker, pseud.]. *Life in the Royal Navy*. Portsmouth: G. Chamberlain, 1891.

Hughes, Thomas. *Tom Brown at Oxford*. New York: H. M. Caldwell Co., 1899 [1861].

Hurd, Archibald. *How our Navy is Run: A Description of Life in the King's Fleet*. London: C. Arthur Pearson, Ltd, 1902.

Jane, Fred T. *The Port Guard Ship: A Romance of the Present Day Navy*. London: Hurst and Blackett Limited, 1900.

——*A Royal Bluejacket*. London: Sampson and Low, 1908.

Kingston, William Henry Giles. *Bluejackets; or, Chips of the Old Block. A Narrative of the Gallant Exploits of British Seamen, and of the Principal Events in the Naval Service, during the Reign of Her Most Gracious Majesty Queen Victoria*. London: Grant and Griffith, 1854.

——*True Blue; or, The Life and Adventures of a British Seaman of the Old School*. London: Griffith and Farran, 1862.

——*The Three Midshipmen*. London: Griffith and Farran, 1873.

——*A Popular History of the British Navy from the Earliest Times to the Present*. London: Gall and Inglis, 1876.

——*From Powder Monkey to Admiral: A Story of Naval Adventure*. New York: A. C. Armstrong and Son, 1884.

Kipling, Rudyard. *A Fleet in Being*. In *The Bombay Edition of the Works of Rudyard Kipling*, volume 5. London: Macmillan, 1913.

——*The Complete Verse*. With a foreword by M. M. Kaye. London: Kyle Cathie, 1990.

Knock, Sidney. *'Clear Lower Deck', An Intimate Study of the Men of the Royal Navy*. London: Philip Allan, 1932.

Laughton, John Knox. *The Study of Naval History*. London: Royal United Service Institution, 1896.

Lyne, Thomas J. Spence. *Something of a Sailor: From Sailor Boy to Admiral*. London: Jarrolds, 1940.

MacKenzie, John M. *Propaganda and Empire: The Manipulation of British Public Opinion, 1880–1960*. Manchester: Manchester University Press, 1985.

——ed. *Imperialism and Popular Culture*. Manchester: Manchester University Press, 1986.

[Maclean, Alastair]. *Fifty World Famous Heroic Deeds*. London, Odhams Press, 1938.

Mahan, Alfred T. *The Influence of Sea Power upon History, 1660–1783*. New York: Sagamore Press, 1957 [1890].

Masefield, John, ed. *A Sailor's Garland*. London: Methuen and Co., 1906.

Matthew, H. C. G., ed. *The Gladstone Diaries with Cabinet Minutes and Prime Ministerial Correspondence*. Oxford: Clarendon Press, 1982.

McHardy, C. McL. *British Seamen, Boy Seamen, and Light Dues*. London: Navy League, 1899.

Noble, Sam. *Sam Noble, Able Seaman: 'Tween Decks in the Seventies*. New York: Frederick A. Stokes, Co., 1926.

Orwell, George. *The Collected Essays, Journalism and Letters of George Orwell: An Age Like This, 1920–1940*, volume 1, edited by Sonia Orwell and Ian Angus. New York: Harcourt, Brace, and World, 1968.

Oxenham, John. *Selected Poems of John Oxenham*. London: T. F. Unwin, 1924.

Reynolds, Stephen. *The Lower Deck, the Navy, and the Nation*. London: J. M. Dent and Sons, 1912.

Riley, Patrick. *Memories of a Bluejacket*. London: Sampson Low, Marston, 1931.

Rowe, Richard. *Jack Afloat and Ashore*. London: Smith, Elder and Co., 1875.

Russell, W. Clark. *Sailors' Language*. London: Sampson, Low, Marston, 1883.

Salisbury, Frank O. *Sarum Chase: New and Enlarged Edition of Portrait and Pageant*, revd edn. London: John Murray, 1953.

Smiles, Samuel. *Self-Help*, revd edn. Chicago: Belford, Clarke and Co, 1886.

——*Duty: With Illustrations of Courage, Patience, and Endurance*. Chicago: Belford, Clarke, and Co, 1881.

Tennyson, Alfred Lord. *Poems of Alfred Lord Tennyson*, volume 3, edited by Christopher Ricks. Berkeley: University of California Press, 1987.

Thring, Theodore. *A Treatise on the Criminal Law of the Navy*. London: V. & R. Stevens and Sons, 1861.

West, Alfred. *Life in Our Navy and Our Army: A Synopsis of the Life-Work of Alfred West*. Portsmouth: Wessex Press, 1912.

Weston, Agnes. *Temperance Work in the Royal Navy*. London: Hodder & Stoughton, 1879.

——*Personal Work among Our Blue Jackets Ashore and Afloat*. Devonport: A. H. Swiss Printers, 1880.

——*One Flag, One Fleet, One Throne*, 1902.

——*A True Blue! What is He?* Portsmouth: Royal Sailors' Rests, 1904.

——*Signals of Distress!* Portsmouth, 1905.

——*For the Glory of God and the Good of the Service*. Portsmouth, 1905.

——*England Home and Duty*. Portsmouth, 1909.

——*My Life Among the Bluejackets*. London: Nisbet, 1911.

——*From One Generation to Another*. Portsmouth, 1913.

White, Arnold. 'The Feeding of the Fleet'. In *Navy League Guide to the Coronation Review, June 28, 1902*, edited by H. W. Wilson. London: A. Constable and Co. for the Navy League, 1902.

—— *The Navy League and the Public.* London: Navy League, circa 1914.

Wilkinson, Spencer. *The Secret of the Sea.* London: Swan, 1895.

Wilson, H. W., ed. *Navy League Guide to the Coronation Review, June 28, 1902.* London: A. Constable and Co. for the Navy League, 1902.

Wintz, Sophia. *Our Blue Jackets: Miss Weston's Life and Work among our Sailors.* London: Hodder & Stoughton, 1890.

Yexley, Lionel [James Woods]. *The Inner Life of the Navy.* London: Pitman, 1908.

—— *Our Fighting Seamen.* London: Stanley Paul, 1911.

—— *Charity and the Navy.* London: The Fleet Ltd, 1911.

Secondary sources

Adams, Paul, ed. *Seamen in Society.* Bucharest: Proceedings of the Conference of the International Commission of Maritime History, 1980.

Anderson, Olive. 'The Growth of Christian Militarism in mid-Victorian Britain'. *English Historical Review* 86 (January 1971): 46–72.

Ashplant, T. G., Graham Dawson and Michael Roper, eds. *The Politics of War Memory and Commemoration.* London: Routledge, 2000.

Bailey, Victor. *Delinquency and Citizenship: Reclaiming the Young Offender, 1914–1948.* Oxford: Clarendon Press, 1987.

Barnett, Correlli. *Britain and Her Army, 1509–1970.* New York: William Morrow, 1970.

Baynham, Henry. *From the Lower Deck: The Old Navy, 1780–1840.* London: Hutchinson, 1969.

—— *Before the Mast: Naval Ratings in the Nineteenth Century.* London: Hutchinson, 1971.

—— *Men from the Dreadnoughts.* London: Hutchinson, 1976.

Bederman, Gail. *Manliness and Civilization: A Cultural History of Gender and Race in the United States, 1880–1917.* Chicago: University of Chicago Press, 1995.

Behrman, Cynthia. *Victorian Myths of the Sea.* Athens, Ohio: Ohio University Press, 1977.

Bolster, W. Jeffrey. *Black Jacks: African American Seamen in the Age of Sail.* Cambridge: Harvard University Press, 1997.

Bourke, Joanna. *Working-Class Cultures in Britain, 1890–1960: Gender, Class and Ethnicity.* London: Routledge, 1994.

—— *Dismembering the Male: Men's Bodies, Britain, and the Great War.* Chicago: University of Chicago Press, 1996.

Boyd, Kelly. 'Exemplars and Ingrates: Imperialism and the Boys' Story Paper, 1880–1930'. *Historical Research* 67, no. 163 (June 1994): 143–55.

—— *Manliness and the Boys' Story Paper in Britain: A Cultural History, 1855–1940.* Houndmills, Basingstoke: Palgrave Macmillan, 2003.

Bradley, Ian. *The Call to Seriousness: The Evangelical Impact on the Victorians.* London: J. Cape, 1976.

Brady, Sean. *Masculinity and Male Homosexuality in Britain, 1861–1913.* Houndmills, Basingstoke: Palgrave Macmillan, 2005.

Brantlinger, Patrick. *Rule of Darkness: British Literature and Imperialism, 1830–1914*. Ithaca: Cornell University Press, 1988.

Bratton, J. S. *The Impact of Victorian Children's Fiction*. London: Croom Helm, 1981.

Briggs, Asa. *Victorian People: A Reassessment of Persons and Themes, 1851–67*. Chicago: University of Chicago Press, 1972.

Bristow, Joseph. *Empire Boys: Adventures in a Man's World*. London: HarperCollins Academic, 1991.

Brown, David. 'Wood, Sail, and Cannonballs to Steel, Steam, and Shells, 1815–1895'. In *The Oxford Illustrated History of the Royal Navy*, edited by J. R. Hill. Oxford: Oxford University Press, 1995, pp. 200–6.

Burnett, John. *Useful Toil: Autobiographies of Working People from the 1820s to the 1920s*. London: Routledge, 1994 [1974].

Burton, Antoinette. *At the Heart of the Empire: Indians and the Colonial Encounter in Late-Victorian Britain*. Berkeley: University of California Press, 1998.

Burton, Valerie. 'The Myth of Bachelor Jack: Masculinity, Patriarchy and Seafaring Labour'. In *Jack Tar in History: Essays in the History of Maritime Life and Labour*, edited by Colin Howell and Richard J. Twomey. Fredericton, New Brunswick: Acadiensis Press, 1991, pp. 179–98.

Carew, Anthony. *The Lower Deck of the Royal Navy, 1900–1939*. Manchester: Manchester University Press, 1981.

Castle, Kathryn. *Britannia's Children: Reading Colonialism through Children's Books and Magazines*. Manchester: Manchester University Press, 1996.

Chamberlain, Muriel. *'Pax Britannica'? British Foreign Policy, 1789–1914*. London: Longman, 1988.

Clark, Anna. *Struggle for the Breeches: Gender and the Making of the British Working Class*. Berkeley: University of California Press, 1997.

Cocks, H. G. *Nameless Offences: Homosexual Desire in the Nineteenth Century*. London: I. B. Tauris, 2003.

Coetzee, Frans. *For Party or Country: Nationalism and the Dilemmas of Popular Conservatism in Edwardian England*. Oxford: Oxford University Press, 1990.

Colley, Linda. *Britons: Forging the Nation 1707–1837*. New Haven: Yale University Press, 1992.

Connell, R. W. *Masculinities*, 2nd edn. Berkeley: University of California Press, 2005.

Connelly, Mark and David Welch, eds. *War and the Media: Reportage and Propaganda, 1900–2003*. London: I. B. Tauris, 2005.

Coombes, Annie E. *Reinventing Africa: Museums, Material Culture and Popular Imagination in Late Victorian and Edwardian England*. New Haven: Yale University Press, 1994.

Creighton, Margaret S. and Lisa Norling, eds. *Iron Men, Wooden Women: Gender and Seafaring the Atlantic World, 1700–1920*. Baltimore: Johns Hopkins University Press, 1996.

Cunningham, Hugh. 'The Language of Patriotism'. In *Patriotism: The Making and Unmaking of British National Identity*, volume 1, edited by Raphael Samuel. London: Routledge, 1989.

Davidoff, Leonore and Catherine Hall. *Family Fortunes: Men and Women of the English Middle Class, 1780–1850*. London: Hutchinson, 1987.

Davin, Anna. 'Imperialism and Motherhood'. *History Workshop* 5 (Spring 1978): 9–66.

Davis, David Brion. *The Problem of Slavery in the Age of Revolution, 1770–1823*. Ithaca, NY: Cornell University Press, 1975.

Dawson, Graham. 'The Blond Bedouin: Lawrence of Arabia, Imperial Adventure and the Imagining of English-British Masculinity'. In *Manful Assertions: Masculinities in Britain since 1800*, edited by Michael Roper and John Tosh. London: Routledge, 1991, pp. 113–44.

——*Soldier Heroes: British Adventure, Empire and the Imagining of Masculinities*. London: Routledge, 1994.

Deslandes, Paul R. *Oxbridge Men: British Masculinity and the Undergraduate Experience, 1850–1920*. Bloomington: Indiana University Press, 2005.

Donajgrodzki, A. P., ed. *Social Control in Nineteenth Century Britain*. London: Croom Helm, 1977.

Drotner, Kirsten. *English Children and their Magazines, 1751–1945*. New Haven: Yale University Press, 1988.

Dudink, Karen Hagemann and John Tosh, eds. 'Hegemonic masculinity and the history of gender'. In *Masculinities in Politics and War*. Manchester: Manchester University Press, 2004.

Eby, Cecil Degrotte. *The Road to Armageddon: The Martial Spirit in Boy's Literature, 1870–1914*. Durham: Duke University Press, 1988.

Eley, Geoff. *Reshaping the German Right: Radical Nationalism and Political Change after Bismarck*. New Haven: Yale University Press, 1980.

Emy, H. V. 'The Impact of Financial Policy on English Party Politics before 1914'. *Historical Journal* 15, no. 1 (March 1972): 103–31.

Fahey, David M. *Temperance and Racism: John Bull, Johnny Reb, and the Good Templars*. Lexington, KY: University of Kentucky Press, 1996.

Fest, Wilfried. 'Jingoism and Xenophobia in the Electioneering Strategies of British Ruling Elites before 1914'. In *Nationalist and Racialist Movements in Britain and Germany Before 1914*, edited by Paul Kennedy and Anthony Nicholls. London: Macmillan Press, Ltd, 1981, pp. 171–89.

Fingard, Judith. *Jack in Port*. Toronto: University of Toronto Press, 1982.

Fletcher, Commandant M. H. *The WRNS: A History of the Women's Royal Naval Service*. Annapolis: Naval Institute Press, 1989.

Foley, Timothy, Lionel Pilkington, Sean Ryder and Elizabeth Tilley, eds. *Gender and Colonialism*. Galway: Galway University Press, 1995.

Frantzen, Allen J. *Bloody Good: Chivalry, Sacrifice, and the Great War*. Chicago: University of Chicago Press, 2004.

Friedberg, Aaron L. *The Weary Titan: Britain and the Experience of Relative Decline, 1895–1905*. Princeton: Princeton University Press, 1988.

Fussell, Paul. *The Great War and Modern Memory*. Oxford: Oxford University Press, 1975.

Gagnier, Regenia. *Subjectivities: A History of Self-Representation in Britain, 1832–1920.* New York: Oxford University Press, 1991.

Gilbert, Arthur N. 'The *Africaine* courts-martial: A study of buggery and the Royal Navy'. *Journal of Homosexuality* 1, no. 1 (1974): 11–22.

——'Buggery and the British Navy, 1700–1861'. *Journal of Social History* 10, no. 1 (Autumn 1976): 72–98.

Gillis, John. *Youth and History: Tradition and Change in European Age Relations.* New York: Academic Press, 1975

——*For Better, For Worse: British Marriages, 1600 to the Present.* New York: Oxford University Press, 1985.

——, ed. *The Militarization of the Western World.* New Brunswick: Rutgers University Press, 1989.

Gilmore, David D. *Manhood in the Making: Cultural Concepts of Masculinity.* London: Yale University Press, 1990.

Girouard, Mark. *The Return to Camelot: Chivalry and the English Gentleman.* New Haven: Yale University Press, 1981.

Goldrick, James. 'The Battleship Fleet: The Test of War, 1895–1919'. In *The Oxford Illustrated History of the Royal Navy*, edited by J. R. Hill and Bryan Ranft. Oxford: Oxford University Press, 1995, pp. 280–318.

Gordon, Andrew. *The Rules of the Game. Jutland and British Naval Command.* Annapolis: Naval Institute Press, 1996.

Green, E. H. H. *The Crisis of Conservatism: The Politics, Economics, and Ideology of the British Conservative Party, 1880–1914.* London: Routledge, 1995.

Grove, Eric J. *The Royal Navy since 1815: A New Short History.* Houndmills, Basingstoke: Palgrave Macmillan, 2005.

Gullace, Nicoletta F. *'The Blood of Our Sons': Men, Women, and the Renegotiation of British Citizenship during the Great War.* Houndmills, Basingstoke: Palgrave Macmillan, 2002.

Gulliver, Doris. *Dame Agnes Weston.* London: Phillimore, 1971.

Hall, Catherine. *Civilising Subjects: Metropole and Colony in the English Colonial Imagination, 1830–1867.* Chicago: University of Chicago Press, 2002.

Hall, Catherine and Sonya Rose, eds. *At Home with the Empire: Metropolitan Culture and the Imperial World.* Cambridge: Cambridge University Press, 2006.

Hall, Catherine, Keith McClelland and Jane Rendall, eds. *Defining the Victorian Nation: Class, Race, Gender and the British Reform Act of 1867.* Cambridge: Cambridge University Press, 2000.

Hall, Donald, ed. *Muscular Christianity: Embodying the Victorian Age.* Cambridge: Cambridge University Press, 1994.

Hamilton, C. I. 'Naval Hagiography and the Victorian Hero'. *Historical Journal* 23 (1980): 381–98.

Hamilton, W. Mark. *The Nation and the Navy: Methods and Organization of British Navalist Propaganda, 1889–1914.* New York: Garland Publishing, 1986.

——'The "New Navalism" and the British Navy League, 1895–1914'. *Mariner's Mirror* 64 (February 1978).

Harrison, Brian. 'Philanthropy and the Victorians'. *Victorian Studies* 9, no. 4 (June 1966): 353–74.

——*Drink and the Victorians: The Temperance Question in England: 1815–1872*. London: Faber & Faber, 1971.

Hayter, Charles. *Gilbert and Sullivan*. New York: St Martin's Press, 1987.

Heathorn, Stephen. *For Home, Country, and Race: Constructing Gender, Class and Englishness in the Elementary School, 1880–1914*. Toronto: University of Toronto Press, 2000.

——'Representations of War and Martial Heroes in English Elementary School Reading and Rituals, 1885–1914'. In *Children and War*, edited by James Marten. New York: New York University Press, 2002, pp. 108–9.

Hendrick, Harry. *Images of Youth: Age, Class, and the Male Youth Problem, 1880–1920*. Oxford: Clarendon Press, 1990.

Herman, Arthur. *To Rule the Waves: How the British Navy Shaped the Modern World*. New York: HarperCollins, 2004.

Hill, J. R. and Brian Ranft, eds. *The Oxford Illustrated History of the Royal Navy*. Oxford: Oxford University Press, 1995.

Hilton, Boyd. *The Age of Atonement: the Influence of Evangelicalism on Social and Economic Thought, 1785–1865*. Oxford: Clarendon Press, 1991.

Hobsbawm, E. J. *Age of Empire*. New York: Vintage, 1989.

——*Industry and Empire: From 1750 to the Present Day*. London: Penguin Books, 1990.

——and Terence Ranger, eds. *The Invention of Tradition*. Cambridge: Cambridge University Press, 1983.

Houghton, Walter. *Victorian Frame of Mind, 1830–1870*. New Haven: Yale University Press, 1957.

Howell, Colin and Richard J. Twomey, eds. *Jack Tar in History: Essays in the History of Maritime Life and Labour*. Fredericton, New Brunswick: Acadiensis Press, 1991.

Hynes, Samuel. *The Edwardian Turn of Mind*. Princeton: Princeton University Press, 1968.

——*A War Imagined: The First World War and English Culture*. New York: Atheneum, 1991.

Jenks, Tim. *Naval Engagements: Patriotism, Cultural Politics, and the Royal Navy, 1793–1815*. Oxford: Oxford University Press, 2006.

Johnson, Douglas H. 'The Death of Gordon: a Victorian Myth'. *Journal of Imperial and Commonwealth History* 10 (1982): 185–310.

Jones, Gareth Stedman. *Languages of Class*. Cambridge: Cambridge University Press, 1989.

Jones, Greta. *Social Darwinism and English Thought*. Brighton, Sussex: Harvester Press, 1980.

Kemp, Peter, *The British Sailor: A Social History of the Lower Deck*. London: Dent, 1970.

——, ed. *The Papers of Admiral Sir John Fisher*, volume 1. London: Navy Records Society, 1960.

Kennedy, Paul. *Rise and Fall of British Naval Mastery*. London: Allen Lane, 1976.

Kennedy, Paul and Anthony Nicholls, eds. *Nationalist and Racialist Movements in Britain and Germany Before 1914*. London: Macmillan Press, Ltd, 1981.

Kent, Susan Kingsley. *Gender and Power in Britain, 1640–1990*. London: Routledge, 1999.

Kershen, Anne J. *Strangers, Aliens and Asians: Huguenots, Jews and Bangladeshis in Spitalfields, 1660–2000*. London: Routledge, 2005.

Kidd, Alan J. 'Philanthropy and the "Social History Paradigm"'. *Social History* 21, no. 2 (May 1996): 180–92.

Krebs, Paula M. *Gender, Race and the Writing of Empire: Public Discourse and the Boer War*. Cambridge: Cambridge University Press, 1999.

Kverndal, Roald. *Seamen's Missions: Their Origin and Early Growth*. Pasadena: William Carey Library, 1986.

Lambert, Andrew D. *The Crimean War: British Grand Strategy, 1853–56*. Manchester: Manchester University Press, 1990.

Lambert, Nicholas A. *Sir John Fisher's Naval Revolution*. Columbia: University of South Carolina Press, 1999.

Land, Isaac. 'Domesticating the Maritime: Culture, Masculinity, and Empire in Britain, 1770–1820'. Unpublished dissertation, University of Michigan, 1999.

——'The Many-tongued Hydra: Sea Talk, Maritime Culture, and Atlantic Identities', *Journal of American Culture* 25, no. 3–4 (September 2002): 412–17.

Leed, Eric. *No Man's Land: Combat and Identity in World War I*. Cambridge: Cambridge University Press, 1979.

Lemisch, Jesse. 'Jack Tar in the Streets: Merchant Seamen in the Politics of Revolutionary America'. *William and Mary Quarterly* 25 (July 1968): 371–407.

Levine, Philippa. *Prostitution, Race and Politics: Policing Venereal Disease in the British Empire*. New York: Routledge, 2003.

——, ed. *Gender and Empire*. Oxford: Oxford University Press, 2004.

Lewis, Jane. *Women in England, 1870–1950: Sexual Divisions and Social Change*. Sussex: Wheatsheaf Books, 1984.

Lewis, Michael. *The Navy of Britain: A Historical Portrait*. London: George Allen & Unwin Ltd, 1949.

——*The History of the British Navy*. Fair Lawn, NJ: Essential Books, 1959.

——*A Social History of the Navy, 1793–1815*. London: George Allen & Unwin, 1960.

——*The Navy in Transition, 1814–1864: A Social History*. London: Hodder & Stoughton, 1965.

Lincoln, Margarette. *Representing the Royal Navy: British Sea Power, 1750–1815*. Aldershot, Hants: Ashgate, 2002.

Lurie, Alison. *The Language of Clothes*. New York: Random House, 2000.

MacKenzie, John M. *Propaganda and Empire*. Manchester: Manchester University Press, 1985.

——, ed. *Popular Imperialism and the Military*. Manchester: Manchester University Press, 1992.

Mangan, J. A. 'Duty Unto Death: English Masculinity and Militarism in the Age of the New Imperialism'. *International Journal of the History of Sport* 12, no. 2 (1995): 10–38.

Mangan, J. A. and James Walvin, eds. *Manliness and Morality: Middle-Class Masculinity in Britain and America, 1800–1940*. New York: St Martin's Press, 1987.

Marder, Arthur J. *From the Dreadnought to Scapa Flow: The Royal Navy in the Fisher Era, 1904–1919, volume 1: The Road to War*. London: Oxford University Press, 1961.

——*The Anatomy of British Sea Power*. New York: Octagon Books, 1976 [1940].

McCarthy, Kathleen D., ed. *Lady Bountiful Revisited: Women, Philanthropy, and Power*. New Brunswick: Rutgers University Press, 1990.

McClintock, Anne. *Imperial Leather: Race, Gender and Sexuality in the Colonial Contest*. New York: Routledge, 1995.

McDevitt, Patrick F. *May the Best Man Win: Sport, Masculinity, and Nationalism in Great Britain and the Empire, 1880–1935*. Houndmills, Basingstoke: Palgrave Macmillan, 2004.

McKee, Christopher. *Sober Men and True: Sailor Lives in the Royal Navy, 1900–1945*. Cambridge: Harvard University Press, 2002.

Midgley, Clare, ed. *Gender and Imperialism*. Manchester: Manchester University Press, 1998.

Millman, Brock. *Managing Domestic Dissent in First World War Britain*. London: Routledge, 2000.

——*Pessimism and British War Policy, 1916–1918*. London: Frank Cass, 2001.

Morris, A. J. A. *The Scaremongers: The Advocacy of War and Rearmament, 1896–1914*. London: Routledge & Kegan Paul, 1984.

Mosse, George. *Nationalism and Sexuality: Respectability and Abnormal Sexuality in Modern Europe*. New York: H. Fertig, 1985.

——*Fallen Soldiers: Reshaping the Memory of the World Wars*. New York: Oxford University Press, 1990.

Newsome, David. *Godliness and Good Learning: Four Studies on a Victorian Ideal*. London: Cassell, 1961.

Owen, David. *English Philanthropy, 1660–1960*. Cambridge: Harvard University Press, 1964.

Padfield, Peter. *Rule Britannia: The Victorian and Edwardian Navy*. London: Routledge & Kegan Paul, 1981.

Paris, Michael. *Warrior Nation: Images of War in British Popular Culture, 1850–2000*. London: Reaktion Books, 2000.

Pelling, Henry. *A History of British Trade Unionism*. London: Macmillan, 1976.

Porter, Bernard. *The Absent-Minded Imperialists: Empire, Society, and Culture in Britain*. Oxford: Oxford University Press, 2004.

Price, Richard. *An Imperial War and The British Working Class: Working-Class Attitudes and Reactions to the Boer War*. London: Routledge, 1972.

Prochaska, F. K. *Women and Philanthropy in Nineteenth-Century England*. Oxford: Clarendon Press, 1980.

—— *The Voluntary Impulse: Philanthropy in Modern Britain*. London: Faber & Faber, 1988.

—— 'Philanthropy'. In *The Cambridge Social History of Britain, 1750–1950*, volume 3, edited by F. M. L. Thompson. Cambridge: Cambridge University Press, 1993, pp. 357–94.

Pugh, Martin. *State and Society: British Political and Social History, 1870–1992*. London: Edward Arnold, 1994.

Rasor, Eugene. *Reform in the Royal Navy: A Social History of the Lower Deck*. Hamden, Conn.: Archon Books, 1976.

Rediker, Marcus. *Between the Devil and the Deep Blue Sea: Merchant Seamen, Pirates, and the Anglo-American Maritime World, 1700–1750*. Cambridge: Cambridge University Press, 1987.

Rediker, Marcus and Peter Linebaugh. *The Many-Headed Hydra: Sailors, Slaves, Commoners, and the Hidden History of the Revolutionary Atlantic*. London: Verso, 2000.

Richards, Jeffrey, ed. *Imperialism and Juvenile Literature*. Manchester: Manchester University Press, 1989.

Robinson, C. N. *British Tar in Fact and Fiction: The Poetry, Pathos, and Humour of the Sailor's Life*. London: Harper, 1911.

Rodger, N. A. M. *The Wooden World: An Anatomy of the Georgian Navy*. Annapolis, Md.: Naval Institute Press, 1986.

Roper, Michael and John Tosh, eds. *Manful Assertions: Masculinities in Britain since 1800*. London: Routledge, 1991.

Rose, Sonya. *Limited Livelihoods: Gender and Class in Nineteenth-Century England*. Berkeley: University of California Press, 1992.

Rosenthal, Michael. *The Character Factory: Baden-Powell and the Origins of the Boy Scout Movement*. New York: Pantheon Books, 1986.

Rüger, Jan. 'Nation, Empire and Navy: Identity Politics in the United Kingdom 1887–1914'. *Past & Present* 185 (2004): 159–87.

—— *The Great Naval Game: Britain and Germany in the Age of Empire*. Cambridge: Cambridge University Press, 2007.

Sanders, M. L. and Philip Taylor. *British Propaganda during the First World War, 1914–1918*. Houndmills, Basingstoke: Palgrave Macmillan, 1982.

Scott, Joan. *Gender and the Politics of History*. New York: Columbia University Press, 1988.

Searle, G. R. *The Quest for National Efficiency: A Study in British Politics and Political Thought, 1899–1914*. London: Ashfield Press, 1971.

—— *Eugenics and Politics in Britain, 1900–1914*. Leyden: Noordoff International Publishing, 1976.

Semmel, Bernard. *Imperialism and Social Reform: English Social-Imperial Thought, 1895–1914*. Cambridge: Harvard University Press, 1960.

—— *Liberalism and Naval Strategy: Ideology, Interest, and Sea Power during the Pax Britannica*. Boston: Allen & Unwin, 1986.

Shiman, Lilian Lewis. *Crusade against Drink in Victorian England*. London: Macmillan, 1986.

Showalter, Elaine. *The Female Malady: Women, Madness and English Culture, 1830–1980*. London: Virago Press, 1987.

Sillars, Stuart. *Art and Survival in First World War Britain*. Houndmills, Basingstoke: Macmillan, 1987.

Sinha, Mrinalini. *Colonial Masculinity: The 'Manly Englishman' and the 'Effeminate Bengali' in the Late Nineteenth Century*. Manchester: Manchester University Press, 1995.

Smith, Geoffrey. *Savoy Operas*. New York: Universe Books, 1985.

Snelling, Stephen. *Naval VCs of the First World War*. Phoenix Mill: Sutton Publishing, 2002.

Soper, J. Christopher. *Evangelical Christianity in the United States and Great Britain*. New York: New York University Press, 1994.

Springhall, John. 'Building Character in the British Boy: The Attempt to Extend Christian Manliness to Working-class Adolescents, 1880–1914'. In *Manliness and Morality: Middle-Class Masculinity in Britain and America, 1800–1940*, edited by J.A. Mangan and James Walvin. New York: St Martin's Press, 1987, pp. 52–74.

Stedman, Jane. *W. S. Gilbert: A Classic Victorian and his Theatre*. New York: Oxford University Press, 1996.

Stevens, David and John Reeve, eds. *The Navy and the Nation: The Influence of the Navy on Modern Australia*. Crows Nest, Australia: Allen & Unwin, 2005.

Stokesbury, James L. *Navy and Empire*. New York: William Morrow and Co., 1983.

Streets, Heather. *Martial Races: The Military, Race and Masculinity in British Imperial Culture, 1857–1914*. Manchester: Manchester University Press, 2004.

Sumida, Jon. *In Defence of Naval Supremacy: Finance, Technology and British Naval Policy, 1889–1914*. London: Routledge, 1993.

Summers, Anne. 'A Home from Home – Women's Philanthropic Work in the Nineteenth Century'. In *Fit Work for Women*, edited by Sandra Burman. New York: St Martin's Press, 1979, pp. 33–63.

——'The Character of Edwardian Nationalism: Three Popular Leagues'. In *Nationalist and Racialist Movements in Britain and Germany Before 1914*, edited by Paul Kennedy and Anthony Nicholls. London: Macmillan Press, Ltd, 1981, pp. 68–87.

Tabili, Laura. *'We ask for British Justice': Workers and Racial Difference in Late Imperial Britain*. Ithaca: Cornell University Press, 1994.

Thane, Pat. 'The British Imperial State and the Construction of National Identities'. In *Borderlines: Gender and Identities in War and Peace, 1870–1930*, edited by Billie Melman. New York: Routledge, 1998, pp. 29–45.

Thompson, Andrew S. *The Empire Strikes Back? The Impact of Imperialism on Britain from the Mid-Nineteenth Century*. Harlow, England: Pearson Longman, 2005.

——*Imperial Britain: the Empire in British Politics, c.1880–1932.* Harlow, England: Longman, 2000.

Tosh, John. *A Man's Place: Masculinity and the Middle-Class Home in Victorian England.* New Haven: Yale University Press, 1999.

——*Manliness and Masculinities in Nineteenth-Century Britain: Essays on Gender, Family, and Empire.* Harlow, England: Pearson Longman, 2005.

Travers, Tim. *Samuel Smiles and the Victorian Work Ethic.* New York: Garland Publishing, 1987.

Turley, Hans. *Rum, Sodomy, and the Lash.* New York: New York University Press, 1999.

Vance, Norman. 'The Ideal of Manliness'. In *The Victorian Public School: Studies in the Development of an Educational Institution,* edited by B. Simon and I. Bradley. Dublin: Gill and Macmillan, 1975.

——*The Sinews of the Spirit: The Ideal of Christian Manliness in Victorian Literature and Religious Thought.* Cambridge: Cambridge University Press, 1985.

Vicinus, Martha, ed. *Suffer and Be Still, Women in the Victorian Age.* Bloomington: Indiana University Press, 1973.

——*A Widening Sphere: Changing Roles of Victorian Women.* Bloomington: Indiana University Press, 1977.

Vincent, David. *Bread, Knowledge and Freedom: A Study of Nineteenth-Century Working Class Autobiography.* London: Europa Publications Limited, 1981.

——'The Domestic and the Official Curriculum in Nineteenth-Century England'. In *Opening the Nursery Door: Reading, Writing, and Childhood, 1600–1900,* edited by Mary Hilton, Morag Styles and Victor Watson. London: Routledge, 1997.

Walkowitz, Judith R. *Prostitution and Victorian Society.* Cambridge: Cambridge University Press, 1980.

Wells, Captain John. *The Royal Navy: An Illustrated Social History.* Gloucestershire: Alan Sutton, 1994.

Wilson, Kathleen. *Island Race: Englishness, Empire and Gender in the Eighteenth Century.* London: Routledge, 2003.

Winter, Jay. *Sites of Memory, Sites of Mourning: The Great War in European Cultural History.* Cambridge: Cambridge University Press, 1995.

Winton, John. *Hurrah for the Life of a Sailor: Life on the Lower-Deck of the Victorian Navy.* London: Michael Joseph, 1977.

——*Naval Heritage of Portsmouth.* Southampton: Ensign, 1989.

——'Life and Education in a Technically Evolving Navy, 1815–1925'. In *The Oxford Illustrated History of the Royal Navy,* edited by J. R. Hill and Bryan Ranft. Oxford: Oxford University Press, 1995, pp. 250–79.

Woollacott, Angela. *Gender and Empire.* Houndmills, Basingstoke: Palgrave Macmillan, 2006.

INDEX

Note: page numbers in *italic* refer to illustrations, 'n.' after a page number indicates the number of a note on that page.

Ashore and Afloat 74–5, 80, 82, 85–9
Asquith, H. H. 31, 167, 187n.11

Baden-Powell, Robert 152–3, 171, 176–7, *178*, 181, 183
Basford, Walter 38
Battle of Jutland (1916) 13–14, 31, 160, 162–4, 168–9, 172–3, 177, 186
Battle of the Somme (1916) 47, 162–3, 166–7, 173–4, 186
Battle of Trafalgar 12–14, 102, 165, 186
Battle of Verdun (1916) 166
Beatty, David 160, 167–70, 173, 175, 177
Bechervaise, John 3
Beresford, Charles 133–4, 140, 149, 173, 182–3
Berkeley, Maurice 34
Bethell, John 167, 175
Bluejacket 43, 50, 54, 68, 87, 89–90, 125, 127–8, 131, 144, 194
Boer War 5–6, 13, 28, 55, 76, 137, 144, 149, 152
  see also Ladysmith, relief of
Boyce, William 1
Boy Scouts 152, 160–2, 164, 168, 171, 175–8, 181–6
  Cornwell Badge 162, 176, 182
boys' fiction 8–9, 101–2, 104–18
Brabazon, Reginald, Lord Meath 153
Brand, T. S. 136
Brassey, Thomas 133, 136
Brett, Reginald, Viscount Esther 30

Bridge, Cyprian 73
British and Foreign Sailors Society 71
British Army 6, 10–11, 22, 25, 28–9, 32, 36, 40, 49–50, 74, 101, 103–4, 141, 144, 149, 150, 168, 174, 195
British Brothers' League 138
Brooke, Rupert 163
Bullen, Frank 13, 124, 132, 136, 138, 141–3, 147–8, 150
Bulwer-Lytton, Edward 114

Campbell-Bannerman, Henry 31
Capper, Henry 56, 128–30
Carson, Edward 184–5
Casabianca 165, 169–70
Cecil, Robert, Lord Salisbury 26–7
Chamberlain, Austen 29
Chamberlain, Joseph 138
Christian militarism 4, 10, 82, 101, 106–7
Churchill, Winston 31, 37, 45, 49–50, 56, 57
class 28, 42, 55, 57, 71–2, 99, 101–3, 105–18, 125, 128, 133–5, 137–42, 148, 163–6, 176, 180–1, 185
Colomb, Philip and John 25, 134
Committee of Imperial Defence 30
conscription 47, 57, 156, 165–7, 172, 176, 183–4, 186
Contagious Diseases Acts 40–1
Cornwell, John Travers 13, 160–86, 194
  Cornwell Memorial Fund 161, 176–7, 182

 # dreadnought hoax ?

'Jack Cornwell Day' 162, 182
National Memorial Fund 173,
175–7, 184
corporal punishment 36, 37, 148
court martial 36–9, 148
Cox, James 9
Crimean War 10, 12, 22–4, 34
Criminal Law Amendment Act
(1885) 38
Cust, Henry 132

Defence of the Realm Act 171
degeneration, racial 13, 28, 152,
180–3
Dilke, Charles 133, 138
discipline 2, 9, 35–40, 42–3, 45, 49,
53, 69–70, 77–9, 99–100, 103,
111, 124, 131, 135–6, 138,
142–3, 147–8, 152–3, 172, 182–3,
194
see also Naval Discipline Act
(1861)
Disraeli, Benjamin 100
domesticity 3–4, 9, 10, 12, 38, 42,
47, 48, 50, *51*, 52–4, 66–8, 72,
85–7, *88*, 89, 99, 101, 124, 125,
126–7, 128–9, *143*, 145, *146*,
147, 194–5
Doyle, Arthur Conan 133–4
duty 3, 5, 7, 12–14, 27, 37–8, 67, 72,
76, 83–4, 99, 101–7, 109, 100–13,
116, 136, 139, 142, 144–5,
149–50, 152–3, 160–7, 169–73,
176–7, 180–1, 183–4, 186, 194–5

Eardley-Wilmot, S. M. 135, 136
education 8, 36, 39, 41, 44, 72, 77,
90, 103, 110, 118, 123, 130–2,
136–7, 139, 148, 176, 180–1, 195
Education Act (1870) 77, 130, 132
Edward VII 17, 57, 152
Eliot, Gilbert, Earl of Minto 133
Elwell, Frederick 177
Elwes, Geoffrey 183
Entente Cordiale 29
evangelicalism 10, 12, 66, 68–9, 70,
71, 78, 104

exhibitions and fleet reviews 6, 8,
27–8, 47, 73, 91, 138, 140, 149

Fielding, Henry 1
First World War 12–14, 19, 31, 47,
50, 54, 57, 73, 76, 140, 160,
162–4, 194
Fisher, John 24, 29–31, 44–5, 49,
56–7, 134, 141
Fleet 50, 131
fleet reviews *see* exhibitions and
fleet reviews
Ford, Arthur 38
France 4, 21–4, 26, 29, 35, 47,
57, 105, 109–10, 112–13, 124,
166
Froude, James Anthony 106

Galloway, A. A. C. 91
George V 133, 174
Germany 4, 10, 13, 24, 26, 29–31,
134–5, 160, 168, 174
Gilbert, W. S. 20, 114, 117–18,
125
Gladstone, W. E. 25–7, 133
see also HMS *Pinafore*
Gloire 23
Gordon, Charles 165–6, 171
Goschen, George 36
Graham, James R. G. 33, 41
Greenwich Hospital 52

Haig, Douglas 167
'handy man' 3, 147, 149, 151
Hanway, Jonas 2, 41
Havelock, Henry 165, 171
Hemans, Dorothea 169–70
Henty, G. A. 12–13, 106–7, 109–11
Do Your Duty 12–13, 109–11,
113
Heron, Bert 38
Hicks-Beach, Michael 29
HMS Pinafore 20, 114–18, 125
see also Gilbert, W. S. and
Sullivan, Arthur
Hodder-Williams, John Ernest 177
Holman, Thomas 97n, 128–9, 130

Hopkins, Gerald Manley 75
Horton-Smith, L. G. 134
Hughes, Thomas 101
  Tom Brown's School Days 101
Hurd, Archibald 124–5, 132, 141–2, 144–5, 147–50

Imperial Maritime League 132, 134
Indian Mutiny 10, 22, 171
  Relief of Lucknow 171
Interdepartmental Committee on Physical Deterioration 13, 28, 144
International Order of the Good Templars 77
Ireland 7, 43
  Easter Rising (Ireland) 166
  Irish Home Rule 7, 28

Jane, Fred T. 13, 124, 132–4, 151–3, 194
Jellicoe, John 167–8, 172, 177, 185
'Jem Hopeful; or, the Ladder of Life' 112–13
John Bull 125–7, 193

Kennedy, William R. 74
Key, A. C. 43, 49
King-Hall, William 78–9
Kingsley, Charles 101
Kingston, W. H. G. 104–7
  Three Midshipmen 105
  True Blue 105–6, 113
Kipling, Rudyard 13, 124, 132–3, 134, 141–2, 147–50, 152, 194
Kitchener, Herbert 167

Labouchere, Henry 62, 133
Ladysmith, relief of 144, 149
  see also Boer War
Lambton, Hedworth 144
Laughton, John Knox 134, 136
Lawrence, T. E. 162
Lawson, Robert 168–71, 177
Lawson, Wilfred 133
Lloyd's Patriotic Fund 53
Login, Spencer 141

lower-deck discontent and grievances 34–5, 48, 50, 54–7, 195
  see also Naval Magna Carta, A
Lyne, Thomas J. Spence 55, 130–1

Macassey, Lynden 184
McKenna naval programme 31
Macnamara, T. J. 161, 165, 177, 184
Madame Tussaud's 161, 177
Mafeking 144
Mahan, Alfred T. 25, 124
Marine Society 2, 41
Marryat, Frederick 105
Matania Fortunio 177
Maxse, Leo 133
merchant service 2, 7, 11, 20, 25, 32, 34–5, 41, 43, 49, 52, 66, 77, 104, 132, 135–8, 141
militarism 4–5, 7, 11, 13, 26–7, 31, 82
Military Service Acts (1916) *see* conscription
Milner, Alfred 133

Napier, Charles 34
Napier, Trevelyan 169
Napoleonic Wars 12–13, 20–1, 23, 32–3, 37, 44, 105, 108–9
National Temperance League 71–2, 79
Naval and Military Bible Society 71
Naval Correspondence Mission 71
Naval Defence Act (1889) 26, 31, 43, 44, 57
naval disasters and disaster relief 66, 69, 72–6
Naval Discipline Act (1861) 35–8
naval efficiency 29, 30, 40–1
naval estimates and budgets 20, 22, 24–7, 29–33, 57, 59n, 133, 134
naval families 38, 42, 47, 48, 50, 51, 52–4, 66–9, 72–5, 79, 82–5, 87, 89, 99, 101, 125, 128, 194
  see also naval marriages

naval films 9, 47
  see also West, Alfred
navalism 5, 13, 25, 27, 31, 84,
  123–4, 129, 132–42, 151, 153,
  163
Naval Magna Carta, A 54
  see also lower-deck discontent
  and grievances
naval marriages 47, 54, 85, 87, 89
naval recruitment 2, 5, 7, 9, 12, 16n,
  20, 33, 42–7, 49–50, 53, 56,
  76–7, 81, 128, 130–1, 136, 138
naval reviews *see* exhibitions and
  fleet reviews
naval scares and races 6, 13, 19,
  23–4, 30, 57, 83, 123–4, 132–3,
  137, 153
Naval Scripture Society 72
naval ships
  HMS *Britannia* 121
  HMS *Caesar* 87
  HMS *Chester* 160, 161, 163, 165,
    168–9, 177, 182
  HMS *Devastation* 23–4, 131
  HMS *Dreadnought* 30–1, 44–5,
    131
  HMS *Excellent* 24
  HMS *Falmouth* 169
  HMS *Fisgard* 44
  HMS *Hampshire* 167
  HMS *Illustrious* 41
  HMS *Invincible* 30, 45
  HMS *Mars* 141, 148
  HMS *Powerful* 144
  HMS *Prosephone* 89
  HMS *Reindeer* 78
  HMS *Serpent* 74
  HMS *Warrior* 23
naval songs 7, 118
navy
  boys in 20, 23, 27, 33–4, 40–5, 52,
    56, 58, 75, 79, 81–2, 90, 147,
    160–1, 165, 175
  brigades 137, 144, 149, 150
  comparison between Georgian and
    Victorian sailors 2–4, 125–8,
    194
  composition of 7, 16
  continuous service 7, 19, 20, 32–5,
    41, 45, 48, 52, 57, 76, 136, 148,
    193–4
  'hire and discharge' 19, 32–3, 48
  homosexuality in 37–40
  impressment 19, 33, 35, 100, 128,
    148
  pay and benefits 20, 33–6, 42–3,
    45, 47–50, 52, 55, 57, 73–5, 129,
    195
  pensions 20, 33–5, 43–4, 48–55,
    57, 76, 136, 195
  promotion 20, 34–5, 54, 55–7,
    130
  Royal Naval Division 47
  Royal Naval Reserve 30, 35, 44,
    47, 136–7
  Royal Naval Volunteer Reserve
    138
  rum ration 77–8, 80–1, 128
  stokers 33, 45–7, 49, 54, 148
  uniform 19, 34, 89, 145, 147
  venereal disease in 40–1
Navy League 9, 13, 91, 123–5,
  132–41, 145, 149, 150–1, 161,
  162, 164, 173, 175–7, 181–3, 186
  efforts to recruit boys into
    merchant service 136–7
Navy Records Society 134
Nelson, Horatio 12, 14, 20, 28,
  101–2, 107–10, 113, 125, 127–8,
  161, 165–6
Noble, Sam 43

Orwell, George 9, 17
Oxenham, John 162, 171, 177

Pakington John 34
Palmer, William, Lord Selborne 44,
  138
Parry, W. Edward 2
Pax Britannica 20, 22, 24–5
press 8, 39, 100, 101, 144, 160, 162,
  164, 170–1, 174–5, 180
Primrose, Archibald, Lord Rosebery
  27, 31

Queen's Regulations 8
Quiller-Couch, Arthur 1

Reynolds, Stephen 54, 128
Roberts, Frederick 133, 153
Royal Naval Benevolent Society 72
Royal Naval Christian Union 67, 68
Royal Naval Exhibition 9, 27, 73, 91
Royal Naval Friendly Union of Sailors' Wives 72
Royal Naval Fund 73
Royal Naval Provident Fund 7–6
Royal Naval Temperance Society 67–8, 72, 79–81
Royal Patriotic Fund 73
Royal Sailors' Rests see sailors' homes and rests
Russell, Charles 180

sacrifice 5–8, 13–14, 102, 111, 130, 160–71, 173, 175–7, 182–6
sailor suits 9, 17
  see also navy: uniform
sailors' homes and rests 67–9, 72–4, 80–1, 85, 87, 91–2
St. George 81
Salisbury, Frank O. 162, 175–7, 179, 184, 185
Selborne Memorandum 44
self-help 73, 101–7, 111, 115, 118
  see also Smiles, Samuel
Smiles, Samuel 102–4
  Duty 103–4
  Self-Help 102, 104
Smith, Humphrey H. 25
social Darwinism 4, 10, 13, 71, 180, 183
socialism 57, 139–40, 151
social purity movement 40, 67
Society for the Promotion of Christian Knowledge (SPCK) 104
sodomy 37–9
  see also navy: homosexuality in
Soldiers' and Sailors' Family Association (SSFA) 72–4, 76

Spencer programme 26–7
Stables, Gordon 101
Stanley, Edward, Lord Derby 33
Stead, W. T. 24–5, 132
Stevens, Thomas, Bishop of Barking 161, 165
stokers' mutiny (1906) 45, 92
  see also lower-deck discontent and grievances
Sullivan, Arthur 114, 125
Sullivan, James 78

Tariff Reform League 138
technology 7, 19, 21, 23–4, 26, 30–2, 57, 84, 130–2, 141, 194
temperance 12, 66–72, 74, 76–92, 128, 148, 168
Tennyson, Alfred 124, 171
'Tommy Atkins' 5–6, 11, 193
total war 163–6, 172–3, 176, 185–6
Tryon, George 48

Union Jack Club 72

Victoria, Queen 77, 104
Victoria Cross 13, 162, 173–4, 177

West, Alfred 9, 28, 47
Westminster Abbey 172
Weston, Agnes 12, 66–74, 79–92, 195
White, Arnold 13, 124, 133, 140–1
Wilkinson, Spenser 124
Wilson, H. W. 124, 133, 139
Women's Royal Naval Service (WRNS) 47
Wyatt, Harold Frazer 134

xenophobia 138

Yerburgh, Robert 140
Yexley, Lionel 50, 57, 74, 76, 87, 89–90, 128–31, 144
youth 6, 8–9, 99, 102, 104–5, 107, 109–11, 118, 125, 127, 130, 137, 143, 145, 147, 152, 162–7, 169–73, 177–86